Photograph by Horydczak

BEN JONSON

From the portrait ascribed to Isaac Oliver at the Folger Shakespeare Library

ELIZABETHAN PLAYS,

Written by

Shakespeare's Friends, Colleagues,

Rivals, and Successors; to wit:

Christopher Marlowe, John Lyly,
Robert Greene, Thomas Kyd, Ben Jonson,
George Chapman, Thomas Dekker, John Marston,
Thomas Heywood, Francis Beaumont, John Fletcher,
John Webster, Thomas Middleton, William Rowley,
Philip Massinger, John Ford, and James Shirley.

Edited, with new *Texts* based on the *original folios, quartos,* and *octavos,* by

HAZELTON SPENCER,
Associate Professor of English in The Johns Hopkins University.

BOSTON:
Published by LITTLE, BROWN, AND COMPANY.

M.CM.XXXIII.

PREFATORY NOTE

The twenty-eight plays of this collection have been chosen primarily for their merit as masterpieces of English drama, and secondarily to represent the leading Elizabethan playwrights and the main currents of drama in Shakespeare's time and just after. The selection has been made without regard to the contents of similar anthologies; but it is a pleasant duty to acknowledge that the first of these, President Neilson's, remains, in the matter of selection, a monument to his taste and judgment.

Almost every play in the present volume, even the crude but powerful *Spanish Tragedy*, is in its way a masterpiece. *Endymion* is an exception; in none of his plays does Lyly manifest either a genuine *vis comica*, or that indispensable possession of the great serious dramatist, profound sympathy with the inner life of sensitive men and women and with its occasional revelation, under the pressure of circumstance, in the manifestations of human passion. But the court plays must be illustrated; and, superficial as Lyly is, he was one of Shakespeare's teachers. Peele on the other hand was not, and has been omitted without much regret. *The Old Wife's Tale* has a few charming passages, but most of it is sad stuff; *David and Bethsabe* opens with one of the age's most amazing bursts of lyrical genius, and then turns into an inferior history play, less dramatic than its source. *Friar Bacon and Friar Bungay* is at least sustained; and, if not quite a masterpiece, it is thoroughly delightful and shows Greene at his best. *Dr. Faustus* and *The Jew of Malta* have come down to us in forms worse than the mutilated statues of antiquity, for they have been debased by the adapter's hand. Yet, mangled as they are, they are mangled masterpieces.

Marlowe, Jonson, and the Beaumont-Fletcher collaboration are illustrated by four plays each; the last two because, except for Webster's masterpiece, their works are nearest Shakespeare's in excellence. And Marlowe's development as a dramatist is so illuminating for the student of Shakespeare's that it seems desirable to afford copious materials for tracing it. Interesting as is Jonson's *Sejanus*, his mastery was in comedy. *Every Man in His Humor* is required by historical considerations, and it seems better to give, in addition to that play, all three of the great comedies than to omit one for the sake of a second-rate tragedy. Dekker is perhaps unduly favored. *The Shoemakers' Holiday* could not be left out, though it is inferior, as a serious work of art, to *The Honest Whore;* and one part of that strangely beautiful drama is not enough. *Part II* is the masterpiece, but its power would be impaired without *Part I*. Toward the end of our period comedy becomes more significant than tragedy, both for its superior vitality, and for its greater influence on the drama of the Restoration and the eighteenth century. The selections from Massinger and Shirley have been made in accordance with this fact. The Editor thought of including less familiar examples of the lighter vein of Fletcher and of Middleton, but was forced to recognize that *The Wild-Goose Chase* and *A Trick to Catch the Old One*, while not indisputably the best of their authors' comedies, are clearly best for the purposes this volume is designed to serve.

These are, of course, chiefly to introduce university students and general readers to the riches of the non-Shakespearean drama of the English Renaissance. Yet care has been taken to make the texts as accurate as possible. For only four of these, precisely specified in the introductory notes, has the Editor been obliged to rely on reprints; and even such exceptions to the general rule of first-hand collation of the old editions have been carefully cross-checked, since for each of these four plays at least two scholarly reprints were available. In several cases (chiefly among the works of those dramatists who have not appeared in collected editions for half a century or more) the present texts, granted their "modernization", probably constitute the closest approximation to the authors' original MSS ever printed (under this category *i Honest Whore* is perhaps the most interesting example); in many others they are considerably more faithful to the earliest editions than the texts of similar undertakings; for errors arising from reliance on derivative texts, and the tampering, whether or not acknowledged, by the nineteenth-century editors, have been incorporated in anthologies to a surprising extent, the more surprising because so often silently.

Departures from the basic texts are here enclosed in square brackets. It has not been thought necessary to record such insignificant changes as "re-enter" for "enter", nor the expansion of abbreviations, nor inconsequential variations in the spelling of proper names and in speech-tags, nor altered word-order in stage directions (though in these a special effort has been made to retain the flavor of the Elizabethan theatre), nor the correction of turned letters and similarly obvious printer's blunders. Rearrangement of lines of verse has not always been indicated, nor arrangement of (printed) prose as verse, etc. It is often quite impossible to say that a given passage is one or the other. It would, however, be folly to hope that the pains taken in collation and proof-reading have eliminated error; the Editor will be grateful for corrections from users of the book. No attempt has been made to supply a complete apparatus of variant readings, but the most suggestive are given. Nor have the old texts been violated in order to wrench them into conformity with pedantic conceptions of metrical regularity. Much of the beauty of spoken blank verse depends upon slight deviations from the norm. Though editors have professed the contrary, the practice has been far too general of forcing lines into the mold of strict regularity by indicating the suppression of vowels which were probably slurred or even pronounced distinctly but rapidly on the stage, and of giving too little heed to the metrical value of dramatic pauses by insisting on the pronunciation of syllables that were probably elided. The evidence afforded by the original editions is by no means conclusive on these matters; but it is about all the evidence we have, and the Editor has followed it.

The present texts, then, are notably conservative, save in two particulars: scholars would rather read an exact reprint of an original quarto, with all variants footnoted; but it seems inadvisable to risk distracting the beginner from the plays as plays and as literature by sticking to archaic spelling and punctuation. With the same end in view, and at the cost of making the book considerably larger, a legible type (nine-point Modern Number 8 Monotype on ten-point body) has been used. The Editor hopes that the owner of this book will enjoy it and that, continuing his reading far beyond it, he will permanently join the good company of those who have found delight in these robust old plays.

The Editor has rejected the theory that annotation is necessarily a nuisance and assumed that such active and inquiring minds as choose to read this book will enjoy the plays more if they understand the meaning of the words the dramatists composed them in. It is patently impossible, however, to note within the limits of an anthology that "still" means "always" and that "friend" often means "lover", every time the words occur; such expressions are glossed scatteringly. The same principle has been adopted in noticing unfamiliar accentuation.

It remains to acknowledge the receipt of many courtesies, which have facilitated the labors of collation and annotation, from the staffs of the Harvard College Library, the Boston Public Library, the Library of Congress, and the Library of The Johns Hopkins University; from the Elizabethan Club of Yale University; and from the Supervisor of Research and his assistants at the Folger Shakespeare Library. To the last of these institutions special thanks is due for permission to reproduce its portrait of Jonson; and, as well as to several of the libraries already mentioned, the Editor is indebted for various favors (especially for the facsimiles of the old title pages) to the British Museum, the Bodleian Library, and the Huntington Library. For the constant coöperation of his publishers the Editor is particularly grateful. The format was designed by Arthur F. Williams of their staff. The coat of arms on the cover was redrawn from a copy of the Gospels bound for Queen Elizabeth and now in the British Museum. The ornaments on the shelf-back are details (cuirasses) from the elaborate design of which the coat of arms is the central feature.

So many critical, historical, and lexicographical works have been levied on that to list them is out of the question. Excellent bibliographies for this field are now so numerous and so accessible that it seems inadvisable to sacrifice precious space by including another. Yet special mention ought to be made of the help received from E. K. Chambers's *Elizabethan Stage*, W. W. Greg's *List of English Plays*, Skeat and Mayhew's *Glossary of Tudor and Stuart Words*, and, most constantly, the *New English Dictionary*. The annotation has been strengthened at a number of points by several of the Editor's colleagues at The Johns Hopkins, who have given him the benefit of their learning in a wide variety of fields. With characteristic liberality the Editor's master, George Lyman Kittredge, entered into a correspondence which continued for several months on certain problems of special difficulty. To Professor Kittredge's incomparable understanding of words and their ways in Elizabethan speech is due the illumination of a number of dark passages which all previous commentators had ignored, given up, or left in confusion worse confounded. Professor Fred N. Robinson kindly lent his aid in the handling of several Gaelic expressions. To the generosity and accuracy of Dr. W. Lee Ustick the Editor is under particular obligations, for the checking of many readings in copies of the early editions which were temporarily out of his reach. These acknowledgments would be incomplete without an allusion to prentice years under Professor John Tucker Murray, as his assistant in his course on these dramatists. The most general indebtedness, however, is to the noble army of Elizabethan play editors, both the living and the slain, to whom salute and thanks.

H. S.

Baltimore, April 15, 1933

CONTENTS

ELIZABETHAN PLAYS

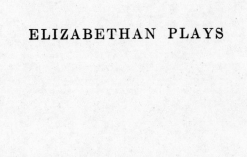

Tamburlaine

the Great.

Who, from a Scythian Shepearde,

by his rare and woonderfull Conquests,
became a most puissant and migh-
tye Monarque.

And (for his tyranny, and terrour in
Warre) was tearmed,

The Scourge of God.

Deuided into two Tragicall Dis-
courses, as they were sundrie times
shewed vpon Stages in the Citie
of London.

By the right honorable the Lord
Admyrall, his seruauntes.

Now first, and newlie published.

LONDON.
Printed by Richard Ihones: at the signe
of the Rose and Crowne neere Hol-
borne Bridge. 1590.

INTRODUCTORY NOTE

The production of *Tamburlaine, Part I*, probably in 1587–88, definitely inaugurated the earlier of the two great ages of British drama. Never before had first-rate genius been devoted to the making of an English play. When Shakespeare came to London, a few years later, he found a highly imaginative drama, bold and passionate, and couched in a ringing blank verse, in possession of the boards. In his tragedies and histories he applied himself to perfecting what Marlowe had begun.

Though a university man, Marlowe succeeded in freeing his work from the smell of the lamp which spoils most tragedies of the 1580's. Taking his theme from the past, he swings it straight into the main current of the Renaissance; Tamburlaine personifies and voices its boundless aspiration. In fact, the form of the play suffers from the author's preoccupation with his hero; Marlowe's later works are better dramas. Outwardly, *Tamburlaine* is a ten-act history play; essentially, it is a soaring piece of almost epical poetry, often wildly extravagant, but adorned with moments of dazzling lyric beauty.[1] In *Part II* the hero extends his conquests, though he is somewhat shaken by the loss of Zenocrate and the cowardice of one of their sons. At last, glutted with blood, intoxicated with success, and broken in health, he madly orders an assault on the powers of Heaven. But now his armies are helpless; he is beaten at last; Death is the final victor.

Marlowe read widely for his materials; in *Tamburlaine* he is something of the scholar, as well as poet. His chief sources are Pedro Mexía's *Silva de Varia Lección* and Petrus Perondinus's *Magni Tamerlanis Scytharum Imperatoris Vita.* But there are many others, both geographical and historical, as Miss Ethel Seaton has shown (see introduction to Miss Ellis-Fermor's edition for references and summaries). Marlowe's great contribution is his crediting the brutal conqueror with the " undeviating pursuit of a vision "; at least this is true of *Part I*, though in the sequel there is more recognition of the horrible futility of what the hero has done.

The gigantic Edward Alleyn was famous in the title rôle, but little is known of the early stage history of the play. It was being acted with great success by the Admiral's Men in 1594 and 1595, and there are many literary allusions up to the closing of the theatres in 1642. The standard editions of Marlowe's works are those of Tucker Brooke (1910), and R. H. Case as general editor (1930–). *Tamburlaine* was edited for the latter by Miss U. M. Ellis-Fermor (1930). Albrecht Wagner published an edition in 1885. *Part I* originally appeared, in octavo, in 1590 (reprinted 1593?, 1597, 1605); on that text, as given by Brooke and Miss Ellis-Fermor, the present edition is based. None of the old editions ascribes the play to Marlowe, but his authorship is certain both from internal evidence and in the light of Thomas Heywood's plain statement in a prologue (1633) to *The Jew of Malta.*

[1] It may seem to a reader new to Marlowe that the opening lines do not bear out this statement; if so, he is advised to whet his appetite by turning to I, ii, 87, ff., or V, ii, 72, ff.

TAMBURLAINE THE GREAT

BY

CHRISTOPHER MARLOWE

THE FIRST PART

[DRAMATIS PERSONAE

MYCETES,[1] King of Persia.
COSROE, his brother.
MEANDER, THERIDAMAS, ORTYGIUS, CENEUS, MENAPHON, } Persian lords.
TAMBURLAINE, a Scythian shepherd.
TECHELLES, USUMCASANE, } his followers.
BAJAZETH, Emperor of the Turks.
KING of FEZ.
KING of MOROCCO.
KING of ARGIER.[2]
KING of ARABIA.
SOLDAN of EGYPT.
GOVERNOR of DAMASCUS.
AGYDAS, MAGNETES, } Median lords.
CAPOLIN, an Egyptian.
PHILEMUS, a messenger.
Bassoes, Lords, Citizens, Moors, Soldiers, and Attendants.

ZENOCRATE, daughter to the Soldan of Egypt.
ANIPPE, her maid.
ZABINA, wife to Bajazeth.
EBEA, her maid.
Virgins of Damascus.]

THE PROLOGUE

FROM jigging veins of rhyming mother wits,
And such conceits as clownage keeps in pay,
We'll lead you to the stately tent of war,
Where you shall hear the Scythian Tamburlaine
Threat'ning the world with high astounding terms,
And scourging kingdoms with his conquering sword.
View but his picture in this tragic glass,
And then applaud his fortunes as you please.

ACT I — SCENE I[3]

[*Enter*] MYCETES, COSROE, MEANDER, THERIDAMAS, ORTYGIUS, CENEUS, [MENAPHON,] *with others.*

MYC. Brother Cosroe, I find myself aggriev'd,
Yet insufficient to express the same,
For it requires a great and thund'ring speech.
Good Brother, tell the cause unto my lords;
I know you have a better wit than I.

COS. Unhappy Persia, that in former age
Hast been the seat of mighty conquerors,
That, in their prowess and their policies,
Have triumph'd over Afric and the bounds
Of Europe,[4] where the sun dares scarce appear
For freezing meteors and congealed cold,
Now to be rul'd and governed by a man
At whose birthday Cynthia with Saturn join'd,
And Jove, the Sun, and Mercury denied
To shed [their][5] influence in his fickle brain.

[1] Some of these names are invented, some historical though unrelated to Tamburlaine, and some (like Bajazeth) both historical and related.
[2] Algiers.
[3] Unlocated by the dramatist, but presumably a camp near Persepolis.
[4] Referring to Cambyses's conquest of Egypt and the expedition of Darius I across the Danube.
[5] Emend. Dyce; old eds. *his*, which may possibly be right, referring to Jove, whose agents are the Sun and Mercury.

Now Turks and Tartars shake their swords at thee,
Meaning to mangle all thy provinces.

MYC. Brother, I see your meaning well enough,
And thorough your planets I perceive you think
I am not wise enough to be a king;
But I refer me to my noblemen,
That know my wit and can be witnesses.
I might command you to be slain for this;
Meander, might I not?

MEAND. Not for so small a fault, my sovereign Lord.

MYC. I mean it not, but yet I know I might;
Yet live; yea, live; Mycetes wills it so. —
Meander, thou, my faithful counsellor,
Declare the cause of my conceived grief,
Which is, God knows, about that Tamburlaine,
That, like a fox in midst of harvest time,
Doth prey upon my flocks of passengers,
And, as I hear, doth mean to pull my plumes;
Therefore 't is good and meet for to be wise.

MEAND. Oft have I heard your Majesty complain
Of Tamburlaine, that sturdy Scythian thief,
That robs your merchants of Persepolis
[Trading] [6] by land unto the Western Isles,
And in your confines with his lawless train
Daily commits incivil [7] outrages,
Hoping (misled by dreaming prophecies)
To reign in Asia, and with barbarous arms
To make himself the monarch of the East;
But ere he march in Asia, or display
His vagrant ensign in the Persian fields,
Your Grace hath taken order by Theridamas,[8]
Charg'd with a thousand horse, to apprehend
And bring him captive to your Highness' throne.

MYC. Full true thou speak'st, and like thyself, my Lord,
Whom I may term a Damon for thy love.
Therefore 't is best, if so it like you all,
To send my thousand horse incontinent [9]
To apprehend that paltry Scythian.
How like you this, my honorable Lords?
Is it not a kingly resolution? [10]

COS. It cannot choose, because it comes from you.

MYC. Then hear thy charge, valiant Theridamas,
The chiefest captain of Mycetes' host,
The hope of Persia, and the very legs
Whereon our state doth lean as on a staff,
That holds us up, and foils our neighbor foes:
Thou shalt be leader of this thousand horse,
Whose foaming gall with rage and high disdain
Have sworn the death of wicked Tamburlaine.
Go frowning forth; but come thou smiling home,
As did Sir Paris with the Grecian dame;
Return with speed: time passeth swift away;
Our life is frail, and we may die to-day.

THER. Before the moon renew her borrowed light,
Doubt not, my lord and gracious sovereign,
But Tamburlaine and that Tartarian rout
Shall either perish by our warlike hands,
Or plead for mercy at your Highness' feet.

MYC. Go, stout Theridamas; thy words are swords,
And with thy looks thou conquerest all thy foes.
I long to see thee back return from thence,
That I may view these milk-white steeds of mine
All loaden with the heads of killed men,
And from their knees even to their hoofs below
Besmear'd with blood that makes a dainty show.

THER. Then now, my Lord, I humbly take my leave.

MYC. Theridamas, farewell ten thousand times. — *Exit* [THERIDAMAS].
Ah, Menaphon, why stayest thou thus behind,
When other men press forward for renown?
Go, Menaphon, go into Scythia;
And foot by foot follow Theridamas.

COS. Nay, pray you let him stay; a greater [task] [11]
Fits Menaphon than warring with a thief.
Create him Prorex [12] of [13] Africa,
That he may win the Babylonians' hearts,
Which will revolt from Persian government
Unless they have a wiser king than you.

MYC. "Unless they have a wiser king than you!"
These are his words; Meander, set them down.

COS. And add this to them: that all Asia
Lament to see the folly of their king.

[6] O_2; O_1 *treading*. [7] Uncivilized.
[8] A twelve-syllable line, but not an Alexandrine, the last two syllables being here lightly pronounced, though in l. 57 (and elsewhere) the last receives a stress.
[9] At once.
[10] "Is it not" forms the first foot of this line; "resolution" has five syllables. The suffix is common as a dissyllable.
[11] Add. Robinson.
[12] Viceroy. [13] O_4 adds *all*.

MYC. Well, here I swear by this my royal seat —
COS. You may do well to kiss it then.
MYC. Emboss'd with silk as best beseems my state,
To be reveng'd for these contemptuous words.
Oh, where is duty and allegiance now?
Fled to the Caspian or the Ocean main?
What shall I call thee? Brother? No, a foe,
Monster of nature, shame unto thy stock,
That dar'st presume thy sovereign for to mock. —
Meander, come; I am abus'd, Meander.
[*Exeunt all but*] COSROE *and* MENAPHON.
MEN. How now, my Lord? What, mated [14] and amaz'd
To hear the King thus threaten like himself?
COS. Ah, Menaphon, I pass not for [15] his threats;
The plot is laid by Persian noblemen
And captains of the Median garrisons
To crown me Emperor of Asia;
But this it is that doth excruciate
The very substance of my vexed soul:
To see our neighbors, that were wont to quake
And tremble at the Persian monarch's name,
Now sits and laughs our regiment [16] to scorn;
And, that which might resolve [17] me into tears,
Men from the farthest equinoctial line
Have swarm'd in troops into the Eastern India,
Lading their ships with gold and precious stones,
And made their spoils from all our provinces.
MEN. This should entreat your Highness to rejoice,
Since Fortune gives you opportunity
To gain the title of a conqueror
By curing of this maimed empery.
Afric and Europe bordering on your land,
And continent to your dominions,
How easily may you, with a mighty host,
Pass into Græcia,[18] as did Cyrus once,
And cause them to withdraw their forces home,
Lest you subdue the pride of Christendom!
COS. But, Menaphon, what means this trumpet's sound?
MEN. Behold, my Lord, Ortygius and the rest
Bringing the crown to make you emperor.

Enter ORTYGIUS *and* CENEUS *bearing a crown, with others.*

ORTY. Magnificent and mighty Prince Cosroe,
We, in the name of other Persian states [19]
And commons of this mighty monarchy,
Present thee with th' imperial diadem.
CEN. The warlike soldiers and the gentlemen,
That heretofore have fill'd Persepolis
With Afric captains taken in the field,
Whose ransom made them march in coats of gold,
With costly jewels hanging at their ears,
And shining stones upon their lofty crests,
Now living idle in the walled towns,
Wanting both pay and martial discipline,
Begin in troops to threaten civil war,
And openly exclaim against the King.
Therefore, to stay all sudden mutinies,
We will invest your Highness emperor;
Whereat the soldiers will conceive more joy
Than did the Macedonians at the spoil
Of great Darius [20] and his wealthy host.
COS. Well, since I see the state of Persia droop
And languish in my brother's government,
I willingly receive th' imperial crown,
And vow to wear it for my country's good,
In spite of them shall malice my estate.
ORTY. And in assurance of desir'd success,
We here do crown thee monarch of the East,
Emperor of Asia and Persia,[21]
Great Lord of Media and Armenia;
Duke of Africa and Albania,[22]
Mesopotamia and of Parthia,
East India and the late-discovered isles;
Chief Lord of all the wide, vast Euxine sea,
And of the ever-raging Caspian lake.
Long live Cosroe, mighty emperor!
COS. And Jove may [23] never let me longer live
Than I may seek to gratify your love,
And cause the soldiers that thus honor me
To triumph over many provinces;
By whose desires of discipline in arms
I doubt not shortly but to reign sole king,
And with the army of Theridamas

[14] Discomfited.
[15] Care not for, am unmoved by.
[16] Rule.
[17] Dissolve.
[18] *I.e.*, the Ionian cities of Asia Minor, reduced, after Cyrus had conquered Lydia, by his generals.
[19] Nobles, men of high estate.
[20] Darius III, defeated by Alexander the Great at Issus.
[21] "Emperor" is practically a trochee; "Asia" and "Persia" are here trisyllables.
[22] West of the Caspian and north of the Caucasus.
[23] May Jove.

(Whither we presently will fly, my Lords)
To rest secure against my brother's force.

ORTY. We knew, my Lord, before we brought the crown,
Intending your investion[24] so near
The residence of your despised brother,
The lords would not be too exasperate
To injure or suppress your worthy title;
Or, if they would, there are in readiness
Ten thousand horse to carry you from hence,
In spite of all suspected enemies.

COS. I know it well, my Lord, and thank you all.

ORTY. Sound up the trumpets then. God save the King! *Exeunt.*

SCENE II[25]

[*Enter*] TAMBURLAINE *leading* ZENOCRATE; TECHELLES, USUMCASANE, [AGYDAS, MAGNETES, *and*] *other* Lords, *and* Soldiers *loaden with treasure.*

TAMB. Come, lady, let not this appall your thoughts;
The jewels and the treasure we have ta'en
Shall be reserv'd, and you in better state
Than if you were arriv'd in Syria,
Even in the circle of your father's arms,
The mighty Soldan of Egyptia.

ZENO. Ah, shepherd, pity my distressed plight,
If, as thou seem'st, thou art so mean a man,
And seek not to enrich thy followers
By lawless rapine from a silly[26] maid,
Who, travelling with these Median lords
To Memphis, from my uncle's country of Media,
Where all my youth I have been governed,
Have pass'd the army of the mighty Turk,
Bearing his privy signet and his hand
To safe conduct us thorough Africa.

MAG. And since we have arriv'd in Scythia,[27]
Besides rich presents from the puissant Cham,
We have his Highness' letters to command
Aid and assistance if we stand in need.

TAMB. But now you see these letters and commands
Are countermanded by a greater man;
And through my provinces you must expect
Letters of conduct from my Mightiness,
If you intend to keep your treasure safe.
But, since I love to live at liberty,
As easily may you get the Soldan's crown
As any prizes out of my precinct;
For they are friends that help to wean[28] my state
Till men and kingdoms help to strengthen it,
And must maintain my life exempt from servitude.
But, tell me, madam, is your Grace betroth'd?

ZENO. I am, my Lord, — for so you do import.

TAMB. I am a lord, for so my deeds shall prove,
And yet a shepherd by my parentage.
But, lady, this fair face and heavenly hue
Must grace his bed that conquers Asia,
And means to be a terror to the world,
Measuring the limits of his empery
By east and west, as Phœbus doth his course.—
Lie here, ye weeds that I disdain to wear;
This complete[29] armor and this curtle-axe[30]
Are adjuncts more beseeming Tamburlaine.
And, madam, whatsoever you esteem
Of this success and loss unvalued,[31]
Both may invest you Empress of the East;
And these that seem but silly[32] country swains
May have the leading of so great an host
As with their weight shall make the mountains quake,
Even as when windy exhalations
Fighting for passage, tilt within the earth.

TECH. As princely lions, when they rouse themselves,
Stretching their paws, and threat'ning herds of beasts,
So in his armor looketh Tamburlaine.
Methinks I see kings kneeling at his feet,
And he, with frowning brows and fiery looks,
Spurning their crowns from off their captive heads.

USUM. And making thee and me, Techelles, kings,
That even to death will follow Tamburlaine.

TAMB. Nobly resolv'd, sweet friends and followers.
These lords, perhaps, do scorn our estimates,
And think we prattle with distempered spirits;
But since they measure our deserts so mean,
That in conceit[33] bear empires on our spears,
Affecting thoughts coequal with the clouds,

[24] Investiture.
[25] A hill in Scythia.
[26] Innocent, harmless.
[27] Part of it was north of Media, which lay between the upper Tigris and the Caspian.
[28] *I.e.*, mature.
[29] Accented on first syllable.
[30] Cutlass; *i.e.*, scimitar.
[31] Invaluable.
[32] Simple, harmless.
[33] Imagination.

They shall be kept our forced followers,
Till with their eyes they view us emperors.
ZENO. The gods, defenders of the innocent,
Will never prosper your intended drifts,
That thus oppress poor friendless passengers.
Therefore at least admit us liberty,
Even as thou hop'st to be eternized
By living Asia's mighty emperor.
AGYD. I hope our lady's treasure and our own
May serve for ransom to our liberties.
Return our mules and empty camels back,
That we may travel into Syria,
Where her betrothed lord, Alcidamus,
Expects th' arrival of her Highness' person.
MAG. And wheresoever we repose ourselves,
We will report but well of Tamburlaine.
TAMB. Disdains Zenocrate to live with me?
Or you, my Lords, to be my followers?
Think you I weigh this treasure more than you?
Not all the gold in India's wealthy arms
Shall buy the meanest soldier in my train. —
Zenocrate, lovelier than the love of Jove,
Brighter than is the silver Rhodope,[34]
Fairer than whitest snow on Scythian hills,
Thy person is more worth to Tamburlaine
Than the possession of the Persian crown,
Which gracious stars have promis'd at my birth.
A hundred Tartars shall attend on thee,
Mounted on steeds swifter than Pegasus;
Thy garments shall be made of Median silk,
Enchas'd with precious jewels of mine own,
More rich and valurous [35] than Zenocrate's.
With milk-white harts upon an ivory sled,
Thou shalt be drawn amidst the frozen pools,
And scale the icy mountains' lofty tops,
Which with thy beauty will be soon resolv'd.[36]
My martial prizes with five hundred men,
Won on the fifty-headed Volga's waves,
Shall all we offer to Zenocrate,
And then myself to fair Zenocrate.
TECH. What now? in love?
TAMB. Techelles, women must be flattered;
But this is she with whom I am in love.

Enter a Soldier.

SOLD. News! news!
TAMB. How now, what's the matter?
SOLD. A thousand Persian horsemen are at hand,
Sent from the King to overcome us all.
TAMB. How now, my Lords of Egypt, and Zenocrate!
Now must your jewels be restor'd again,
And I that triumph'd so be overcome —
How say you, lordings, is not this your hope?
AGYD. We hope yourself will willingly restore them.
TAMB. Such hope, such fortune, have the thousand horse.
Soft ye, my Lords, and sweet Zenocrate.
You must be forced from me ere you go.
A thousand horsemen! We five hundred foot!
An odds too great for us to stand against.
But are they rich? And is their armor good?
SOLD. Their plumed helms are wrought with beaten gold,
Their swords enamell'd, and about their necks
Hangs massy chains of gold down to the waist,
In every part exceeding brave [37] and rich.
TAMB. Then shall we fight courageously with them,
Or look you I should play the orator?
TECH. No; cowards and faint-hearted runaways
Look for orations when the foe is near.
Our swords shall play the orators for us.
USUM. Come, let us meet them at the mountain foot,[38]
And with a sudden and an hot alarm,
Drive all their horses headlong down the hill.
TECH. Come, let us march.
TAMB. Stay, Techelles, ask a parley first.

The Soldiers *enter.*

Open the mails,[39] yet guard the treasure sure;
Lay out our golden wedges to the view,
That their reflections may amaze the Persians;
And look we friendly on them when they come.
But if they offer word or violence,
We'll fight five hundred men at arms to one,
Before we part with our possession;
And 'gainst the general we will lift our swords,
And either lance his greedy thirsting throat,
Or take him prisoner, and his chain shall serve
For manacles, till he be ransom'd home.
TECH. I hear them come; shall we encounter them?

[34] Emend. Dyce; old eds. *Rhodolfe*. These snow-capped Thracian mountains contained silver.
[35] Valuable.
[36] Dissolved.
[37] Fine.
[38] O_4 *top*.
[39] Trunks, baggage.

TAMB. Keep all your standings and not stir a foot;
Myself will bide the danger of the brunt.

Enter THERIDAMAS *with others.*

THER. Where is this Scythian Tamburlaine?

TAMB. Whom seek'st thou, Persian? I am Tamburlaine.

THER. [*aside*] Tamburlaine! A Scythian shepherd so embellished
With nature's pride and richest furniture,
His looks do menace Heaven and dare the gods!
His fiery eyes are fix'd upon the earth,
As if he now devis'd some stratagem,
Or meant to pierce Avernus' darksome vaults
To pull the triple-headed dog from hell.

TAMB. [*aside*] Noble and mild this Persian seems to be,
If outward habit judge the inward man.

TECH. [*aside*] His deep affections [40] make him passionate.

TAMB. [*aside*] With what a majesty he rears his looks! —
In thee, thou valiant man of Persia,
I see the folly of thy emperor.
Art thou but captain of a thousand horse,
That by characters [41] graven in thy brows,
And by thy martial face and stout aspect,
Deserv'st to have the leading of an host?
Forsake thy king, and do but join with me,
And we will triumph over all the world.
I hold the Fates bound fast in iron chains,
And with my hand turn Fortune's wheel about;
And sooner shall the sun fall from his sphere [42]
Than Tamburlaine be slain or overcome.
Draw forth thy sword, thou mighty man at arms,
Intending but to raze my charmed skin,
And Jove himself will stretch his hand from Heaven
To ward the blow and shield me safe from harm.
See how he rains down heaps of gold in showers,
As if he meant to give my soldiers pay;
And as a sure and grounded argument
That I shall be the monarch of the East,
He sends this Soldan's daughter, rich and brave,[43]
To be my queen and portly [44] emperess.
If thou wilt stay with me, renowmed man,
And lead thy thousand horse with my conduct,[45]
Besides thy share of this Egyptian prize,
Those thousand horse shall sweat with martial spoil
Of conquered kingdoms and of cities sack'd.
Both we will walk upon the lofty cliffs,[46]
And Christian merchants [47] that with Russian stems
Plough up huge furrows in the Caspian sea,
Shall vail [48] to us, as lords of all the lake.
Both we will reign as consuls of the earth,
And mighty kings shall be our senators.
Jove sometimes masked in a shepherd's weed,
And by those steps that he hath scal'd the Heavens
May we become immortal like the gods.
Join with me now in this my mean estate
(I call it mean because, being yet obscure,
The nations far remov'd admire me not),
And when my name and honor shall be spread
As far as Boreas claps his brazen wings,
Or fair Boötes sends his cheerful light,
Then shalt thou be competitor [49] with me,
And sit with Tamburlaine in all his majesty.

THER. Not Hermes, prolocutor to the gods,
Could use persuasions more pathetical.[50]

TAMB. Nor are Apollo's oracles more true
Than thou shalt find my vaunts substantial.

TECH. We are his friends, and if the Persian King
Should offer present dukedoms to our state,[51]
We think it loss to make exchange for that
We are assured of by our friend's success.

USUM. And kingdoms at the least we all expect,
Besides the honor in assured conquests,
Where kings shall crouch unto our conquering swords,
And hosts of soldiers stand amaz'd at us,
When with their fearful tongues they shall confess
These are the men that all the world admires.

[40] Feelings.
[41] Accented on second syllable.
[42] Marlowe's astronomy is Ptolemaic.
[43] Fine.
[44] Stately. — "Renowmed" = renowned.
[45] Accented on second syllable.
[46] O_2; other old eds. *clifts*.
[47] Merchantmen.
[48] Strike the topsail or dip the ensign as a mark of submission.
[49] Colleague.
[50] Moving.
[51] For our rank or estate.

THER. What strong enchantments 'tice my yielding soul?
Are these resolved [nobles] [52] Scythians?
But shall I prove a traitor to my king?

TAMB. No, but the trusty friend of Tamburlaine.

THER. Won with thy words, and conquered with thy looks,
I yield myself, my men and horse, to thee,
To be partaker of thy good or ill,
As long as life maintains Theridamas.

TAMB. Theridamas, my friend, take here my hand,
Which is as much as if I swore by Heaven
And call'd the gods to witness of my vow.
Thus shall my heart be still combin'd with thine
Until our bodies turn to elements,
And both our souls aspire celestial thrones.
Techelles and Casane, welcome him.

TECH. Welcome, renowmed Persian, to us all.

USUM. Long may Theridamas remain with us.

TAMB. These are my friends, in whom I more rejoice
Than doth the King of Persia in his crown;
And by the love of Pylades and Orestes,
Whose statutes [53] we adore in Scythia,
Thyself and them shall never part from me
Before I crown you kings in Asia.
Make much of them, gentle Theridamas,
And they will never leave thee till the death.

THER. Nor thee nor them, thrice noble Tamburlaine,
Shall want my heart to be with gladness pierc'd
To do you honor and security.

TAMB. A thousand thanks, worthy Theridamas.
And now fair madam, and my noble Lords,
If you will willingly remain with me
You shall have honors [54] as your merits be;
Or else you shall be forc'd with slavery.

AGYD. We yield unto thee, happy Tamburlaine.

TAMB. For you then, madam, I am out of doubt.

ZENO. I must be pleas'd, perforce. Wretched Zenocrate! *Exeunt.*

[52] Emend. Neilson; old eds. *noble*.
[53] Oo 3, 4, *statues*.
[54] O1 *herors*. (Ellis-Fermor, but neither Wagner nor Brooke.)

ACT II — SCENE I [1]

[*Enter*] COSROE, MENAPHON, ORTYGIUS, CENEUS, *with other* Soldiers.

COS. Thus far are we towards Theridamas,
And valiant Tamburlaine, the man of fame,
The man that in the forehead of his fortune
Bears figures of renown and miracle.
But tell me, that hast seen him, Menaphon,
What stature wields he, and what personage?

MEN. Of stature tall, and straightly fashioned,
Like his desire, lift upwards and divine;
So large of limbs, his joints so strongly knit,
Such breadth of shoulders as might mainly bear
Old Atlas' burden; 'twixt his manly pitch,[2]
A pearl, more worth than all the world, is plac'd,
Wherein by curious sovereignty of art
Are fix'd his piercing instruments of sight,
Whose fiery circles bear encompassed
A heaven of heavenly bodies in their spheres,
That guides his steps and actions to the throne,
Where honor sits invested royally;
Pale of complexion, wrought in him with passion,
Thirsting with sovereignty, with [3] love of arms,
His lofty brows in folds do figure death,
And in their smoothness amity and life;
About them hangs a knot of amber hair,
Wrapped in curls, as fierce Achilles' was,
On which the breath of heaven delights to play,
Making it dance with wanton majesty;
His arms and fingers long and [sinewy],[4]
Betokening valor and excess of strength:
In every part proportioned like the man
Should make the world subdued to Tamburlaine.

COS. Well hast thou portray'd in thy terms of life
The face and personage of a wondrous man;
Nature doth strive with Fortune and his stars
To make him famous in accomplish'd worth;
And well his merits show him to be made
His fortune's master and the king of men,
That could persuade at such a sudden pinch,
With reasons of his valor and his life,

[1] Unlocated by the dramatist; perhaps a road in Media.
[2] Projection of the body; here, shoulders.
[3] Oo 3, 4, *and*.
[4] Emend. Dyce; old eds. *snowy*.

A thousand sworn and overmatching foes.
Then, when our powers in points of swords are join'd
And clos'd in compass of the killing bullet,
Though strait the passage and the port[5] be made
That leads to palace of my brother's life,
Proud is his fortune if we pierce it not.
And when the princely Persian diadem
Shall overweigh his weary, witless head,
And fall like mellowed fruit with shakes of death,
In fair Persia noble Tamburlaine[6]
Shall be my regent and remain as king.

ORTY. In happy hour we have set the crown
Upon your kingly head, that seeks our honor
In joining with the man ordain'd by Heaven,
To further every action to the best.

CEN. He that with shepherds and a little spoil
Durst, in disdain of wrong and tyranny,
Defend his freedom 'gainst a monarchy,
What will he do supported by a king,
Leading a troop of gentlemen and lords,
And stuff'd[7] with treasure for his highest thoughts!

COS. And such shall wait on worthy Tamburlaine.
Our army will be forty thousand strong,
When Tamburlaine and brave Theridamas
Have met us by the river Araris;[8]
And all conjoin'd to meet the witless King,
That now is marching near to Parthia,
And with unwilling soldiers faintly arm'd,
To seek revenge on me and Tamburlaine,
To whom, sweet Menaphon, direct me straight.

MEN. I will, my Lord.

Exeunt.

SCENE II[9]

[*Enter*] MYCETES, MEANDER, *with other* Lords *and* Soldiers.

MYC. Come, my Meander, let us to this gear.[10]
I tell you true, my heart is swoln with wrath
On this same thievish villain, Tamburlaine,
And of that false Cosroe, my traitorous brother.
Would it not grieve a king to be so abus'd
And have a thousand horsemen ta'en away?
And, which is worst, to have his diadem
Sought for by such scald[11] knaves as love him not?
I think it would; well then, by Heavens I swear,
Aurora shall not peep out of her doors,
But I will have Cosroe[12] by the head,
And kill proud Tamburlaine with point of sword.
Tell you the rest, Meander; I have said.

MEAND. Then having pass'd Armenian deserts now,
And [pitch'd][13] our tents under the Georgian hills,
Whose tops are covered with Tartarian[14] thieves,
That lie in ambush, waiting for a prey,
What should we do but bid them battle straight,
And rid the world of those detested troops,
Lest, if we let them linger here awhile,
They gather strength by power of fresh supplies?
This country swarms with vile, outrageous men
That live by rapine and by lawless spoil,
Fit soldiers for the wicked Tamburlaine;
And he that could with gifts and promises
Inveigle him that led a thousand horse,
And make him false his faith unto his king,
Will quickly win such as are like himself.
Therefore cheer up your minds; prepare to fight;
He that can take or slaughter Tamburlaine
Shall rule the province of Albania.
Who brings that traitor's head, Theridamas,
Shall have a government in Media,
Beside the spoil of him and all his train.
But if Cosroe as our spials[15] say,
And as we know, remains with Tamburlaine,
His Highness' pleasure is that he should live,
And be reclaim'd with princely lenity.

[*Enter a* Spy.]

A SPY. An hundred horsemen of my company

[5] Portal.
[6] This line can be regularized by pronouncing "fair" as a dissyllable, or "Persia" as a trisyllable accented on the "i"; but if "fair Persia" be read sonorously with natural emphasis, the line will give no trouble.
[7] Supplied.
[8] Old maps show the river Araxes in Armenia; Herodotus so calls the Oxus. (Ellis-Fermor.)
[9] A camp in Georgia.
[10] Business, affair.
[11] Scurvy.
[12] Here, as often, a trisyllable.
[13] O_2; O_1 *pitch.*
[14] Scythians and Tartars are undistinguished by Marlowe.
[15] Spies.

Scouting abroad upon these champaign plains
Have view'd the army of the Scythians,
Which make reports it far exceeds the King's.

MEAND. Suppose they be in number infinite,
Yet, being void of martial discipline,
All running headlong after greedy spoils
And more regarding gain than victory,
Like to the cruel brothers of the earth,
Sprung of the teeth of dragons venomous,
Their careless swords shall lance their fellows' throats,
And make us triumph in their overthrow.

MYC. Was there such brethren, sweet Meander, say,
That sprung of teeth of dragons venomous?

MEAND. So poets say, my Lord.

MYC. And 't is a pretty toy to be a poet.
Well, well, Meander, thou art deeply read;
And, having thee, I have a jewel sure.
Go on, my Lord, and give your charge, I say;
Thy wit will make us conquerors to-day.

MEAND. Then, noble soldiers, to entrap these thieves,
That live confounded in disordered troops,
If wealth or riches may prevail with them,
We have our camels laden all with gold,
Which you that be but common soldiers
Shall fling in every corner of the field;
And while the baseborn Tartars take it up,
You, fighting more for honor than for gold,
Shall massacre those greedy-minded slaves;
And when their scattered army is subdu'd,
And you march on their slaughtered carcases,
Share equally the gold that bought their lives,
And live like gentlemen in Persia.
Strike up the drum and march courageously;
Fortune herself doth sit upon our crests.

MYC. He tells you true, my masters,[16] so he does.—
Drums, why sound ye not, when Meander speaks?

Exeunt.

SCENE III[17]

[*Enter*] COSROE, TAMBURLAINE, THERIDAMAS, TECHELLES, USUMCASANE, ORTYGIUS, *with others.*

COS. Now, worthy Tamburlaine, have I repos'd
In thy approved[18] fortunes all my hope.
What think'st thou, man, shall come of our attempts?
For, even as from assured oracle,
I take thy doom for satisfaction.

TAMB. And so mistake you not a whit, my Lord;
For fates and oracles [of][19] Heaven have sworn
To royalize the deeds of Tamburlaine,
And make them blest that share in his attempts.
And doubt you not but, if you favor me
And let my fortunes and my valor sway
To some direction in your martial deeds,
The world will strive with hosts of men at arms,
To swarm unto the ensign I support.
The host of Xerxes, which by fame is said
To drink the mighty Parthian Araris,
Was but a handful to that we will have.
Our quivering lances, shaking in the air,
And bullets, like Jove's dreadful thunderbolts,
Enroll'd in flames and fiery smoldering mists,
Shall threat the gods more than Cyclopian[20] wars;
And, with our sun-bright armor as we march,
We'll chase the stars from Heaven and dim their eyes
That stand and muse at our admired arms.

THER. You see, my Lord, what working words he hath;
But when you see his actions [top][21] his speech,
Your speech will stay or so extol his worth
As I shall be commended and excus'd
For turning my poor charge to his direction.
And these his two renowmed friends, my Lord,
Would make one thrust and strive to be retain'd
In such a great degree of amity.

TECH. With duty [and][22] with amity we yield
Our utmost service to the fair Cosroe.

COS. Which I esteem as portion of my crown.
Usumcasane and Techelles both,
When she that rules in Rhamn[u]s'[23] golden gates,
And makes a passage for all prosperous arms,
Shall make me solely Emperor of Asia,
Then shall your meeds and valors be advanc'd
To rooms of honor and nobility.

[16] Gentlemen.
[17] Tamburlaine's camp in the Georgian hills.
[18] Tested.

[19] Add. Robinson.
[20] *I.e.*, the Titans'.
[21] Emend. Dyce; old eds. *stop*.
[22] O_4; earlier eds. *not*.
[23] In Attica; Nemesis had a temple there.

TAMB. Then haste, Cosroe, to be king alone,
That I with these, my friends, and all my men
May triumph in our long-expected fate.
The King, your brother, is now hard at hand;
Meet with the fool, and rid your royal shoulders
Of such a burden as outweighs the sands
And all the craggy rocks of Caspia.

[*Enter a* Messenger.]

MES. My Lord, we have discovered the enemy
Ready to charge you with a mighty army.
COS. Come, Tamburlaine, now whet thy winged sword,
And lift thy lofty arm into the clouds,
That it may reach the King of Persia's crown,
And set it safe on my victorious head.
TAMB. See where it is, the keenest cu[r]tle-axe
That e'er made passage thorough Persian arms.
These are the wings shall make it fly as swift
As doth the lightning or the breath of Heaven,
And kill as sure[24] as it swiftly flies.
COS. Thy words assure me of kind success;
Go, valiant soldier, go before and charge
The fainting army of that foolish king.
TAMB. Usumcasane and Techelles, come;
We are enough to scare the enemy,
And more than needs to make an emperor.
[*Exeunt.*]

[SCENE IV][25]

To the battle, and MYCETES *comes out alone with his crown in his hand, offering*[26] *to hide it.*

MYC. Accurs'd be he that first invented war!
They knew not, ah, they knew not, simple men,
How those[27] were hit by pelting cannon shot
Stand staggering like a quivering aspen leaf
Fearing the force of Boreas' boist'rous blasts.
In what a lamentable case were I
If Nature had not given me wisdom's lore!
For kings are clouts[28] that every man shoots at,
Our crown the pin that thousands seek to cleave;
Therefore in policy I think it good
To hide it close, a goodly stratagem,
And far from any man that is a fool.
So shall I not be known; or, if I be,
They cannot take away my crown from me. —
Here will I hide it in this simple hole.

Enter TAMBURLAINE.

TAMB. What fearful coward, straggling from the camp,
When kings themselves are present in the field?
MYC. Thou liest.
TAMB. Base villain, dar'st thou give the lie?
MYC. Away; I am the King; go, touch me not.
Thou break'st the law of arms unless thou kneel
And cry me, "Mercy, noble King."
TAMB. Are you the witty[29] King of Persia?
MYC. Ay, marry am I; have you any suit to me?
TAMB. I would entreat you speak but three wise words.
MYC. So I can when I see my time.
TAMB. Is this your crown?
MYC. Ay, didst thou ever see a fairer?
TAMB. You will not sell it, will ye?
MYC. Such another word and I will have thee executed. Come, give it me.[30]
TAMB. No; I took it prisoner.
MYC. You lie; I gave it you.
TAMB. Then 't is mine.
MYC. No; I mean, I let you keep it.
TAMB. Well, I mean you shall have it again.
Here, take it for a while; I lend it thee,
Till I may see thee hemm'd with armed men.
Then shalt thou see me pull it from thy head;
Thou art no match for mighty Tamburlaine.
[*Exit.*]
MYC. O gods! Is this Tamburlaine the thief?
I marvel much he stole it not away.
Sound trumpets to the battle, and he runs in.

[24] Pronounce as dissyllable.
[25] A battlefield.
[26] Attempting.
[27] Understand "who."
[28] The white centres of archery targets. The *pin* was the peg at the dead centre of the target.

[29] Clever, sagacious.
[30] This departure from blank verse looks suspicious. We may have here a fragment of a longer comic scene, perhaps not composed by Marlowe; or perhaps we have merely actors' gags here. The publisher of O_1 states that he has "left out some fond and frivolous gestures" which "were showed upon the stage in their graced deformities."

[Scene V] [31]

[*Enter*] Cosroe, Tamburlaine, Theridamas, Menaphon, Meander, Ortygius, Techelles, [*and*] Usumcasane, *with others.*

Tamb. Hold thee, Cosroe; wear two imperial crowns.
Think thee invested now as royally,
Even by the mighty hand of Tamburlaine,
As if as many kings as could encompass thee [32]
With greatest pomp, had crown'd thee emperor.

Cos. So do I, thrice renowmed man at arms,
And none shall keep the crown but Tamburlaine:
Thee do I make my regent of Persia,
And general-lieutenant of my armies. —
Meander, you, that were our brother's guide,
And chiefest counsellor in all his acts,
Since he is yielded to the stroke of war,
On your submission we with thanks excuse,
And give you equal place in our affairs.

Meand. Most happy Emperor, in humblest terms,
I vow my service to your Majesty,
With utmost virtue of my faith and duty.

Cos. Thanks, good Meander; then, Cosroe, reign
And govern Persia in her former pomp.
Now send embassage to thy neighbor kings,
And let them know the Persian king is chang'd —
From one that knew not what a king should do,
To one that can command what 'longs thereto.
And now we will to fair Persepolis,
With twenty thousand expert soldiers.
The lords and captains of my brother's camp
With little slaughter take Meander's course
And gladly yield them to my gracious rule.
Ortygius and Menaphon, my trusty friends, [33]
Now will I gratify [34] your former good,
And grace your calling with a greater sway.

Orty. And as we ever [aim'd] [35] at your behoof,
And sought your state [36] all honor it deserv'd,
So will we with our powers and our lives
Endeavor to preserve and prosper it.

Cos. I will not thank thee, sweet Ortygius;
Better replies shall prove my purposes.
And now, Lord Tamburlaine, my brother's camp
I leave to thee and to Theridamas,
To follow me to fair Persepolis.
Then will we march to all those Indian mines
My witless brother to the Christians lost,
And ransom them with fame and usury.
And till thou overtake me, Tamburlaine,
Staying to order all the scattered troops,
Farewell, Lord Regent and his happy friends!
I long to sit upon my brother's throne.

Meand. Your Majesty shall shortly have your wish,
And ride in triumph through Persepolis.

Exeunt [*all but*] Tamburlaine, Techelles, Theridamas, [*and*] Usumcasane.

Tamb. "And ride in triumph through Persepolis!"
Is it not brave to be a king, Techelles?
Usumcasane and Theridamas,
Is it not passing brave to be a king,
"And ride in triumph through Persepolis"?

Tech. Oh, my Lord, 't is sweet and full of pomp.

Usum. To be a king is half to be a god.

Ther. A god is not so glorious as a king.
I think the pleasure they enjoy in Heaven
Can not compare with kingly joys in earth.
To wear a crown enchas'd with pearl and gold,
Whose virtues carry with it life and death;
To ask and have, command and be obeyed;
When looks breed love, with looks to gain the prize —
Such power attractive shines in princes' eyes.

Tamb. Why say, Theridamas, wilt thou be a king?

Ther. Nay, though I praise it, I can live without it.

Tamb. What says my other friends? Will you be kings?

Tech. Ay, if I could, with all my heart, my Lord.

Tamb. Why, that 's well said, Techelles; so would I,
And so would you, my masters, would you not?

Usum. What then, my Lord?

Tamb. Why then, [Casane,] [37] shall we wish for aught
The world affords in greatest novelty,
And rest attemptless, faint, and destitute?
Methinks we should not: I am strongly mov'd
That, if I should desire the Persian crown,
I could attain it with a wondrous ease.

[31] The same.
[32] Another "apparent" Alexandrine.
[33] Not an Alexandrine.
[34] Reward.
[35] Cor. O_3; Oo 1, 2, *and.*
[36] Rank, place.
[37] Old eds. *Casanes.*

And would not all our soldiers soon consent,
If we should aim at such a dignity?

THER. I know they would with our persuasions.

TAMB. Why then, Theridamas, I 'll first assay
To get the Persian kingdom to myself;
Then thou for Parthia, they for Scythia and Media;
And, if I prosper, all shall be as sure
As if the Turk, the Pope, Afric, and Greece,
Came creeping to us with their crowns apace.[38]

TECH. Then shall we send to this triumphing[39] king,
And bid him battle for his novel crown?

USUM. Nay, quickly, then, before his room be hot.

TAMB. 'T will prove a pretty jest, in faith, my friends.

THER. A jest to charge on twenty thousand men?
I judge the purchase[40] more important far.

TAMB. Judge by thyself, Theridamas, not me;
For presently Techelles here shall haste
To bid him battle ere he pass too far,
And lose more labor than the gain will quit.[41]
Then shalt thou see the Scythian Tamburlaine
Make but a jest to win the Persian crown.
Techelles, take a thousand horse with thee,
And bid him turn [him][42] back to war with us,
That only made him king to make us sport.
We will not steal upon him cowardly,
But give him warning and more warriors.
Haste thee, Techelles; we will follow thee.
What saith Theridamas?

THER. Go on, for me.[43]

Exeunt.

SCENE VI[44]

[*Enter*] COSROE, MEANDER, ORTYGIUS, MENAPHON, *with other* Soldiers.

COS. What means this devilish shepherd to aspire
With such a giantly[45] presumption
To cast up hills against the face of Heaven,
And dare the force of angry Jupiter?
But as he thrust them underneath the hills
And press'd out fire[46] from their burning jaws,
So will I send this monstrous slave to hell,
Where flames shall ever feed upon his soul.

MEAND. Some powers divine, or else infernal, mix'd
Their angry seeds at his conception;
For he was never sprung of human race,
Since with the spirit of his fearful pride
He dares so doubtlessly resolve of rule,
And by profession be ambitious.

ORTY. What god or fiend or spirit of the earth,
Or monster turned to a manly shape,
Or of what mold or mettle he be made,
What star or state soever govern him,
Let us put on our meet encount'ring minds
And, in detesting such a devilish thief,
In love of honor and defence of right,
Be arm'd against the hate of such a foe,
Whether from earth, or hell, or Heaven, he grow.

COS. Nobly resolv'd, my good Ortygius;
And since we all have suck'd one wholesome air,
And with the same proportion of elements
Resolve,[47] I hope we are resembled,
Vowing our loves to equal death and life.
Let 's cheer our soldiers to encounter him,
That grievous image of ingratitude,
That fiery thirster after sovereignty,
And burn him in the fury of that flame,
That none can quench but blood and empery.
Resolve, my Lords and loving soldiers, now
To save your king and country from decay.
Then strike up, drum; and all the stars that make
The loathsome circle of my dated life,
Direct my weapon to his barbarous heart
That thus opposeth him against the gods
And scorns the powers that govern Persia.

[*Exeunt.*]

[SCENE VII][48]

Enter to the battle; and after the battle, enter COSROE *wounded,* THERIDAMAS, TAMBURLAINE, TECHELLES, USUMCASANE, *with others.*

COS. Barbarous and bloody Tamburlaine,
Thus to deprive me of my crown and life!
Treacherous and false Theridamas,
Even at the morning of my happy state,

[38] Oo 3, 4, *apeece.*
[39] Accented on the second syllable.
[40] Undertaking.
[41] Repay, requite.
[42] Emend. Robinson; old eds. *his.*
[43] For all of me, as far as I'm concerned.
[44] Unlocated, but presumably on the borders of Armenia.
[45] *I.e.*, like the Titans.
[46] A dissyllable here.
[47] Dissolve; *i.e.*, when we die we shall disintegrate into the same elements.
[48] A battlefield.

Scarce being seated in my royal throne,
To work my downfall and untimely end!
An uncouth pain torments my grieved soul,
And Death arrests the organ of my voice,
Who, ent'ring at the breach thy sword hath made,
Sacks every vein and artier of my heart,
Bloody and insatiate Tamburlaine!

TAMB. The thirst of reign and sweetness of a crown,
That caus'd the eldest son of heavenly Ops
To thrust his doting father from his chair
And place himself in the imperial Heaven,
Mov'd me to manage arms against thy state.
What better precedent than mighty Jove?
Nature that fram'd us of four elements,
Warring within our breasts for regiment,[49]
Doth teach us all to have aspiring minds.
Our souls, whose faculties can comprehend
The wondrous architecture of the world
And measure every wand'ring planet's course,
Still climbing after knowledge infinite,
And always moving as the restless spheres,
Wills us to wear ourselves and never rest
Until we reach the ripest fruit of all,
That perfect bliss and sole felicity,
The sweet fruition of an earthly crown.

THER. And that made me to join with Tamburlaine;
For he is gross and like the massy earth
That moves not upwards, nor by princely deeds
Doth mean to soar above the highest sort.

TECH. And that made us the friends of Tamburlaine,
To lift our swords against the Persian king.

USUM. For as, when Jove did thrust old Saturn down,
Neptune and Dis gain'd each of them a crown,
So do we hope to reign in Asia,
If Tamburlaine be plac'd in Persia.

COS. The strangest men that ever nature made!
I know not how to take their tyrannies.
My bloodless body waxeth chill and cold,
And with my blood my life slides through my wound;
My soul begins to take her flight to hell,
And summons all my senses to depart.
The heat and moisture, which did feed each other,
For want of nourishment to feed them both,
Is dry and cold; and now doth ghastly death
With greedy talents [50] gripe my bleeding heart,

[49] Rule. [50] Talons.

And like a harpy [51] tires [52] on my life.
Theridamas and Tamburlaine, I die;
And fearful vengeance light upon you both!
[COSROE *dies*. TAMBURLAINE] *takes the crown and puts it on.*

TAMB. Not all the curses which the Furies breathe
Shall make me leave so rich a prize as this.
Theridamas, Techelles, and the rest,
Who think you now is King of Persia?

ALL. Tamburlaine! Tamburlaine!

TAMB. Though Mars himself, the angry god of arms,
And all the earthly potentates, conspire
To dispossess me of this diadem,
Yet will I wear it in despite of them,
As great commander of this eastern world,
If you but say that Tamburlaine shall reign.

ALL. Long live Tamburlaine and reign in Asia!

TAMB. So now it is more surer on my head,
Than if the gods had held a parliament
And all pronounc'd me King of Persia.
[*Exeunt.*]

ACT III — SCENE I[1]

[*Enter*] BAJAZETH, *the* KINGS *of* FEZ, MOROCCO, *and* ARGIER,[2] *with others, in great pomp.*

BAJ. Great Kings of Barbary and my portly bassoes,[3]
We hear the Tartars and the eastern thieves,
Under the conduct of one Tamburlaine,
Presume a bickering with your emperor,
And thinks to rouse us from our dreadful siege
Of the famous Grecian Constantinople.
You know our army is invincible;
As many circumcised Turks we have,
And warlike bands of Christians renied,[4]
As hath the ocean or the Terrene [5] sea
Small drops of water when the moon begins
To join in one her semicircled horns.
Yet would we not be brav'd with foreign power,
Nor raise our siege before the Grecians yield,
Or breathless lie before the city walls.

K. OF FEZ. Renowmed Emperor, and mighty general,
What if you sent the bassoes of your guard

[51] O_2 *Harpye;* other old eds. *Harpyr, Harper.*
[52] Preys, tears. A dissyllable here.
[1] The Turkish camp before Constantinople.
[2] Algiers.
[3] Stately pashas.
[4] Apostate; cf. "reneged."
[5] Mediterranean.

To charge him to remain in Asia,
Or else to threaten death and deadly arms
As from the mouth of mighty Bajazeth?

BAJ. Hie thee, my basso, fast to Persia;
Tell him thy lord, the Turkish Emperor,
Dread Lord of Afric, Europe, and Asia,
Great King and conqueror of Græcia,
The ocean, Terrene, and the Coal-black sea,
The high and highest monarch of the world,
Wills and commands (for say not I entreat),
Not once to set his foot in Africa,
Or spread his colors [6] in Græcia,
Lest he incur the fury of my wrath.
Tell him I am content to take a truce,
Because I hear he bears a valiant mind.
But if, presuming on his silly power,
He be so mad to manage arms with me,
Then stay thou with him; say I bid thee so.
And if, before the sun have measured heaven
With triple circuit, thou regreet us not,
We mean to take his morning's next arise
For messenger he will not be reclaim'd,
And mean to fetch thee in despite of him.

BAS. Most great and puissant monarch of the earth,
Your basso will accomplish your behest
And show your pleasure to the Persian,
As fits the legate of the stately Turk.

Exit Basso.

K. OF ARG. They say he is the King of Persia;
But, if he dare attempt to stir your siege,
'T were requisite he should be ten times more,
For all flesh quakes at your magnificence.

BAJ. True, Argier, and tremble [7] at my looks.

K. OF MOR. The spring is hind'red by your smothering host,
For neither rain can fall upon the earth
Nor sun reflex his virtuous [8] beams thereon,
The ground is mantled with such multitudes.

BAJ. All this is true as holy Mahomet;
And all the trees are blasted with our breaths.

K. OF FEZ. What thinks your Greatness best to be achiev'd
In pursuit of the city's overthrow?

BAJ. I will the captive pioners of Argier
Cut off the water that by leaden pipes
Runs to the city from the mountain Carnon.
Two thousand horse shall forage up and down,
That no relief or succor come by land;
And all the sea my galleys countermand.[9]
Then shall our footmen lie within the trench,
And with their cannons, mouth'd like Orcus' gulf,[10]
Batter the walls, and we will enter in;
And thus the Grecians shall be conquered.

Exeunt.

SCENE II [11]

[*Enter*] AGYDAS, ZENOCRATE, ANIPPE, *with others.*

[AGYD.] Madam Zenocrate, may I presume
To know the cause of these unquiet fits,
That work such trouble to your wonted rest?
'T is more than pity such a heavenly face
Should by heart's sorrow wax so wan and pale,
When your offensive rape [12] by Tamburlaine,
Which of your whole displeasures should be most,
Hath seem'd to be digested long ago.

ZENO. Although it be digested long ago,
As his exceeding favors have deserv'd,
And might content the Queen of Heaven,[13] as well
As it hath chang'd my first conceiv'd disdain,
Yet, since, a farther passion feeds my thoughts
With ceaseless and disconsolate conceits,
Which dyes my looks so lifeless as they are,
And might, if my extremes had full events,
Make me the ghastly counterfeit of death.

AGYD. Eternal Heaven sooner be dissolv'd,
And all that pierceth Phœbe's silver eye,
Before such hap fall to Zenocrate.

ZENO. Ah, life and soul, still hover in his breast
And leave my body senseless as the earth;
Or else unite you to his life and soul,
That I may live and die with Tamburlaine.

Enter [*behind*] TAMBURLAINE, *with* TECHELLES *and others.*

AGYD. With Tamburlaine! Ah, fair Zenocrate,
Let not a man so vile and barbarous,
That holds you from your father in despite
And keeps you from the honors of a queen,
Being suppos'd his worthless concubine,
Be honored with your love but for necessity.
So, now the mighty Soldan hears of you,
Your Highness needs not doubt but in short time

[6] Mod. eds. add a monosyllable, but if the "r" be rolled the metre comes right.
[7] The "r" should be rolled, or a trisyllable be made of "Argier."
[8] Powerful.

[9] Control.
[10] Hell-mouth.
[11] Unlocated; perhaps the palace at Persepolis.
[12] Capture.
[13] Juno.

He will with Tamburlaine's destruction
Redeem you from this deadly servitude.

ZENO. [Agydas,] [14] leave to wound me with these words,
And speak of Tamburlaine as he deserves.
The entertainment we have had of him
Is far from villainy or servitude,
And might in noble minds be counted princely.

AGYD. How can you fancy [15] one that looks so fierce,
Only dispos'd to martial stratagems;
Who, when he shall embrace you in his arms,
Will tell how many thousand men he slew;
And, when you look for amorous discourse,
Will rattle forth his facts of war and blood,
Too harsh a subject for your dainty ears?

ZENO. As looks the Sun through Nilus' flowing stream,
Or when the Morning holds him in her arms,
So looks my lordly love, fair Tamburlaine;
His talk much sweeter than the Muses' song
They sung for honor 'gainst Pierides,[16]
Or when Minerva did with Neptune strive [17];
And higher would I rear my estimate
Than Juno, sister to the highest god,
If I were match'd with mighty Tamburlaine.

AGYD. Yet be not so inconstant in your love,
But let the young Arabian live in hope
After your rescue to enjoy his choice.
You see, though first the King of Persia,
Being a shepherd, seem'd to love you much,
Now in his majesty he leaves those looks,
Those words of favor, and those comfortings,
And gives no more than common courtesies.

ZENO. Thence rise the tears that so distain my cheeks,
Fearing [18] his love through my unworthiness.

TAMBURLAINE *goes to her and takes her away lovingly by the hand, looking wrathfully on* AGYDAS, *and says nothing.* [*Exeunt all but* AGYDAS.]

AGYD. Betray'd by fortune and suspicious love,
Threat'ned with frowning wrath and jealousy,
Surpris'd with fear of hideous revenge,
I stand aghast; but most astonied [19]
To see his choler shut in secret thoughts,
And wrapp'd in silence of his angry soul.
Upon his brows was portray'd ugly death;
And in his eyes the fury of his heart,
That shine as comets, menacing revenge,
And casts a pale complexion on his cheeks.
As when the seaman sees the Hyades
Gather an army of Cimmerian [20] clouds,
(Auster and Aquilon with winged steeds,
All sweating, tilt about the watery Heavens,
With shivering spears enforcing thunderclaps,
And from their shields strike flames of lightening,)
All fearful folds his sails and sounds the main,
Lifting his prayers to the Heavens for aid
Against the terror of the winds and waves;
So fares Agydas for the late-felt frowns,
That sent a tempest to my daunted thoughts,
And makes my soul divine her overthrow.

Re-enter TECHELLES *with a naked dagger.*

TECH. See you, Agydas, how the King salutes you.
He bids you prophesy what it imports. *Exit.*[21]

AGYD. I prophesied before, and now I prove
The killing frowns of jealousy and love.
He needed not with words confirm my fear,
For words are vain where working tools present
The naked action of my threat'ned end:
It says, Agydas, thou shalt surely die,
And of extremities elect the least;
More honor and less pain it may procure
To die by this resolved hand of thine,
Than stay [22] the torments he and Heaven have sworn.
Then haste, Agydas, and prevent the plagues
Which thy prolonged fates may draw on thee.
Go, wander, free from fear of tyrant's rage,
Removed from the torments and the hell
Wherewith he may excruciate thy soul;
And let Agydas by Agydas die,
And with this stab slumber eternally.
[*Stabs himself.*] [23]

[*Re-enter* TECHELLES *with* USUMCASANE.] [24]

TECH. Usumcasane, see, how right the man
Hath hit the meaning of my Lord, the King.

USUM. Faith, and, Techelles, it was manly done;
And since he was so wise and honorable,

[14] Add. Dyce.
[15] Fall in love with.
[16] The daughters of Pierus.
[17] Alluding to the strife of Athene and Poseidon for the possession of Athens.
[18] Fearing for.
[19] Astonished.
[20] *I.e.*, black.
[21] Om. $Oo_{3,4}$.
[22] Await.
[23] Add. O_4.
[24] Add. Neilson.

Let us afford him now the bearing hence,
And crave his triple-worthy burial.
TECH. Agreed, Casane; we will honor him.
[*Exeunt bearing out the body.*]

SCENE III [25]

[*Enter*] TAMBURLAINE, TECHELLES, USUMCASANE, THERIDAMAS, BASSO, ZENOCRATE, [ANIPPE,] *with others.*

TAMB. Basso, by this thy lord and master knows
I mean to meet him in Bithynia.
See how he comes! Tush, Turks are full of brags,
And menace more than they can well perform.
He meet me in the field, and fetch thee hence?
Alas, poor Turk, his fortune is too weak
T' encounter with the strength of Tamburlaine.
View well my camp, and speak indifferently; [26]
Do not my captains and my soldiers look
As if they meant to conquer Africa?
BAS. Your men are valiant, but their number few,
And cannot terrify his mighty host.
My lord, the great commander of the world,
Besides fifteen contributory kings
Hath now in arms ten thousand Janissaries,
Mounted on lusty Mauritanian steeds,
Brought to the war by men of Tripoli;
Two hundred thousand footmen that have serv'd
In two set battles fought in Græcia;
And, for the expedition of this war,
If he think good, can from his garrisons
Withdraw as many more to follow him.
TECH. The more he brings the greater is the spoil;
For, when they perish by our warlike hands,
We mean to seat our footmen on their steeds,
And rifle all those stately Janisars.
TAMB. But will those kings accompany your lord?
BAS. Such as his Highness please; but some must stay
To rule the provinces he late subdu'd.
TAMB. Then fight courageously: their crowns are yours.
This hand shall set them on your conquering heads,
That made me Emperor of Asia.
USUM. Let him bring millions infinite of men,
Unpeopling Western Africa and Greece;
Yet we assure us of the victory.
THER. Even he that in a trice vanquish'd two kings,
More mighty than the Turkish Emperor,
Shall rouse him out of Europe, and pursue
His scattered army till they yield or die.
TAMB. Well said, Theridamas; speak in that mood;
For "will" and "shall" best fitteth Tamburlaine,
Whose smiling stars gives him assured hope
Of martial triumph ere he meet his foes.
I that am term'd the scourge and wrath of God,
The only fear and terror of the world,
Will first subdue the Turk, and then enlarge
Those Christian captives, which you keep as slaves,
Burdening their bodies with your heavy chains
And feeding them with thin and slender fare,
That naked row about the Terrene sea,
And when they chance to breathe and rest a space,
Are punish'd with bastones [27] so grievously
That they lie panting on the galley's side
And strive for life at every stroke they give.
These are the cruel pirates of Argier,
That damned train, the scum of Africa,
Inhabited with straggling runagates,[28]
That make quick havoc of the Christian blood;
But, as I live, that town shall curse the time
That Tamburlaine set foot in Africa.

Enter BAJAZETH *with his* BASSOES *and contributory* KINGS [*of* FEZ, MOROCCO, *and* ARGIER; ZABINA *and* EBEA].

BAJ. Bassoes and Janissaries of my guard,
Attend upon the person of your lord,
The greatest potentate of Africa.
TAMB. Techelles and the rest, prepare your swords;
I mean t' encounter with that Bajazeth.
BAJ. Kings of Fez, Moroccus, and Argier,
He calls me Bajazeth, whom you call Lord!
Note the presumption of this Scythian slave!
I tell thee, villain, those that lead my horse
Have to their names titles of dignity;
And dar'st thou bluntly call me Bajazeth?
TAMB. And know, thou Turk, that those which lead my horse

[25] A battlefield in Bithynia.
[26] Impartially.
[27] Sticks.
[28] Vagabonds, deserters.

Shall lead thee captive thorough Africa ;
And dar'st thou bluntly call me Tamburlaine?

BAJ. By Mahomet my kinsman's sepulchre,
And by the holy Alc[o]r[a]n, I swear
He shall be made a chaste and lustless eunuch,
And in my sarell [29] tend my concubines ;
And all his captains, that thus stoutly stand,
Shall draw the chariot of my emperess,
Whom I have brought to see their overthrow.

TAMB. By this my sword, that conquer'd Persia,
Thy fall shall make me famous through the world.
I will not tell thee how I 'll handle thee,
But every common soldier of my camp
Shall smile to see thy miserable state.

K. OF FEZ. What means the mighty Turkish Emperor,
To talk with one so base as Tamburlaine?

K. OF MOR. Ye Moors and valiant men of Barbary,
How can ye suffer these indignities?

K. OF ARG. Leave words, and let them feel your lances' points,
Which glided through the bowels of the Greeks.

BAJ. Well said, my stout contributory kings ;
Your threefold army and my hugy host
Shall swallow up these baseborn Persians.

TECH. Puissant, renowmed, and mighty Tamburlaine,
Why stay we thus prolonging all their lives?

THER. I long to see those crowns won by our swords,
That we may reign as kings of Africa.

USUM. What coward would not fight for such a prize?

TAMB. Fight all courageously and be you kings ;
I speak it, and my words are oracles.

BAJ. Zabina, mother of three braver boys
Than Hercules, that in his infancy
Did pash [30] the jaws of serpents venomous ;
Whose hands are made to gripe a warlike lance,
Their shoulders broad for complete armor fit,
Their limbs more large, and of a bigger size,
Than all the brats ysprung from Typhon's loins ;
Who, when they come unto their father's age,
Will batter turrets with their manly fists ;
Sit here upon this royal chair of state,
And on thy head wear my imperial crown,
Until I bring this sturdy Tamburlaine
And all his captains bound in captive chains.

ZAB. Such good success happen to Bajazeth.

TAMB. Zenocrate, the loveliest maid alive,
Fairer than rocks of pearl and precious stone,
The only paragon of Tamburlaine,
Whose eyes are brighter than the lamps of Heaven
And speech more pleasant than sweet harmony,
That with thy looks canst clear the darkened sky,
And calm the rage of thund'ring Jupiter,
Sit down by her, adorned with my crown,
As if thou wert the Empress of the world.
Stir not, Zenocrate, until thou see
Me march victoriously with all my men,
Triumphing over him and these his kings,
Which I will bring as vassals to thy feet.
Till then take thou my crown, vaunt of my worth,
And manage words with her, as we will arms.

ZENO. And may my love, the King of Persia,
Return with victory and free from wound.

BAJ. Now shalt thou feel the force of Turkish arms,
Which lately made all Europe quake for fear.
I have of Turks, Arabians, Moors, and Jews,
Enough to cover all Bithynia.
Let thousands die ; their slaughtered carcasses
Shall serve for walls and bulwarks to the rest ;
And as the heads of Hydra, so my power,
Subdued, shall stand as mighty as before.
If they should yield their necks unto the sword,
Thy soldiers' arms could not endure to strike
So many blows as I have heads for thee.
Thou knowest not, foolish-hardy Tamburlaine,
What 't is to meet me in the open field,
That leave no ground for thee to march upon.

TAMB. Our conquering swords shall marshal us the way
We use to march upon the slaughtered foe,
Trampling their bowels with our horses' hoofs,
Brave horses bred on the white Tartarian hills.
My camp is like to Julius Cæsar's host,
That never fought but had the victory ;
Nor in Pharsalia was there such hot war
As these, my followers, willingly would have.
Legions of spirits fleeting [31] in the air
Direct our bullets and our weapons' points,
And make [your] [32] strokes to wound the senseless [air] ; [33]

[29] Seraglio.
[30] Smash.
[31] Floating.
[32] Cor. Dyce ; old eds. *our*.
[33] Conj. Dyce ; $O_{1,3,4}$ *lure;* O_2 *lute.*

And, when she sees our bloody colors spread,
Then Victory begins to take her flight,
Resting herself upon my milk-white tent. —
But come, my Lords, to weapons let us fall;
The field is ours, the Turk, his wife, and all.

Exit with his followers.

BAJ. Come, kings and bassoes, let us glut our swords,
That thirst to drink the feeble Persians' blood.

Exit with his followers.

ZAB. Base concubine, must thou be plac'd by me,
That am the empress of the mighty Turk?

ZENO. Disdainful Turkess and unreverend boss,[34]
Call'st thou me concubine, that am betroth'd
Unto the great and mighty Tamburlaine?

ZAB. To Tamburlaine, the great Tartarian thief?

ZENO. Thou wilt repent these lavish words of thine,
When thy great basso-master and thyself
Must plead for mercy at his kingly feet,
And sue to me to be your advocates.

ZAB. And sue to thee! I tell thee, shameless girl,
Thou shalt be laundress to my waiting maid!—
How lik'st thou her, Ebea? Will she serve?

EBEA. Madam, she thinks, perhaps, she is too fine;
But I shall turn her into other weeds,
And make her dainty fingers fall to work.

ZENO. Hear'st thou, Anippe, how thy drudge doth talk?
And how my slave, her mistress, menaceth?
Both for their sauciness shall be employed
To dress the common soldiers' meat and drink,
For we will scorn they should come near ourselves.

ANIP. Yet sometimes let your Highness send for them
To do the work my chambermaid disdains.

They sound the battle within, and stay.

ZENO. Ye gods and powers that govern Persia,
And made my lordly love her worthy king,
Now strengthen him against the Turkish Bajazeth,
And let his foes, like flocks of fearful roes
Pursu'd by hunters, fly his angry looks,
That I may see him issue conqueror.

ZAB. Now, Mahomet, solicit God himself,
And make him rain down murdering[35] shot from Heaven
To dash the Scythians' brains and strike them dead
That dare to manage arms with him
That offered jewels to thy sacred shrine,
When first he warr'd against the Christians.

[They sound] to the battle again.

ZENO. By this the Turks lie welt'ring in their blood,
And Tamburlaine is Lord of Africa.

ZAB. Thou art deceiv'd. I heard the trumpets sound
As when my emperor overthrew the Greeks,
And led them captive into Africa.
Straight will I use thee as thy pride deserves;
Prepare thyself to live and die my slave.

ZENO. If Mahomet should come from Heaven and swear
My royal lord is slain or conquered,
Yet should he not persuade me otherwise
But that he lives and will be conqueror.

BAJAZETH *flies and* [TAMBURLAINE] *pursues him. The battle short, and they enter;* BAJAZETH *is overcome.*

TAMB. Now, King of bassoes, who is conqueror?

BAJ. Thou, by the fortune of this damned [foil].[36]

TAMB. Where are your stout contributory kings?

Re-enter TECHELLES, THERIDAMAS, [*and*] USUMCASANE.

TECH. We have their crowns; their bodies strow the field.

TAMB. Each man a crown! Why, kingly fought, i' faith.
Deliver them into my treasury.

ZENO. Now let me offer to my gracious Lord
His royal crown again so highly won.

TAMB. Nay, take the Turkish crown from her, Zenocrate,
And crown me Emperor of Africa.

ZAB. No, Tamburlaine; though now thou gat the best
Thou shalt not yet be Lord of Africa.

THER. Give her the crown, Turkess, you were best.

He takes it from her, and gives it ZENOCRATE.

[34] Fat woman.

[35] From "murderers", a species of small cannon used to scatter shot at close range.

[36] Repulse; emend. Dyce. Old eds. *soile*. Cf. l. 235.

ZAB. Injurious villains! thieves! runagates!
How dare you thus abuse my Majesty?
THER. Here, madam, you are Empress; she is none.
TAMB. Not now, Theridamas; her time is past.
The pillars that have bolstered up those terms
Are fall'n in clusters at my conquering feet.
ZAB. Though he be prisoner, he may be ransomed.
TAMB. Not all the world shall ransom Bajazeth.
BAJ. Ah, fair Zabina, we have lost the field;
And never had the Turkish emperor
So great a foil by any foreign foe.
Now will the Christian miscreants be glad,
Ringing with joy their superstitious bells
And making bonfires for my overthrow.
But, ere I die, those foul idolaters
Shall make me bonfires with their filthy bones;
For, though the glory of this day be lost,
Afric and Greece have garrisons enough
To make me sovereign of the earth again.
TAMB. Those walled garrisons will I subdue,
And write myself great Lord of Africa.
So from the East unto the furthest West
Shall Tamburlaine extend his puissant arm.
The galleys and those pilling[37] brigandines
That yearly sail to the Venetian gulf
And hover in the Straits for Christians' wrack
Shall lie at anchor in the isle Asant,[38]
Until the Persian fleet and men-of-war,
Sailing along the oriental sea,
Have fetch'd about the Indian continent,
Even from Persepolis to Mexico
And thence unto the straits of Jubalter;[39]
Where they shall meet and join their force in one,
Keeping in awe the bay of Portingale,[40]
And all the ocean by the British shore;
And by this means I'll win the world at last.
BAJ. Yet set a ransom on me, Tamburlaine.
TAMB. What, think'st thou Tamburlaine esteems thy gold?
I'll make the kings of India, ere I die,
Offer their mines, to sue for peace, to me,
And dig for treasure to appease my wrath.
Come, bind them both, and one lead in the Turk;
The Turkess let my love's maid lead away.
They bind them.

[37] Robbing, pillaging.
[38] Zante. (Bullen.)
[39] Gibraltar.
[40] Bay of Biscay.

BAJ. Ah, villains, dare ye touch my sacred arms?
O Mahomet! O sleepy Mahomet!
ZAB. O cursed Mahomet, that makest us thus
The slaves to Scythians rude and barbarous!
TAMB. Come, bring them in; and, for this happy conquest,
Triumph and solemnize a martial feast.
Exeunt.

ACT IV — SCENE I[1]

[*Enter the*] SOLDAN *of* EGYPT, *with three or four* Lords, CAPOLIN, [*and a* Messenger].

SOLD. Awake, ye men of Memphis! Hear the clang
Of Scythian trumpets, — hear the basilisks[2]
That, roaring, shake Damascus' turrets down.
The rogue of Volga holds Zenocrate,
The Soldan's daughter, for his concubine,
And with a troop of thieves and vagabonds
Hath spread his colors to our high disgrace;
While you faint-hearted, base Egyptians
Lie slumbering on the flow'ry banks of Nile,
As crocodiles that unaffrighted rest
While thund'ring cannons rattle on their skins.
MESS. Nay, mighty Soldan, did your Greatness see
The frowning looks of fiery Tamburlaine,
That with his terror and imperious eyes
Commands the hearts of his associates,
It might amaze your royal Majesty.
SOLD. Villain, I tell thee, were that Tamburlaine
As monstrous[3] as Gorgon,[4] prince of hell,
The Soldan would not start a foot from him.
But speak, what power[5] hath he?
MESS. Mighty Lord,
Three hundred thousand men in armor clad,
Upon their prancing steeds disdainfully
With wanton paces trampling on the ground;
Five hundred thousand footmen, threat'ning shot,
Shaking their swords, their spears, and iron bills,
Environing their standard round, that stood
As bristle-pointed as a thorny wood.

[1] Unlocated; presumably the Soldan's palace at Memphis.
[2] A kind of cannon.
[3] Here a trisyllable.
[4] Demogorgon.
[5] Army.

Their warlike engines and munition
Exceed the forces of their martial men.

SOLD. Nay, could their numbers countervail the stars,
Or ever-drizzling drops of April showers,
Or withered leaves that autumn shaketh down,
Yet would the Soldan by his conquering power
So scatter and consume them in his rage
That not a man should live to rue their fall.

CAPO. So might your Highness, had you time to sort
Your fighting men and raise your royal host;
But Tamburlaine, by expedition,
Advantage takes of your unreadiness.

SOLD. Let him take all th' advantages he can.
Were all the world conspir'd to fight for him,
Nay, were he devil, as he is no man,
Yet in revenge of fair Zenocrate,
Whom he detaineth in despite of us,
This arm should send him down to Erebus,
To shroud his shame in darkness of the night.

MESS. Pleaseth your Mightiness to understand,
His resolution far exceedeth all.
The first day when he pitcheth down his tents,
White is their hue, and on his silver crest
A snowy feather spangled white he bears,
To signify the mildness of his mind,
That, satiate with spoil, refuseth blood.
But, when Aurora mounts the second time,
As red as scarlet is his furniture;
Then must his kindled wrath be quench'd with blood,
Not sparing any that can manage arms.
But if these threats move not submission,
Black are his colors; black, pavilion;
His spear, his shield, his horse, his armor, plumes,
And jetty feathers menace death and hell:
Without respect of sex, degree, or age,
He razeth all his foes with fire and sword.

SOLD. Merciless villain, peasant, ignorant
Of lawful arms or martial discipline!
Pillage and murder are his usual trades;
The slave usurps the glorious name of war.
See, Capolin, the fair Arabian king,
That hath been disappointed by this slave
Of my fair daughter and his princely love,
May have fresh warning to go war with us,
And be reveng'd for her disparagement.

[*Exeunt.*]

SCENE II [6]

[*Enter*] TAMBURLAINE, TECHELLES, THERIDAMAS, USUMCASANE, ZENOCRATE, ANIPPE, *two* Moors *drawing* BAJAZETH *in his cage, and his wife* [ZABINA] *following him.*

TAMB. Bring out my footstool.

They take him out of the cage.

BAJ. Ye holy priests of heavenly Mahomet,
That, sacrificing, slice and cut your flesh,
Staining his altars with your purple blood,
Make Heaven to frown and every fixed star
To suck up poison from the moorish fens
And pour it in this glorious [7] tyrant's throat.

TAMB. The chiefest God, first mover of that sphere
Enchas'd with thousands ever-shining lamps,
Will sooner burn the glorious frame of Heaven
Than it should so conspire my overthrow.
But, villain, thou that wishest this to me,
Fall prostrate on the low disdainful earth,
And be the footstool of great Tamburlaine,
That I may rise into my royal throne.

BAJ. First shalt thou rip my bowels with thy sword
And sacrifice my heart to death and hell,
Before I yield to such a slavery.

TAMB. Base villain, vassal, slave to Tamburlaine,
Unworthy to embrace or touch the ground
That bears the honor of my royal weight,
Stoop, villain, stoop! — Stoop! for so he bids [8]
That may command thee piecemeal to be torn,
Or scattered like the lofty cedar trees
Struck with the voice of thund'ring Jupiter.

BAJ. Then, as I look down to the damned fiends,
Fiends, look on me! and thou, dread god of hell,
With ebon sceptre strike this hateful earth
And make it swallow both of us at once!

[TAMBURLAINE] *gets up upon him to his chair.*

TAMB. Now clear the triple [9] region of the air,
And let the Majesty of Heaven behold
Their scourge and terror tread on emperors.
Smile, stars that reign'd at my nativity,
And dim the brightness of their neighbor lamps!
Disdain to borrow light of Cynthia;

[6] Tamburlaine's camp before Damascus.
[7] Boastful, vainglorious.
[8] Note metrical value of pause.
[9] Upper, middle, and lower.

For I, the chiefest lamp of all the earth,
First rising in the East with mild aspect,
But fixed now in the meridian line,[10]
Will send up fire to your turning spheres,
And cause the sun to borrow light of you.
My sword struck fire from his coat of steel,
Even in Bithynia, when I took this Turk;
As when a fiery exhalation,
Wrapp'd in the bowels of a freezing cloud,
Fighting for passage, [makes][11] the welkin crack,
And casts a flash of lightning to the earth.
But, ere I march to wealthy Persia,
Or leave Damascus and th' Egyptian fields,
As was the fame of Clymene's brainsick son,
That almost brent[12] the axletree of Heaven,
So shall our swords, our lances, and our shot
Fill all the air with fiery meteors.
Then, when the sky shall wax as red as blood,
It shall be said I made it red myself,
To make me think of naught but blood and war.

Zab. Unworthy king, that by thy cruelty
Unlawfully usurpest the Persian seat,
Dar'st thou, that never saw an emperor
Before thou met my husband in the field,
Being thy captive, thus abuse his state,
Keeping his kingly body in a cage,
That roofs of gold and sun-bright palaces
Should have prepar'd to entertain his Grace,
And treading him beneath thy loathsome feet,
Whose feet the kings of Africa have kiss'd?

Tech. You must devise some torment worse, my Lord,
To make these captives rein their lavish tongues.

Tamb. Zenocrate, look better to your slave.

Zeno. She is my handmaid's slave, and she shall look
That these abuses flow not from her tongue.
Chide her, Anippe.

Anip. Let these be warnings for you then, my slave,
How you abuse the person of the King;
Or else I swear to have you whipp'd, stark-nak'd.

Baj. Great Tamburlaine, great in my overthrow,
Ambitious pride shall make thee fall as low,
For treading on the back of Bajazeth,
That should be horsed on four mighty kings.

Tamb. Thy names and titles and thy dignities
Are fled from Bajazeth and remain with me,
That will maintain it against a world of kings.
Put him in again.

[*They put him into the cage.*]

Baj. Is this a place for mighty Bajazeth?
Confusion light on him that helps thee thus!

Tamb. There whiles he lives, shall Bajazeth be kept;
And where I go, be thus in triumph drawn;
And thou, his wife, shalt feed him with the scraps
My servitors shall bring thee from my board;
For he that gives him other food than this
Shall sit by him and starve to death himself.
This is my mind and I will have it so.
Not all the kings and emperors of the earth,
If they would lay their crowns before my feet,
Shall ransom him or take him from his cage.
The ages that shall talk of Tamburlaine,
Even from this day to Plato's wondrous year,[13]
Shall talk how I have handled Bajazeth;
These Moors, that drew him from Bithynia
To fair Damascus, where we now remain,
Shall lead him with us wheresoe'er we go. —
Techelles, and my loving followers,
Now may we see Damascus' lofty towers,
Like to the shadows of Pyramides,
That with their beauties grac'd the Memphian fields.
The golden stature[14] of their feathered bird,
That spreads her wings upon the city walls,
Shall not defend it from our battering shot.
The townsmen mask in silk and cloth of gold,
And every house is as a treasury.
The men, the treasure, and the town is ours.

Ther. Your tents of white now pitch'd before the gates,
And gentle flags of amity display'd,
I doubt not but the governor will yield,
Offering Damascus to your Majesty.

Tamb. So shall he have his life, and all the rest.
But if he stay until the bloody flag
Be once advanc'd on my vermilion tent,
He dies, and those that kept us out so long.

[10] *I.e.*, now at my highest (and permanent) point.

[11] Cor. Dyce; old eds. *make*.

[12] Burned. The allusion is to the myth of Phaëthon.

[13] Plato (*Timaeus*) refers to a perfect "year", a period at the close of which all the "seven planets" will be relatively in the same positions as at its beginning. 15,000 solar years was Cicero's estimate of its length, according to Macrobius; but computations varied widely.

[14] Oo 3, 4, *statue*. The bird was the ibis.

And when they see me march in black array,
With mournful streamers hanging down their heads,
Were in that city all the world contain'd,
Not one should scape, but perish by our swords.

ZENO. Yet would you have some pity for my sake,
Because it is my country's, and my father's.

TAMB. Not for the world, Zenocrate, if I have sworn.
Come; bring in the Turk. *Exeunt.*

SCENE III [15]

[*Enter the*] SOLDAN, [*the* KING OF] ARABIA, CAPOLIN, *with streaming colors and* Soldiers.

SOLD. Methinks we march as Meleager did,
Environed with brave Argolian knights,
To chase the savage Cal[y]donian boar;
Or Cephalus with lusty Theban youths
Against the wolf that angry Themis sent
To waste and spoil the sweet Aonian fields,
A monster of five hundred thousand heads,
Compact of rapine, piracy, and spoil.
The scum of men, the hate and scourge of God,
Raves in Egyptia and annoyeth us.
My Lord, it is the bloody Tamburlaine,
A sturdy felon and a base-bred thief,
By murder raised to the Persian crown,
That dares control us in our territories.
To tame the pride of this presumptuous beast,
Join your Arabians with the Soldan's power;
Let us unite our royal bands in one,
And hasten to remove Damascus' siege.
It is a blemish to the majesty
And high estate of mighty emperors,
That such a base usurping vagabond
Should brave a king, or wear a princely crown.

K. of ARAB. Renowmed Soldan, have ye lately heard
The overthrow of mighty Bajazeth
About the confines of Bithynia?
The slavery wherewith he persecutes
The noble Turk and his great emperess?

SOLD. I have, and sorrow for his bad success; [16]
But, noble Lord of great Arabia,
Be so persuaded that the Soldan is
No more dismay'd with tidings of his fall
Than in the haven when the pilot stands
And views a stranger's ship rent in the winds,
And shivered against a craggy rock;
Yet, in compassion of his wretched state,
A sacred vow to Heaven and him I make,
Confirming it with Ibis' holy name,
That Tamburlaine shall rue the day, the hour,
Wherein he wrought such ignominious wrong
Unto the hallowed person of a prince,
Or kept the fair Zenocrate so long
As concubine, I fear, to feed his lust.

K. of ARAB. Let grief and fury hasten on revenge;
Let Tamburlaine for his offences feel
Such plagues as Heaven and we can pour on him.
I long to break my spear upon his crest,
And prove the weight of his victorious arm;
For Fame, I fear, hath been too prodigal
In sounding through the world his partial praise.

SOLD. Capolin, hast thou survey'd our powers?

CAPOL. Great Emperors of Egypt and Arabia,
The number of your hosts united is
A hundred [17] and fifty thousand horse;
Two hundred thousand foot, brave men at arms,
Courageous,[17] and full of hardiness,
As frolic as the hunters in the chase
Of savage beasts amid the desert woods.

K. of ARAB. My mind presageth fortunate success;
And, Tamburlaine, my spirit doth foresee
The utter ruin of thy men and thee.

SOLD. Then rear your standards; let your sounding drums
Direct our soldiers to Damascus' walls. —
Now, Tamburlaine, the mighty Soldan comes,
And leads with him the great Arabian King,
To dim thy baseness and obscurity,
Famous for nothing but for theft and spoil;
To raze and scatter thy inglorious crew
Of Scythians and slavish Persians. *Exeunt.*

SCENE [IV] [18]

The banquet, and to it cometh TAMBURLAINE *all in scarlet*, [ZENOCRATE,] THERIDAMAS, TECHELLES, USUMCASANE, the Turk [BAJAZETH *in his cage*, ZABINA,] *with others.*

TAMB. Now hang our bloody colors by Damascus,
Reflexing hues of blood upon their heads,
While they walk quivering on their city walls,

[15] Unlocated; presumably a camp in Syria.
[16] Outcome, fortune.
[17] Trisyllabic here.
[18] Tamburlaine's camp before Damascus.

Half dead for fear before they feel my wrath.
Then let us freely banquet and carouse
Full bowls of wine unto the god of war
That means to fill your helmets full of gold,
And make Damascus spoils as rich to you
As was to Jason Colchos' golden fleece. —
And now, Bajazeth, hast thou any stomach?[19]

BAJ. Ay, such a stomach, cruel Tamburlaine, as I could willingly feed upon thy blood-raw heart.

TAMB. Nay, thine own is easier to come by; pluck out that, and 't will serve thee and thy wife. — Well, Zenocrate, Techelles, and the rest, fall to your victuals.

BAJ. Fall to, and never may your meat digest.
Ye Furies, that can mask invisible,
Dive to the bottom of Avernus' pool
And in your hands bring hellish poison up
And squeeze it in the cup of Tamburlaine.
Or, winged snakes of Lerna, cast your stings,
And leave your venoms in this tyrant's dish.

ZAB. And may this banquet prove as ominous
As Progne's to th' adulterous Thracian king,
That fed upon the substance of his child.

ZENO. My Lord, how can you[20] suffer these
Outrageous curses by these slaves of yours?

TAMB. To let them see, divine Zenocrate,
I glory in the curses of my foes,
Having the power from the imperial Heaven
To turn them all upon their proper heads.

TECH. I pray you give them leave, madam; this speech is a goodly refreshing to them.

THER. But if his Highness would let them be fed, it would do them more good.

TAMB. Sirrah, why fall you not to? Are you so daintily brought up, you cannot eat your own flesh?

BAJ. First, legions of devils shall tear thee in pieces.

USUM. Villain, knowest thou to whom thou speakest?

TAMB. O, let him alone. Here; eat, sir; take it from my sword's point, or I'll thrust it to thy heart.

[*Bajazeth*] *takes it and stamps upon it.*

THER. He stamps it under his feet, my Lord.

TAMB. Take it up, villain, and eat it; or I will make thee slice the brawns of thy arms into carbonadoes[21] and eat them.

USUM. Nay, 't were better he kill'd his wife, and then she shall be sure not to be starv'd, and he be provided for a month's victual beforehand.

TAMB. Here is my dagger; despatch her while she is fat; for, if she live but a while longer, she will fall into a consumption with fretting, and then she will not be worth the eating.

THER. Dost thou think that Mahomet will suffer this?

TECH. 'T is like he will when he cannot let[22] it.

TAMB. Go to; fall to your meat. — What, not a bit! Belike he hath not been watered today; give him some drink.

They give him water to drink, and he flings it on the ground.

TAMB. Fast, and welcome, sir, while[23] hunger make you eat. — How now, Zenocrate, doth not the Turk and his wife make a goodly show at a banquet?

ZENO. Yes, my Lord.

THER. Methinks 't is a great deal better than a consort[24] of music.

TAMB. Yet music would do well to cheer up Zenocrate. — Pray thee, tell why thou art so sad. If thou wilt have a song, the Turk shall strain his voice. But why is it?

ZENO. My Lord, to see my father's town besieg'd,
The country wasted where myself was born,
How can it but afflict my very soul?
If any love remain in you, my Lord,
Or if my love unto your Majesty
May merit favor at your Highness' hands,
Then raise your siege from fair Damascus' walls,
And with my father take a friendly truce.

TAMB. Zenocrate, were Egypt Jove's own land,
Yet would I with my sword make Jove to stoop.
I will confute those blind geographers
That make a triple region in the world,
Excluding regions which I mean to trace
And with this pen[25] reduce them to a map,

[19] Appetite. Note that the comic passages which follow are in prose. They may be non-Marlovian, or the actors' corruption or amplification of original verse.

[20] A short line; Dyce adds *tamely*.

[21] Steaks.

[22] Hinder.

[23] Until.

[24] Band.

[25] *I.e.*, his sword. The "triple region" was, for Marlowe, Eurasia, Africa, and America. "Trace" = traverse.

Calling the provinces, cities, and towns,
After my name and thine, Zenocrate.
Here at Damascus will I make the point
That shall begin the perpendicular ;[26]
And wouldst thou have me buy thy father's love
With such a loss? Tell me, Zenocrate!

ZENO. Honor still wait on happy Tamburlaine!
Yet give me leave to plead for him, my Lord.

TAMB. Content thyself: his person shall be safe
And all the friends of fair Zenocrate,
If with their lives they will be pleas'd to yield,
Or may be forc'd to make me Emperor;
For Egypt and Arabia must be mine. —
Feed, you slave! Thou mayst think thyself happy to be fed from my trencher.

BAJ. My empty stomach, full of idle heat,
Draws bloody humors[27] from my feeble parts,
Preserving life by hasting cruel death.
My veins are pale, my sinews hard and dry,
My joints benumb'd; unless I eat, I die.

ZAB. Eat, Bajazeth. Let us live in spite of them, looking[28] some happy power will pity and enlarge us.

TAMB. Here, Turk; wilt thou have a clean trencher?

BAJ. Ay, tyrant, and more meat.

TAMB. Soft, sir; you must be dieted; too much eating will make you surfeit.

THER. So it would, my Lord, specially having so small a walk and so little exercise.

Enter a second course of crowns.

TAMB. Theridamas, Techelles, and Casane, here are the cates you desire to finger, are they not?

THER. Ay, my Lord; but none save kings must feed with these.

TECH. 'T is enough for us to see them, and for Tamburlaine only to enjoy them.

TAMB. Well, here is now to the Soldan of Egypt, the King of Arabia, and the Governor of Damascus. — Now take these three crowns, and pledge me, my contributory kings. I crown you here, Theridamas, King of Argier; Techelles, King of Fez; and Usumcasane, King of Moroccus. — How say you to this, Turk? These are not your contributory kings.

BAJ. Nor shall they long be thine, I warrant them.

[26] *I.e.*, longitude 0°. (Ellis-Fermor.)
[27] Moistures, vapors.
[28] Expecting.

TAMB. Kings of Argier, Moroccus, and of Fez,
You that have march'd with happy Tamburlaine
As far as from the frozen [plage][29] of Heaven
Unto the wat'ry morning's ruddy [bower][30]
And thence by land unto the torrid zone,
Deserve these titles I endow you with
By [valor][31] and by magnanimity.
Your births shall be no blemish to your fame,
For virtue[32] is the fount whence honor springs,
And they are worthy she investeth kings.

THER. And since your Highness hath so well vouchsaf'd,
If we deserve them not with higher meeds
Than erst our states and actions have retain'd,
Take them away again and make us slaves.

TAMB. Well said, Theridamas; when holy fates
Shall 'stablish me in strong Egyptia,
We mean to travel to th' anta[rc]tic pole,
Conquering the people underneath our feet,
And be renowm'd as never emperors were. —
Zenocrate, I will not crown thee yet,
Until with greater honors I be grac'd.

[*Exeunt.*]

ACT V — SCENE I[1]

[*Enter*] *the* GOVERNOR *of* DAMASCO, *with three or four* Citizens, *and four* Virgins *with branches of laurel in their hands.*

GOV. Still doth this man, or rather god, of war
Batter our walls and beat our turrets down;
And to resist with longer stubbornness
Or hope of rescue from the Soldan's power,
Were but to bring our wilful overthrow
And make us desperate of our threat'ned lives.
We see his tents have now been altered
With terrors to the last and cruel'st hue.
His coal-black colors everywhere advanc'd
Threaten our city with a general spoil;
And if we should with common rites of arms
Offer our safeties to his clemency,
I fear the custom, proper[2] to his sword,
Which he observes as parcel of his fame,

[29] Shore. Emend. Dyce; old eds. *place*. *Plage* occurs in *Part II*, I, i, 68, in $O_{1, 2}$, rendered by $O_{3, 4}$, *place*.
[30] Cor. O_3; $O_{1, 2}$, *hower*.
[31] Emend. Robinson; old eds. *value*.
[32] Worth, ability.
[1] A holy place in Damascus.
[2] Peculiar, habitual. "Parcel" = part.

Intending so to terrify the world,
By any innovation or remorse[3]
Will never be dispens'd with till our deaths.
Therefore, for these our harmless virgins' sakes,
Whose honors and whose lives rely on him,
Let us have hope that their unspotted prayers,
Their blubbered cheeks, and hearty, humble moans,
Will melt his fury into some remorse,
And use us like a loving conqueror.

[1] VIRG. If humble suits or imprecations,[4]
(Uttered with tears of wretchedness and blood
Shed from the heads and hearts of all our sex,
Some made your wives and some your children)
Might have entreated your obdurate breasts
To entertain some care of our securities
Whiles only danger beat upon our walls,
These more than dangerous warrants of our death
Had never been erected as they be,
Nor you depend on such weak helps as we.

GOV. Well, lovely virgins, think our country's care,
Our love of honor, loath to be enthrall'd
To foreign powers and rough imperious yokes,
Would not with too much cowardice or fear,
Before all hope of rescue were denied,
Submit yourselves and us to servitude.
Therefore in that your safeties and our own,
Your honors, liberties, and lives were weigh'd
In equal care and balance with our own,
Endure as we the malice of our stars,
The wrath of Tamburlaine, and power of wars;
Or be the means the overweighing heavens
Have kept to qualify[5] these hot extremes,
And bring us pardon in your cheerful looks.

2 VIRG. Then here before the Majesty of Heaven
And holy Patrons of Egyptia,
With knees and hearts submissive we entreat
Grace to our words and pity to our looks,
That this device may prove propitious
And through the eyes and ears of Tamburlaine
Convey events of mercy[6] to his heart;
Grant that these signs of victory[7] we yield
May bind the temples of his conquering head,
To hide the folded furrows of his brows,
And shadow his displeased countenance
With happy looks of ruth and lenity.
Leave us, my Lord, and loving countrymen;
What simple virgins may persuade, we will.

GOV. Farewell, sweet virgins, on whose safe return
Depends our city, liberty, and lives.

Exeunt [*all but the* Virgins].

SCENE II[8]

[*To the* Virgins *enter*] TAMBURLAINE, TECHELLES, THERIDAMAS, USUMCASANE, *with others;* TAMBURLAINE *all in black and very melancholy.*

TAMB. What, are the turtles[9] fray'd[10] out of their nests?
Alas, poor fools, must you be first shall feel
The sworn destruction of Damascus?
They know my custom; could they not as well
Have sent ye out when first my milk-white flags,
Through which sweet Mercy threw her gentle beams,
Reflexing them on your disdainful eyes,
As now, when fury and incensed hate
Flings slaughtering terror from my coal-black tents,
And tells for truth submissions comes too late?

1 VIRG. Most happy King and Emperor of the earth,
Image of honor and nobility,
For whom the powers divine have made the world,
And on whose throne the holy Graces sit;
In whose sweet person is compris'd the sum
Of Nature's skill and heavenly majesty;
Pity our plights! O pity poor Damascus!
Pity old age, within whose silver hairs
Honor and reverence evermore have reign'd!
Pity the marriage bed, where many a lord,
In prime and glory of his loving joy,
Embraceth now with tears of ruth and blood
The jealous body of his fearful wife,
Whose cheeks and hearts, so punish'd with conceit
To think thy puissant, never-stayed arm
Will part their bodies, and prevent their souls
From heavens of comfort yet their age might bear,
Now wax all pale and withered to the death,
As well for grief our ruthless governor
[Hath][11] thus refus'd the mercy of thy hand
(Whose sceptre angels kiss and Furies dread)

[3] Pity.
[4] Prayers.
[5] Moderate.
[6] Merciful conclusions.
[7] *I.e.*, the laurel.

[8] Though the Virgins remain on stage, the scene changes to the camp. After l. 343 it changes again, to the battlefield.
[9] Turtledoves.
[10] Frightened.
[11] Oo 3, 4; Oo 1, 2, *haue.*

As for their liberties, their loves, or lives!
O then for these, and such as we ourselves,
For us, for infants, and for all our bloods,
That never nourish'd thought against thy rule,
Pity, O pity, sacred Emperor,
The prostrate service of this wretched town,
And take in sign thereof this gilded wreath,
Whereto each man of rule hath given his hand,
And wish'd, as worthy subjects, happy means
To be investers of thy royal brows
Even with the true Egyptian diadem.

TAMB. Virgins, in vain ye labor to prevent
That which mine honor swears shall be perform'd.
Behold my sword! what see you at the point?

[1] VIRG. Nothing but fear and fatal steel, my Lord.

TAMB. Your fearful minds are thick and misty then;
For there sits Death, there sits imperious Death,
Keeping his circuit [12] by the slicing edge.
But I am pleas'd you shall not see him there;
He now is seated on my horsemen's spears,
And on their points his fleshless body feeds. —
Techelles, straight go charge a few of them
To charge these dames, and show my servant, Death,
Sitting in scarlet on their armed spears.

OMNES. O pity us!

TAMB. Away with them, I say, and show them Death. — *They take them away.*
I will not spare these proud Egyptians,
Nor change my martial observations
For all the wealth of Gihon's golden waves,
Or for the love of Venus, would she leave
The angry god of arms and lie with me.
They have refus'd the offer of their lives;
And know my customs are as peremptory
As wrathful planets, death, or destiny.

Re enter TECHELLES.

What, have your horsemen shown the virgins Death?

TECH. They have, my Lord, and on Damascus' walls
Have hoisted up their slaughtered carcases.

TAMB. A sight as baneful to their souls, I think,
As are Thessalian drugs or mithridate.
But go, my Lords; put the rest to the sword. — *Exeunt* [*all except* TAMBURLAINE].
Ah, fair Zenocrate! divine Zenocrate!
Fair is too foul an epithet for thee,
That in thy passion,[13] for thy country's love,
And fear to see thy kingly father's harm,
With hair dishevell'd wip'st thy watery cheeks;
And, like to Flora in her morning's pride
Shaking her silver tresses in the air,
Rain'st on the earth resolved [14] pearl in showers,
And sprinklest sapphires on thy shining face,
Where Beauty, mother to the Muses, sits
And comments volumes with her ivory pen,
Taking instructions from thy flowing eyes,
Eyes when that Ebena [15] steps to Heaven,
In silence of thy solemn evening's walk,
Making the mantle of the richest night,
The moon, the planets, and the meteors, light;
There angels in their crystal armors fight
A doubtful battle with my tempted thoughts
For Egypt's freedom, and the Soldan's life,
His life that so consumes Zenocrate;
Whose sorrows lay more siege unto my soul,
Than all my army to Damascus' walls,
And neither [Persia's] [16] sovereign nor the Turk
Troubled my senses with conceit of foil [17]
So much by much as doth Zenocrate.
What is beauty, saith my sufferings, then?
If all the pens that ever poets held
Had fed the feeling of their masters' thoughts,
And every sweetness that inspir'd their hearts,
Their minds, and muses on admired themes;
If all the heavenly quintessence they still [18]
From their immortal flowers of poesy,
Wherein, as in a mirror, we perceive
The highest reaches of a human wit;
If these had made one poem's period,
And all combin'd in beauty's worthiness,
Yet should there hover in their restless heads
One thought, one grace, one wonder, at the least,
Which into words no virtue [19] can digest.
But how unseemly is it for my sex,
My discipline of arms and chivalry,
My nature, and the terror of my name,
To harbor thoughts effeminate and faint!
Save only that in beauty's just applause,
With whose instinct the soul of man is touch'd —
And every warrior that is rapt with love

[12] Court.

[13] *I.e.*, sorrow.
[14] Dissolved.
[15] Unidentified; the line is doubtless corrupt.
[16] Emend. Robinson; old eds. *Perseans*.
[17] Idea of defeat.
[18] Distill.
[19] Power.

Of fame, of valor, and of victory,
Must needs have beauty beat on his conceits, —
I thus conceiving and subduing both
That which hath [stoop'd the temper] [20] of the gods,
Even from the fiery-spangled veil of Heaven,
To feel the [lowly] [21] warmth of shepherds' flames,
And [watch] [22] in cottages of strowed [reeds],[23]
Shall give the world to note, for all my birth,
That virtue solely is the sum of glory,
And fashions men with true nobility. —
Who 's within there?

Enter two or three.

Hath Bajazeth been fed to-day?

AN [ATTENDANT]. Ay, my Lord.

TAMB. Bring him forth; and let us know if the town be ransack'd. [*Exeunt* Attendants.]

Enter TECHELLES, THERIDAMAS, USUMCASANE, *and others.*

TECH. The town is ours, my Lord, and fresh supply
Of conquest and of spoil is offered us.

TAMB. That's well, Techelles; what 's the news?

TECH. The Soldan and the Arabian King together
March on us with such eager violence
As if there were no way but one with us.

TAMB. No more there is not, I warrant thee, Techelles.

They bring in the Turk [*and* ZABINA].

THER. We know the victory is ours, my Lord;
But let us save the reverend Soldan's life,
For fair Zenocrate that so laments his state.

TAMB. That will we chiefly see unto, Theridamas,
For sweet Zenocrate, whose worthiness
Deserves a conquest over every heart.
And now, my footstool, if I lose the field,
You hope of liberty and restitution! —
Here let him stay, my masters, from the tents,
Till we have made us ready for the field. —
Pray for us, Bajazeth; we are going.

Exeunt [*all but* BAJAZETH *and* ZABINA].

BAJ. Go, never to return with victory!
Millions of men encompass thee about,
And gore thy body with as many wounds!
Sharp, forked arrows light upon thy horse!
Furies from the black Cocytus lake
Break up the earth, and with their firebrands
Enforce thee run upon the baneful pikes!
Volleys of shot pierce through thy charmed skin,
And every bullet dipp'd in poisoned drugs,
Or roaring cannons sever all thy joints,
Making thee mount as high as eagles soar!

ZAB. Let all the swords and lances in the field
Stick in his breast as in their proper rooms!
At every pore let blood come dropping forth,
That ling'ring pains may massacre his heart
And madness send his damned soul to hell!

BAJ. Ah, fair Zabina, we may curse his power,
The heavens may frown, the earth for anger quake,
But such a star hath influence in his sword
As rules the skies and countermands the gods,
More than Cimmerian Styx or Destiny;
And then shall we in this detested guise,
With shame, with hunger, and with horror aye
Griping our bowels with retorqued [24] thoughts,
And have no hope to end our ecstasies?

ZAB. Then is there left no Mahomet, no God,
No Fiend, no Fortune, nor no hope of end
To our infamous,[25] monstrous slaveries!
Gape, earth, and let the fiends infernal view
[A] [26] hell as hopeless and as full of fear
As are the blasted banks of Erebus,
Where shaking ghosts with ever-howling groans
Hover about the ugly ferryman,
To get a passage to Elysium.[27]
Why should we live? O, wretches, beggars, slaves!
Why live we, Bajazeth, and build up nests
So high within the region of the air
By living long in this oppression,
That all the world will see and laugh to scorn
The former triumphs of our mightiness
In this obscure, infernal servitude?

BAJ. O life, more loathsome to my vexed thoughts
Than noisome parbreak [28] of the Stygian snakes,

[20] Old eds. *stopt the tempest*, certainly corrupt; the reading of this ed. combines guesses of Dyce and Collier.
[21] Conj. Collier; old eds. *louely*.
[22] Emend. present Ed. Old eds. *martch*.
[23] Emend. Dyce; old eds. *weeds*.

[24] *I.e.*, retrospective.
[25] Accented on second syllable.
[26] Cor. Robinson; old eds. *As*.
[27] Old eds. *Elisian*.
[28] Vomit.

Which fills the nooks of hell with standing air,
Infecting all the ghosts with cureless griefs!
O dreary engines [29] of my loathed sight,
That sees my crown, my honor, and my name
Thrust under yoke and thraldom of a thief,
Why feed ye still on day's accursed beams
And sink not quite into my tortur'd soul?
You see my wife, my queen, and emperess,
Brought up and propped by the hand of Fame,
Queen of fifteen contributory queens,
Now thrown to rooms of black abjection,
Smear'd with blots of basest drudgery,
And villeiness [30] to shame, disdain, and misery.
Accursed Bajazeth, whose words of ruth,
(That would with pity cheer Zabina's heart,
And make our souls resolve in ceaseless tears;)
Sharp hunger bites upon, and gripes the root
From whence the issues of my thoughts do break.
O poor Zabina, O my queen, my queen,
Fetch me some water for my burning breast,
To cool and comfort me with longer date;
That in the short'ned sequel of my life
I may pour forth my soul into thine arms
With words of love, whose moaning intercourse
Hath hitherto been stay'd with wrath and hate
Of our expressless bann'd inflictions.

ZAB. Sweet Bajazeth, I will prolong thy life,
As long as any blood or spark of breath
Can quench or cool the torments of my grief.
She goes out.

BAJ. Now, Bajazeth, abridge thy baneful days,
And beat thy brains out of thy conquer'd head,
Since other means are all forbidden me
That may be ministers of my decay.
O highest lamp of ever-living Jove,
Accursed day, infected with my griefs,
Hide now thy stained face in endless night,
And shut the windows of the lightsome heavens!
Let ugly Darkness with her rusty coach,
Engirt with tempests, wrapp'd in pitchy clouds,
Smother the earth with never-fading mists,
And let her horses from their nostrils breathe
Rebellious winds and dreadful thunderclaps,
That in this terror Tamburlaine may live,
And my pin'd soul, resolv'd in liquid [air],[31]
May still excruciate his tormented thoughts!
Then let the stony dart of senseless cold
Pierce through the centre of my withered heart,
And make a passage for my loathed life!
He brains himself against the cage.

Re-enter ZABINA.

ZAB. What do mine eyes behold, my husband dead?
His skull all riven in twain, his brains dash'd out?
The brains of Bajazeth, my lord and sovereign!
O Bajazeth, my husband and my lord,
O Bajazeth, O Turk, O Emperor!

Give him his liquor? Not I. Bring milk and fire, and my blood I bring him again. — Tear me in pieces! Give me the sword with a ball of wildfire upon it. — Down with him! Down with him! — Go to, my child! Away! away! away! Ah, save that infant! save him, save him! — I, even I, speak to her. — The sun was down. Streamers white, red, black, here, here, here! — Fling the meat in his face — Tamburlaine, Tamburlaine! — Let the soldiers be buried. — Hell! Death! Tamburlaine! Hell! — Make ready my coach, my chair, my jewels; I come, I come, I come!
She runs against the cage and brains herself.

[*Enter*] ZENOCRATE *with* ANIPPE.

[ZENO.] Wretched Zenocrate! that livest to see
Damascus' walls dy'd with Egyptian blood,
Thy father's subjects and thy countrymen;
Thy streets strowed with dissevered joints of men
And wounded bodies gasping yet for life.
But most accurs'd, to see the sun-bright troop
Of heavenly virgins and unspotted maids,
Whose looks might make the angry god of arms
To break his sword and mildly treat of love,
On horsemen's lances to be hoisted up
And guiltlessly endure a cruel death;
For every fell and stout Tartarian steed,
That stamp'd on others with their thund'ring hoofs
When all their riders charg'd their quivering spears,
Began to check the ground and rein themselves,
Gazing upon the beauty of their looks.
Ah, Tamburlaine, wert thou the cause of this
That term'st Zenocrate thy dearest love?
Whose lives were dearer to Zenocrate

[29] Instruments.
[30] Serf.
[31] Cor. O3; Oo1, 2, *ay*.

Than her own life, or aught save thine own love.
But see, another bloody spectacle!
Ah, wretched eyes, the enemies of my heart,
How are ye glutted with these grievous objects,
And tell my soul more tales of bleeding ruth!
See, see, Anippe, if they breathe or no.

ANIPPE. No breath, nor sense, nor motion in them both;
Ah, madam, this their slavery hath enforc'd,
And ruthless cruelty of Tamburlaine.

ZENO. Earth, cast up fountains from thy entrails,[32]
And wet thy cheeks for their untimely deaths!
Shake with their weight in sign of fear and grief!
Blush, Heaven, that gave them honor at their birth
And let them die a death so barbarous.
Those that are proud of fickle empery
And place their chiefest good in earthly pomp,
Behold the Turk and his great Emperess!
Ah, Tamburlaine, my love, sweet Tamburlaine,
That fights for sceptres and for slippery crowns,
Behold the Turk and his great Emperess!
Thou, that in conduct of thy happy stars
Sleep'st every night with conquest on thy brows,
And yet wouldst shun the wavering turns of war,
In fear and feeling of the like distress,
Behold the Turk and his great Emperess!
Ah, mighty Jove and holy Mahomet,
Pardon my love! O, pardon his contempt
Of earthly fortune and respect of pity,
And let not conquest, ruthlessly pursu'd,
Be equally against his life incens'd
In this great Turk and hapless Emperess!
And pardon me that was not mov'd with ruth
To see them live so long in misery!
Ah, what may chance to thee, Zenocrate?

ANIPPE. Madam, content yourself, and be resolv'd[33]
Your love hath Fortune so at his command,
That she shall stay and turn her wheel no more,
As long as life maintains his mighty arm
That fights for honor to adorn your head.

Enter [PHILEMUS,] *a* Messenger.

ZENO. What other heavy news now brings Philemus?

PHIL. Madam, your father, and th' Arabian King,
The first affecter[34] of your excellence,
Comes now, as Turnus 'gainst Æneas did,
Armed with lance into the Egyptian fields,
Ready for battle 'gainst my Lord, the King.

ZENO. Now shame and duty, love and fear, presents
A thousand sorrows to my martyred soul.
Whom should I wish the fatal victory,
When my poor pleasures are divided thus
And rack'd by duty from my cursed heart?
My father and my first-betrothed love
Must fight against my life and present love;
Wherein the change I use condemns my faith,
And makes my deeds infamous through the world.
But as the gods, to end the Troyans' toil,
Prevented Turnus of Lavinia
And fatally enrich'd Æneas' love,
So, for a final issue to my griefs,
To pacify my country and my love
Must Tamburlaine by their resistless powers
With virtue of a gentle victory
Conclude a league of honor to my hope;
Then, as the Powers divine have preordain'd,
With happy safety of my father's life
Send like defence of fair Arabia.

They sound to the battle: and TAMBURLAINE *enjoys the victory. After,* [*the* KING OF] ARABIA *enters wounded.*

K. of ARAB. What cursed power guides the murdering hands
Of this infamous tyrant's soldiers;
That no escape may save their enemies,
Nor fortune keep themselves from victory?
Lie down, Arabia, wounded to the death,
And let Zenocrate's fair eyes behold
That, as for her thou bear'st these wretched arms,
Even so for her thou diest in these arms,
Leaving thy blood for witness of thy love.

ZENO. Too dear a witness for such love, my Lord.
Behold Zenocrate, the cursed object,
Whose fortunes never mastered her griefs;
Behold her wounded, in conceit, for thee,
As much as thy fair body is for me.

K. of ARAB. Then shall I die with full contented heart,
Having beheld divine Zenocrate,
Whose sight with joy would take away my life
As now it bringeth sweetness to my wound,

[32] Trisyllabic. [33] Assured. [34] Lover.

If I had not been wounded as I am.
Ah, that the deadly pangs I suffer now
Would lend an hour's license to my tongue,
To make discourse of some sweet accidents
Have chanc'd thy merits in this worthless bondage ;
And that I might be privy to the state
Of thy deserv'd contentment, and thy love ;
But, making now a virtue of thy sight
To drive all sorrow from my fainting soul,
Since death denies me further cause of joy,
Depriv'd of care, my heart with comfort dies,
Since thy desired hand shall close mine eyes.
[*He dies.*]

Re-enter TAMBURLAINE *leading the* SOLDAN, TECHELLES, THERIDAMAS, USUMCASANE, *with others.*

TAMB. Come, happy father of Zenocrate,
A title higher than thy Soldan's name ;
Though my right hand have thus enthralled thee,
Thy princely daughter here shall set thee free ;
She that hath calm'd the fury of my sword,
Which had ere this been bath'd in streams of blood
As vast and deep as Euphrates [35] or Nile.

ZENO. O sight thrice welcome to my joyful soul,
To see the King, my father, issue safe
From dangerous battle of my conquering love !

SOLD. Well met, my only dear Zenocrate,
Though with the loss of Egypt and my crown.

TAMB. 'T was I, my Lord, that gat the victory,
And therefore grieve not at your overthrow,
Since I shall render all into your hands,
And add more strength to your dominions
Than ever yet confirm'd th' Egyptian crown.
The god of war resigns his room to me,
Meaning to make me general of the world.
Jove, viewing me in arms, looks pale and wan,
Fearing my power should pull him from his throne.
Where'er I come the Fatal Sisters sweat,
And grisly Death, by running to and fro,
To do their ceaseless homage to my sword ;
And here in Afric, where it seldom rains,
Since I arriv'd with my triumphant host,
Have swelling clouds, drawn from wide-gasping wounds,
Been oft resolv'd in bloody purple showers,
A meteor that might terrify the earth
And make it quake at every drop it drinks.
Millions of souls sit on the banks of Styx,
Waiting the back return of Charon's boat ;
Hell and Elysium [36] swarm with ghosts of men
That I have sent from sundry foughten fields,
To spread my fame through hell and up to Heaven.
And see, my Lord, a sight of strange import,
Emperors and kings lie breathless at my feet :
The Turk and his great Empress, as it seems,
Left to themselves while we were at the fight,
Have desperately despatch'd their slavish lives ;
With them Arabia, too, hath left his life —
All sights of power to grace my victory !
And such are objects fit for Tamburlaine ;
Wherein, as in a mirror, may be seen
His honor, that consists in shedding blood,
When men presume to manage arms with him.

SOLD. Mighty hath God and Mahomet made thy hand,
Renowmed Tamburlaine, to whom all kings
Of force must yield their crowns and emperies ;
And I am pleas'd with this my overthrow,
If, as beseems a person of thy state,
Thou hast with honor us'd Zenocrate.

TAMB. Her state and person wants no pomp, you see ;
And for all blot of foul inchastity
I record Heaven her heavenly self is clear.
Then let me find no further time to grace
Her princely temples with the Persian crown.
But here these kings that on my fortunes wait,
And have been crown'd for proved worthiness,
Even by this hand that shall establish them,
Shall now, adjoining all their hands with mine,
Invest her here my Queen of Persia.
What saith the noble Soldan and Zenocrate?

SOLD. I yield with thanks and protestations
Of endless honor to thee for her love.

TAMB. Then doubt I not but fair Zenocrate
Will soon consent to satisfy us both.

ZENO. Else should I much forget myself, my Lord.

THER. Then let us set the crown upon her head,
That long hath ling'red for so high a seat.

TECH. My hand is ready to perform the deed,
For now her marriage time shall work us rest.

USUM. And here 's the crown, my Lord ; help set it on.

TAMB. Then sit thou down, divine Zenocrate ;
And here we crown thee Queen of Persia

[35] Accented on first syllable here.

[36] Old eds. *Elisian.*

And all the kingdoms and dominions
That late the power of Tamburlaine subdu'd.
As Juno, when the giants were suppress'd,
That darted mountains at her brother Jove,
So looks my love, shadowing in her brows
Triumphs and trophies for my victories;
Or as Latona's daughter,[37] bent to arms,
Adding more courage to my conquering mind.
To gratify the sweet Zenocrate,
Egyptians, Moors, and men of Asia,
From Barbary unto the western Indie,
Shall pay a yearly tribute to thy sire;
And from the bounds of Afric to the banks
Of Ganges shall his mighty arm extend. —
And now, my Lords and loving followers,
That purchas'd kingdoms by your martial deeds,
Cast off your armor, put on scarlet robes,
Mount up your royal places of estate,
Environed with troop of noblemen,
And there make laws to rule your provinces.
Hang up your weapons on Alcides' post,[38]
For Tamburlaine takes truce with all the world. —
Thy first-betrothed love, Arabia,
Shall we with honor, as beseems, entomb,
With this great Turk and his fair Emperess.
Then, after all these solemn exequies,
We will our [39] rites of marriage solemnize.

[*Exeunt.*]

[37] Diana.

[38] *I.e.*, at the temple door. See Horace, *Epistles*, I, i, 4, 5. (Ellis-Fermor.)

[39] Old eds. add *celebrated*.

THE TRAGICALL History of D. Faustus.

As it hath bene Acted by the Right Honorable the Earle of Nottingham his seruants.

Written by Ch. Marl.

LONDON
Printed by V. S. for Thomas Bushell. 1604.

INTRODUCTORY NOTE

As Tamburlaine aspired to the world's mastery by force of arms, Faustus sought it through knowledge; thus Marlowe exhibits in this play another aspect of the Renaissance will to freedom. In its original form *Doctor Faustus* must have been a sublime poem, and it still retains what *Tamburlaine* lacks, scenes of primarily dramatic power. Unfortunately, though the play was probably produced about 1589 (Boas inclines to 1592 but minimizes the significance of a ballad on Faustus licensed in 1589 and presumably inspired by the play), the first edition appeared only in 1604. By that time, eleven years after the author's death, the piece had been mangled by stage alterations.

In 1602 Henslowe, whose company, the Admiral's (or Nottingham's) Men, acted it, paid £4 to William Bird and Samuel Rowley for additions. And doubtless, both before and after their work, there was fairly constant tampering. The Quarto of 1616 gives us a version widely different from the first edition, and the Quarto of 1663 contains grotesque additions partly adapted from *The Jew of Malta.* The tendency of the early stage was to treat the Devil as a comic character; and as new material was successively introduced for the low comedians, the original was repeatedly pared down to make room for it. *Doctor Faustus,* then, is to be approached like a temple of the antique world; we are the losers if we allow partial collapse, inartistic restoration, and unauthentic and impudent addition to obscure the surviving traces of its beauty. (For a sketch of the probable process of corruption see Percy Simpson's article in *Essays and Studies by Members of the English Association,* VII, 143–155.) Aside from interpolation and excision, the most notable changes are the mangling of metre and the substitution of prose paraphrases for the original verse.

Marlowe's source was evidently not the German *Historia Von D. Johann Fausten* (Frankfurt am Main, 1587), but the not very faithful English translation of it, the *Historie of Doctor Iohn Faustus* (London, 1592), which Marlowe (unless we are to date the play after its appearance) must have read in MS or in an earlier edition. The moral application of the story is a prominent feature of the source, which also shows an anti-Papal bias. The play closely follows selected materials of the English Faust Book; but, as Boas remarks, "it is the questing spirit of the youthful Marlowe that transfigures it." The core of the legend is the compact with the Devil and the consequent retribution. The interval of twenty years is replete in the Faust Book with a great variety of experiences, including the episodes with the Pope, the horse-courser, and the clowns. It is generally believed that Marlowe's soaring pen was incapable of the comic scenes and that a collaborator furnished them. Marlowe was clearly more interested in the aspiration of Faustus, and with that fact in mind the reader must attempt as best he may to hold in his mind's eye the noble outlines of the original structure. "How greatly," said Goethe, "is it all planned."

Whatever the date of the original production, Henslowe records performances of *Doctor Faustus* by the Admiral's Men, with Edward Alleyn in the title rôle, in 1594–97. It continued to be acted, in more and more degraded versions, till well into the eighteenth century. The Case edition of this play is the work of F. S. Boas (1932).[1] Among other editions are Hermann Breymann's parallel texts of Qq 1604 and 1616 (vol. II of the *Historisch-Kritische Ausgabe* of Marlowe's Works, 1889); modernized editions by A. W. Ward (fourth edition, 1901), and I. Gollancz (1897); and a facsimile of Q 1604 by J. S. Farmer (1920). Professor Brooke (*Philological Quarterly,* January, 1933) has supplemented these editions with several valuable bibliographical and exegetical notes.

[1] The present edition has profited, during correction of proofs, by T. M. Parrott's review of Boas (*Modern Language Notes,* June, 1933).

Faustus was first printed, in quarto, in 1604 (reprinted 1609, 1611). In 1616 (reprinted 1619, 1620, 1624, 1628, 1631) a new version added about 550 lines and rewrote much of the play. Since Q 1616 evidently rests in part, not on an earlier quarto, but on independent MS authority, an extremely difficult textual problem is presented. Boas thinks Q 1616 more authentic; but the present edition is based on Breymann's and Brooke's reprints of Q 1604, though with indicated restorations and rearrangements from Q 1616 as given by them; for Q 1604 presents a badly cut and garbled stage version. Q 1616, on the contrary, constantly betrays, in the opinion of the present editor, the hand of an "improver", who smooths out difficult expressions; and it contains a number of new passages that are certainly not Marlovian.

As for the authorship of the version of 1604, Boas's conclusions seem reasonable and may be applied as follows. Marlowe probably wrote the first two acts, through II, ii (the episode of the Seven Deadly Sins is a possible exception); the chorus and the next fifty-three lines of Act III; Act IV, chorus, i, ii (1–9), iii; and Act V. The prose comic scenes may be a collaborator's, subsequently modified, in any case, by the steady pressure of theatrical conditions.

THE TRAGICAL HISTORY OF DOCTOR FAUSTUS

BY

CHRISTOPHER MARLOWE

[DRAMATIS PERSONAE

THE POPE.
CARDINAL OF LORRAINE.
CHARLES V, EMPEROR OF GERMANY.
DUKE OF VANHOLT.[1]
FAUSTUS.
VALDES, } friends to FAUSTUS.
CORNELIUS, }
WAGNER, servant to FAUSTUS.
Clown.
ROBIN.
RALPH.
Vintner.
Horse-Courser.[2]
Knight.
Old Man.

Scholars, Friars, and Attendants.

DUCHESS OF VANHOLT.

LUCIFER.
BELZEBUB.
MEPHISTOPHILIS.
Good Angel.
Evil Angel.
The Seven Deadly Sins.
Devils.
Spirits in the shapes of ALEXANDER THE GREAT, of his Paramour, and of HELEN of TROY.
Chorus.]

[ACT I]

Enter Chorus.

[CHORUS.] Not marching now in fields of Thrasimene,
Where Mars did mate [3] the Carthaginians;
Nor sporting in the dalliance of love,
In courts of kings where state is overturn'd;
Nor in the pomp of proud, audacious deeds,
Intends our Muse to [vaunt] [4] his [5] heavenly verse:—
Only this, gentlemen: we must perform
The form of Faustus' fortunes, good or bad.
To patient judgments we appeal our plaud,[6]
And speak for Faustus in his infancy.
Now is he born, his parents base of stock,
In Germany, within a town call'd Rhodes;[7]
Of riper years to Wittenberg he went,
Whereas his kinsmen chiefly brought him up.
So soon he profits in divinity,
The fruitful plot of scholarism grac'd,[8]
That shortly he was grac'd [9] with doctor's name,
Excelling all whose sweet delight disputes
In heavenly matters of theology;
Till, swoln with cunning,[10] of a self-conceit,
His waxen [11] wings did mount above his reach,
And melting Heavens conspir'd his overthrow;
For, falling to a devilish exercise,
And glutted more [12] with learning's golden gifts,
He surfeits upon cursed necromancy.
Nothing so sweet as magic is to him,
Which he prefers before his chiefest bliss.
And this [13] the man that in his study sits.
Exit.

[1] Anholt.
[2] Horse trader.
[3] Defeat. But Hannibal won this battle. The author may be confused; and the whole speech may be non-Marlovian.
[4] Proudly display; so Q 1616; earlier eds. *daunt.*
[5] Cf. Shakespeare, *Sonnets*, XXI, 1, 2.
[6] For our applause. Q 1616: *And now to patient iudgements we appeale*, typical of that ed.'s efforts to smooth the original version.
[7] Roda, in the Duchy of Saxe-Altenburg.
[8] Full of graces. (Cf. *Macbeth*, III, iv, 41.)
[9] Punning on the official "grace" (at Cambridge) by virtue of which a candidate took his degree.
[10] Puffed up with knowledge.
[11] *I.e.*, insecure, like the wings of Icarus.
[12] Q 1616 *now.*
[13] This is.

[Scene I][14]

Enter Faustus *in his study.*

Faust. Settle thy studies, Faustus, and begin
To sound the depth of that thou wilt profess.
Having commenc'd,[15] be a divine in show;
Yet level[16] at the end of every art,
And live and die in Aristotle's works.
Sweet Analytics,[17] 't is thou hast ravish'd me,
Bene disserere est finis logices.
Is to dispute well logic's chiefest end?
Affords this art no greater miracle?
Then read no more; thou hast attain'd the end —
A greater subject fitteth Faustus' wit.
Bid [ὂν καὶ μὴ ὄν][18] farewell, Galen come:
Seeing *Ubi desinit philosophus, ibi incipit medicus;*[19]
Be a physician, Faustus, heap up gold,
And be eterniz'd for some wondrous cure.
Summum bonum medicinæ sanitas:
The end of physic is our body's health.
Why, Faustus, hast thou not attain'd that end?
Is not thy common talk sound Aphorisms?[20]
Are not thy bills[21] hung up as monuments,
Whereby whole cities have escap'd the plague,
And thousand desp'rate maladies been eas'd?
Yet art thou still but Faustus and a man.
Wouldst thou make man[22] to live eternally,
Or, being dead, raise them to life again?
Then this profession were to be esteem'd.
Physic, farewell. Where is Justinian? [*Reads.*]
Si una eademque res legatur duobus,
Alter rem, alter valorem rei, &c.[23]
A pretty[24] case of paltry legacies! [*Reads.*]
Exhæreditare filium non potest pater nisi. . .[25]
Such is the subject of the Institute
And universal body of the [law].[26]
His[27] study fits a mercenary drudge,
Who aims at nothing but external trash;[28]
[Too servile][29] and illiberal for me.
When all is done, divinity is best;
Jerome's Bible,[30] Faustus, view it well. [*Reads.*]
Stipendium peccati mors est. Ha! *Stipendium, &c.:*
The reward of sin is death. — That 's hard. [*Reads.*]
Si peccasse negamus, fallimur, et nulla est in nobis veritas:
If we say that we have no sin we deceive ourselves, and there 's no truth in us. — Why then,
belike we must sin and so consequently die.
Ay, we must die an everlasting death.
What doctrine call you this, *Che sera, sera:*
"What will be shall be?" — Divinity, adieu!
These metaphysics of magicians
And necromantic books are heavenly;
Lines, circles, scenes,[31] letters, and characters,
Ay, these are those that Faustus most desires.
O what a world of profit and delight,
Of power, of honor, of omnipotence
Is promis'd to the studious artisan!
All things that move between the quiet[32] poles
Shall be at my command. Emperors and kings
Are but obey'd in their several provinces,
Nor can they raise the wind or rend the clouds;
But his dominion that exceeds[33] in this
Stretcheth as far as doth the mind of man.
A sound magician is a mighty god:
Here, Faustus, try thy[34] brains to gain[35] a deity.

Enter Wagner.

Wagner! commend me to my dearest friends,
The German Valdes and Cornelius;[36]
Request them earnestly to visit me.

Wag. I will, sir. *Exit.*

[14] Wittenberg. Faustus is "discovered" on the inner stage.

[15] Taken a degree.

[16] Aim.

[17] Aristotelian logic.

[18] Aristotle's "being and not being"; emend. Bullen; Q1 *Oncaymaeon;* later eds. *Oeconomy.*

[19] Where the philosopher leaves off, there the physician begins. (Adapted from Aristotle, as is l. 16.)

[20] Medical memoranda, so called from the Aphorisms of Hippocrates. (Ward.)

[21] Prescriptions. (Wheeler.)

[22] Qq1, 2; later eds. *men.*

[23] If one and the same thing is bequeathed to two persons, one shall take the thing and the other its value. (An incorrect version of a rule in the *Institutes.*) (Boas.)

[24] Q 1616 *petty.*

[25] A father cannot disinherit his son, except . . (Adapted from the *Institutes* of Justinian, codifier of the Roman law.)

[26] Q 1616; earlier eds. *Church.*

[27] Its.

[28] *I.e.*, money.

[29] Q 1616; earlier eds. *The deuill.*

[30] The Vulgate.

[31] Logeman conj. *schemes.*

[32] *I.e.*, fixed.

[33] Excels.

[34] Q 1616 *tire my.*

[35] Q 1616 *get.*

[36] Marlowe takes this name from Henry Cornelius Agrippa von Nettesheim, a friend of Faustus and a magician; but this character is not Agrippa (see ll. 116, 117). Brooke suggests that "the German Valdes" is a complimentary title for a mythical character, in allusion to the sixteenth-century Spanish humanist, Juan de Valdes.

FAUST. Their conference [37] will be a greater help to me
Than all my labors, plod I ne'er so fast.

Enter the Good Angel *and the* Evil Angel.

G. ANG. O Faustus, lay that damned book aside,
And gaze not on it lest it tempt thy soul
And heap God's heavy wrath upon thy head.
Read, read the Scriptures; that is blasphemy.

E. ANG. Go forward, Faustus, in that famous art,
Wherein all Nature's treasury is contain'd;
Be thou on earth as Jove is in the sky,
Lord and commander of these elements.
Exeunt [Angels.]

FAUST. How am I glutted with conceit of this! [38]
Shall I make spirits fetch me what I please,
Resolve me of all ambiguities,
Perform what desperate enterprise I will?
I'll have them fly to India [39] for gold,
Ransack the ocean for orient [40] pearl,
And search all corners of the new-found world
For pleasant fruits and princely delicates.
I'll have them read me strange philosophy
And tell the secrets of all foreign kings;
I'll have them wall all Germany with brass,
And make swift Rhine circle fair [Wittenberg]; [41]
I'll have them fill the public schools [42] with [silk], [43]
Wherewith the students shall be bravely clad;
I'll levy soldiers with the coin they bring,
And chase the Prince of Parma [44] from our land,
And reign sole king of all our provinces;
Yea, stranger engines for the brunt of war
Than was the fiery keel [45] at Antwerp's bridge,
I'll make my servile spirits to invent.
Come, German Valdes and Cornelius,
And make me blest with your sage conference.

Enter VALDES *and* CORNELIUS.

Valdes, sweet Valdes, and Cornelius,
Know that your words have won me at the last
To practise magic and concealed arts;
Yet not your words only, but mine own fantasy,
That will receive no object; [46] for my head
But ruminates on necromantic skill.
Philosophy is odious and obscure;
Both law and physic are for petty wits;
Divinity is basest of the three,
Unpleasant, harsh, contemptible, and vild; [47]
'T is magic, magic, that hath ravish'd me.
Then, gentle friends, aid me in this attempt;
And I that have with concise syllogisms
Gravell'd the pastors of the German church,
And made the flow'ring pride of Wittenberg
Swarm to my problems, [48] as the infernal spirits
On sweet Musæus, when he came to hell,
Will be as cunning as Agrippa was,
Whose shadows [49] made all Europe honor him.

VALD. Faustus, these books, thy wit, and our experience
Shall make all nations to canonize us.
As Indian Moors [50] obey their Spanish lords,
So shall the subjects [51] of every element
Be always serviceable to us three;
Like lions shall they guard us when we please;
Like Almain rutters [52] with their horsemen's staves,
Or Lapland giants, trotting by our sides;
Sometimes like women or unwedded maids,
Shadowing [53] more beauty in their airy [54] brows
Than in [the] [55] white breasts of the Queen of Love:
[From] [56] Venice shall they drag huge argosies, [57]
And from America the golden fleece

[37] Conversation.
[38] How am I filled with this notion.
[39] Probably, the West Indies, America.
[40] Lustrous.
[41] For the *Wittenberge* of Q 1616, Q1 has *Wertenberge*. Brooke suggests that Marlowe thought of the university town as the capital of Würtemberg.
[42] University lecture-halls.
[43] Emend. Dyce; old eds. *skill.* Brooke cites Cambridge regulations which forbade the wearing of silk by the students.
[44] The Spanish governor-general (1579–1592) of the Netherlands, nominally a part of the Empire.
[45] A Dutch "devil-ship" (filled with explosives) which damaged Parma's bridge at the siege of Antwerp.
[46] *I.e.*, my own fancy, which will entertain no regular academic subject — nor anything else but necromancy. Brooke differs from mod. eds., who insert the semicolon and omit the old texts' comma after "head"; but the antithesis is between "words" and "fantasy."
[47] Vile.
[48] Mathematical and logical lectures. (Ward.)
[49] Shades raised from the dead.
[50] American Indians.
[51] Q 1616 *spirits.*
[52] German troopers.
[53] Shadowing forth, portraying.
[54] Because insubstantial.
[55] Q 1616; Q1 *their.* Q 1616 reads *has* for *in.*
[56] Cor. Q 1609; Q1 *For.*
[57] Large merchantmen.

That yearly stuffs [58] old Philip's treasury;
If learned Faustus will be resolute.

FAUST. Valdes, as resolute am I in this
As thou to live; therefore object it not.

CORN. The miracles that magic will perform
Will make thee vow to study nothing else.
He that is grounded in astrology,
Enrich'd with tongues, well seen [59] [in] [60] minerals,
Hath all the principles magic doth require.
Then doubt not, Faustus, but to be renowm'd,
And more frequented for this mystery
Than heretofore the Delphian oracle.
The spirits tell me they can dry the sea
And fetch the treasure of all foreign wracks,
Ay, all the wealth that our forefathers hid
Within the massy entrails of the earth;
Then tell me, Faustus, what shall we three want?

FAUST. Nothing, Cornelius. O, this cheers my soul!
Come, show me some demonstrations magical,
That I may conjure in some lusty [61] grove,
And have these joys in full possession.

VALD. Then haste thee to some solitary grove,
And bear wise Bacon's [62] and Albanus' [63] works,
The Hebrew Psalter and New Testament;
And whatsoever else is requisite
We will inform thee ere our conference cease.

CORN. Valdes, first let him know the words of art;
And then, all other ceremonies learn'd,
Faustus may try his cunning by himself.

VALD. First I'll instruct thee in the rudiments,
And then wilt thou be perfecter than I.

FAUST. Then come and dine with me, and after meat
We'll canvass every quiddity [64] thereof;
For ere I sleep I'll try what I can do:
This night I'll conjure though I die therefore.

Exeunt.

[58] Q 1616 *stuff'd,* altered after the death of Philip II. Note inconsistency with the appearance of Charles V in this play.

[59] Versed.

[60] Add. Q_2.

[61] Pleasant. Qq $_{2, 3}$, *little*; Q 1616 *bushy.*

[62] Roger Bacon's.

[63] Possibly Pietro d'Albano, a thirteenth-century alchemist; or, misprinted, Albertus Magnus, the German Dominican of the same century, supposed to be a magician.

[64] Essential point.

[SCENE II] [65]

Enter two Scholars.

1 SCHOL. I wonder what's become of Faustus, that was wont to make our schools ring with *sic probo?* [66]

2 SCHOL. That shall we know, for see here comes his boy.

Enter WAGNER.

1 SCHOL. How now, sirrah! Where's thy master?

WAG. God in Heaven knows.

2 SCHOL. Why, dost not thou know?

WAG. Yes, I know; but that follows not.

1 SCHOL. Go to, sirrah; leave your jesting, and tell us where he is.

WAG. That follows not necessary by force of argument, that you, being licentiate, [67] should stand upon 't; therefore acknowledge your error and be attentive.

2 SCHOL. Why, didst thou not say thou knew'st?

WAG. Have you any witness on 't?

1 SCHOL. Yes, sirrah, I heard you.

WAG. Ask my fellow if I be a thief.

2 SCHOL. Well, you will not tell us?

WAG. Yes, sir, I will tell you; yet if you were not dunces, you would never ask me such a question; for is not he *corpus naturale?* [68] and is not that *mobile?* Then wherefore should you ask me such a question? But that I am by nature phlegmatic, slow to wrath, and prone to lechery — to love, I would say, — it were not for you to come within forty foot of the place of execution, [69] although I do not doubt to see you both hang'd the next sessions. Thus having triumph'd over you, I will set my countenance like a precisian, [70] and begin to speak thus: — Truly, my dear brethren, my master is within at dinner, with Valdes and Cornelius, as this wine, if it could speak, it would inform your Worships; and so the Lord bless you, preserve you, and keep you, my dear brethren, my dear brethren. *Exit.*

1 SCHOL. Nay, then, I fear he has fall'n into

[65] Before Faustus's house.

[66] Thus I prove (a scholastic formula).

[67] Licensed to ascend to a Master's or Doctor's degree. (Boas.)

[68] "'Corpus naturale seu mobile' is the current scholastic expression for the subject-matter of physics." (Ward.)

[69] *I.e.,* the dining-room. (Wagner.)

[70] Puritan.

that damned art, for which they two are infamous through the world.

2 SCHOL. Were he a stranger, and not allied to me, yet should I grieve for him. But come, let us go and inform the Rector,[71] and see if he by his grave counsel can reclaim him.

1 SCHOL. O, but I fear me nothing can reclaim him.

2 SCHOL. Yet let us try what we can do.

Exeunt.

[SCENE III] [72]

Enter FAUSTUS *to conjure.*

FAUST. Now that the gloomy shadow of the earth,[73]
Longing to view Orion's drizzling look,
Leaps from th' antar[c]tic world unto the sky
And dims the welkin with her pitchy breath,
Faustus, begin thine incantations,
And try if devils will obey thy hest,
Seeing thou hast pray'd and sacrific'd to them.
Within this circle is Jehovah's name,
Forward and backward anagrammatiz'd,
The breviated names of holy saints,
Figures of every adjunct to [74] the Heavens,
And characters of signs and erring stars,[75]
By which the spirits are enforc'd to rise.
Then fear not, Faustus, but be resolute,
And try the uttermost magic can perform.

Sint mihi Dei Acherontis propitii! Valeat numen triplex Iehovae! Ignei, aerii, aquatani [76] *spiritus, salvete! Orientis Princeps Belzebub, inferni ardentis monarcha, et Demogorgon, propitiamus vos, ut appareat et surgat Mephistophilis.* [*Quid tu moraris?*] [77] *Per Iehovam, Gehennam, et consecratam aquam quam nunc spargo, signumque crucis quod nunc facio, et per vota nostra, ipse nunc surgat nobis dicatus* [78] *Mephistophilis!* [79]

Enter [MEPHISTOPHILIS,] [80] *a* Devil.

I charge thee to return and change thy shape;
Thou art too ugly to attend on me.
Go, and return an old Franciscan friar;
That holy shape becomes a devil best.

Exit Devil.

I see there's virtue in my heavenly words;
Who would not be proficient in this art?
How pliant is this Mephistophilis,
Full of obedience and humility!
Such is the force of magic and my spells.
[Now,] [81] Faustus, thou art conjuror laureate;
Thou canst command great Mephistophilis:
Quin regis Mephistophilis fratris imagine.[82]

Re-enter MEPHISTOPHILIS [*like a Franciscan Friar*].

MEPH. Now, Faustus, what wouldst thou have me do?

FAUST. I charge thee wait upon me whilst I live,
To do whatever Faustus shall command,
Be it to make the moon drop from her sphere
Or the ocean to overwhelm the world.

MEPH. I am a servant to great Lucifer,
And may not follow thee without his leave;
No more than he commands must we perform.

FAUST. Did he not charge thee to appear to me?

MEPH. No, I came now hither of mine own accord.

FAUST. Did not my conjuring speeches raise thee? Speak!

MEPH. That was the cause, but yet per accident;
For when we hear one rack [83] the name of God,

[71] The head of the university.

[72] A grove.

[73] Q 1616 *night*. But, as Brooke notes, Orion is a winter constellation (hence "drizzling"), and when it is visible the sun is below the equator; thus the earth's shadow "can be said to be projected from the southern hemisphere . . unto the sky."

[74] Every star joined to.

[75] Planets.

[76] So old eds. Emend. Brooke *aquatici*.

[77] Conj. Schröer; old eds. *quod tumeraris*. For *Mephastophilis* of the earlier eds., Qq 1616 *et seq.* have *Mephostophilis Dragon*. Boas conj. *Enter Dragon above*. This is unlikely, but there may have been a note anticipatory of some feature of the entrance of "a Devil" immediately after this speech. The whole question is discussed by Root, *Englische Studien*, XLIII, 144–149.

[78] Cor. Q 1620; earlier eds. *dicatis*.

[79] Unto me be the gods of Acheron propitious. May the triple name of Jehovah prevail. Spirits of fire, air, and water, hail! Belzebub, Prince of the East, Sovereign of burning Hell, and Demogorgon, we propitiate you, that Mephistophilis may appear and rise. Why delayest thou? By Jehovah, Gehenna, and the holy water which now I sprinkle, and the sign of the cross which now I make, and by our prayer, may Mephistophilis, by us summoned, now arise.

[80] But not the actor who played Mephistophilis. Cf. on l. 21. In the Faust Book "a mighty Dragon" appears at this point.

[81] Emend. Albers; old eds. *No*.

[82] Indeed thou rulest Mephistophilis in his likeness of a friar. (Boas, who adopts, however, Taylor's emendation, *redis* for *regis*.)

[83] Torture into anagrams.

Abjure the Scriptures and his Savior Christ,
We fly, in hope to get his glorious soul;
Nor will we come, unless he use such means
Whereby he is in danger to be damn'd.
Therefore the shortest cut for conjuring
Is stoutly to abjure the Trinity,
And pray devoutly to the Prince of Hell.

FAUST. So Faustus hath
Already done, and holds this principle:
There is no chief but only Belzebub,
To whom Faustus doth dedicate himself.
This word "damnation" terrifies not him,
For he confounds hell in [84] Elysium;
His ghost be with the old philosophers!
But, leaving these vain trifles of men's souls,
Tell me what is that Lucifer, thy lord?

MEPH. Arch-regent and commander of all spirits.

FAUST. Was not that Lucifer an angel once?

MEPH. Yes, Faustus, and most dearly lov'd of God.

FAUST. How comes it then that he is prince of devils?

MEPH. Oh, by aspiring pride and insolence,
For which God threw him from the face of Heaven.

FAUST. And what are you that live with Lucifer?

MEPH. Unhappy spirits that fell with Lucifer,
Conspir'd against our God with Lucifer,
And are for ever damn'd with Lucifer.

FAUST. Where are you damn'd?

MEPH. In hell.

FAUST. How comes it then that thou art out of hell?

MEPH. Why this is hell, nor am I out of it!
Think'st thou that I, who saw the face of God,
And tasted the eternal joys of Heaven,
Am not tormented with ten thousand hells
In being depriv'd of everlasting bliss?
O Faustus, leave these frivolous demands,
Which strike a terror to my fainting soul.

FAUST. What, is great Mephistophilis so passionate [85]
For being depriv'd of the joys of Heaven?
Learn thou of Faustus manly fortitude,
And scorn those joys thou never shalt possess.
Go bear [these] [86] tidings to great Lucifer:
Seeing Faustus hath incurr'd eternal death
By desp'rate thoughts against Jove's [87] deity,
Say he surrenders up to him his soul,
So [88] he will spare him four-and-twenty years,
Letting him live in all voluptuousness,
Having thee ever to attend on me,
To give me whatsoever I shall ask,
To tell me whatsoever I demand,
To slay mine enemies, and aid my friends,
And always be obedient to my will.
Go, and return to mighty Lucifer,
And meet me in my study at midnight,
And then resolve [89] me of thy master's mind.

MEPH. I will, Faustus. *Exit.*

FAUST. Had I as many souls as there be stars,
I'd give them all for Mephistophilis.
By him I'll be great emp'ror of the world,
And make a bridge through [90] the moving air,
To pass the ocean with a band of men;
I'll join the hills that bind the Afric shore,
And make that [country] [91] continent to [92] Spain,
And both contributory to my crown.
The Emperor shall not live but by my leave,
Nor any potentate of Germany.
Now that I have obtain'd what I desire,
I'll live in speculation [93] of this art
Till Mephistophilis return again. *Exit.*

[SCENE IV] [94]

Enter WAGNER *and the* Clown.

WAG. Sirrah boy, come hither.

CLOWN. How, "boy"! Swowns,[95] "boy"! I hope you have seen many boys with such pickadevaunts [96] as I have. "Boy," quotha!

WAG. Tell me, sirrah, hast thou any comings in?

CLOWN. Ay, and goings out too. You may see else.

WAG. Alas, poor slave! See how poverty jesteth in his nakedness! The villain is bare and out of service, and so hungry that I know he would give his soul to the Devil for a shoulder of mutton, though it were blood-raw.

CLOWN. How? My soul to the Devil for a shoulder of mutton, though 't were blood-raw! Not so, good friend. By'r Lady, I had need

[84] Makes no distinction between hell and.
[85] Emotionally disturbed, grieved.
[86] Cor. Q 1616; earlier eds. *those.*
[87] Common in Elizabethan literature for the Christian God.
[88] Provided that.
[89] Inform.
[90] Dissyllabic.
[91] Q 1616; earlier eds. *land.*
[92] Adjoining.
[93] Contemplative study.
[94] Unlocated; perhaps a field or wood near Wittenberg.
[95] Zounds, God's wounds.
[96] Pointed beards.

have it well roasted and good sauce to it, if I pay so dear.

WAG. Well, wilt thou serve me, and I'll make thee go like *Qui mihi discipulus?*[97]

CLOWN. How, in verse?

WAG. No, sirrah; in beaten silk[98] and stavesacre.[99]

CLOWN. How, how, Knave's acre![100] Ay, I thought that was all the land his father left him. Do ye hear? I would be sorry to rob you of your living.

WAG. Sirrah, I say in stavesacre.

CLOWN. Oho! Oho! Stavesacre! Why, then, belike, if I were your man I should be full of vermin.

WAG. So thou shalt, whether thou beest with me or no. But, sirrah, leave your jesting, and bind yourself presently unto me for seven years, or I'll turn all the lice about thee into familiars, and they shall tear thee in pieces.

CLOWN. Do you hear, sir? You may save that labor; they are too familiar with me already. Swowns! they are as bold with my flesh as if they had paid for my meat and drink.

WAG. Well, do you hear, sirrah? Hold, take these guilders.

CLOWN. Gridirons! what be they?

WAG. Why, French crowns.

CLOWN. Mass, but for the name of French crowns, a man were as good have as many English counters. And what should I do with these?

WAG. Why, now, sirrah, thou art at an hour's warning, whensoever or wheresoever the Devil shall fetch thee.

CLOWN. No, no. Here, take your gridirons again.

WAG. Truly, I'll none of them.

CLOWN. Truly, but you shall.

WAG.[101] Bear witness I gave them him.

CLOWN. Bear witness I give them you again.

WAG. Well, I will cause two devils presently to fetch thee away — Baliol[102] and Belcher.

CLOWN. Let your Baliol and your Belcher come here, and I'll knock them, they were never so knock'd since they were devils. Say I should kill one of them, what would folks say? "Do ye see yonder tall[103] fellow in the round slop?[104] — he has kill'd the Devil." So I should be call'd Kill-devil all the parish over.

WAG. Baliol and Belcher! (*Enter two* Devils *and the* Clown *runs up and down crying.*) Spirits, away! *Exeunt* [Devils].

CLOWN. What, are they gone? A vengeance on them; they have vild long nails! There was a he-devil, and a she-devil; I'll tell you how you shall know them: all he-devils has horns, and all she-devils has clifts and cloven feet.

WAG. Well, sirrah, follow me.

CLOWN. But, do you hear — if I should serve you, would you teach me to raise up Banios and Belcheos?

WAG. I will teach thee to turn thyself to anything; to a dog, or a cat, or a mouse, or a rat, or anything.

CLOWN. How? a Christian fellow to a dog or a cat, a mouse, or a rat? No, no, sir; if you turn me into anything, let it be in the likeness of a little pretty frisking flea, that I may be here and there and everywhere. O, I'll tickle the pretty wenches' plackets[105]; I'll be amongst them, i' faith.

WAG. Well, sirrah, come.

CLOWN. But, do you hear, Wagner?

WAG. How! — Baliol and Belcher!

CLOWN. O Lord! I pray, sir, let Banio and Belcher go sleep.

WAG. Villain, call me Master Wagner, and let thy left eye be diametarily fix'd upon my right heel, with *quasi vestigias nostras insistere.*[106] *Exit.*

CLOWN. God forgive me, he speaks Dutch fustian![107] Well, I'll follow him; I'll serve him; that's flat. *Exit.*

[ACT II — SCENE I]

Enter FAUSTUS *in his study.*

FAUST. Now, Faustus, must
Thou needs be damn'd,[1] and canst thou not be saved!
What boots it then to think of God or Heaven?
Away with such vain fancies, and despair
Despair in God, and trust in Belzebub.

[97] The first words of W. Lily's *Ad discipulos carmen de moribus.* (Dyce.)
[98] Silk with metal embroidery hammered into it.
[99] A kind of larkspur, used to kill lice.
[100] Poultney Street, Soho, where junk-dealers were established.
[101] To the audience.
[102] Belial.
[103] Valiant.
[104] Loose breeches.
[105] Slits in skirts and petticoats.
[106] As if to tread my tracks.
[107] Highfalutin.
[1] Dyce's line division; in old eds. l. 1 ends here.

Now go not backward; no, Faustus, be resolute.
Why waverest thou? O, something soundeth in mine ears,
"Abjure this magic; turn to God again."
Ay, and Faustus will turn to God again.
To God? — He loves thee not;
The God thou servest is thine own appetite,
Wherein is fix'd the love of Belzebub;
To him I'll build an altar and a church,
And offer lukewarm blood of newborn babes.

Enter Good Angel *and* Evil [Angel].

G. Ang. Sweet Faustus, leave that execrable art.
[E. Ang. Go forward, Faustus, in that famous art.[2]]
Faust. Contrition, prayer, repentance! What of them?
G. Ang. O, they are means to bring thee unto Heaven.
E. Ang. Rather illusions, fruits of lunacy,
That makes men foolish that do trust them most.
G. Ang. Sweet Faustus, think of Heaven, and heavenly things.
E. Ang. No, Faustus, think of honor and[3] wealth. *Exeunt* [Angels].
Faust. Of wealth!
Why, the signiory of Emden[4] shall be mine.
When Mephistophilis shall stand by me,
What God can hurt thee, Faustus? Thou art safe;
Cast[5] no more doubts. Come, Mephistophilis,
And bring glad tidings from great Lucifer! —
Is 't not midnight? — Come, Mephistophilis:
Veni, veni, Mephistophile!

Enter Mephistophilis.

Now tell [me],[6] what says Lucifer, thy lord?
Meph. That I shall wait on Faustus while [he lives],[7]
So[8] he will buy my service with his soul.
Faust. Already Faustus hath hazarded that for thee.
Meph. But, Faustus, thou must bequeath it solemnly
And write a deed of gift with thine own blood,
For that security craves great Lucifer.
If thou deny it, I will back to hell.
Faust. Stay, Mephistophilis! and tell me what good
Will my soul do thy lord.
Meph. Enlarge his kingdom.
Faust. Is that the reason [why][9] he tempts us thus?
Meph. *Solamen miseris socios habuisse doloris.*[10]
Faust. [Why],[11] have you any pain, that tortures others?
Meph. As great as have the human souls of men.
But tell me, Faustus, shall I have thy soul?
And I will be thy slave, and wait on thee,
And give thee more than thou hast wit to ask.
Faust. Ay, Mephistophilis, I give it thee.
Meph. Then, [Faustus],[12] stab thine arm courageously,
And bind thy soul that at some certain day
Great Lucifer may claim it as his own;
And then be thou as great as Lucifer.
Faust. Lo, Mephistophilis, for love of thee
I cut mine arm, and with my proper blood
Assure my soul to be great Lucifer's,
Chief lord and regent of perpetual night.
View here the blood that trickles from mine arm,
And let it be propitious for my wish.
Meph. But, Faustus, thou must
Write it in manner of a deed of gift.
Faust. Ay, so I will. [*Writes.*] But, Mephistophilis,
My blood congeals, and I can write no more.
Meph. I'll fetch thee fire to dissolve it straight. *Exit.*
Faust. What might the staying of my blood portend?
Is it unwilling I should write this bill?
Why streams it not that I may write afresh?
"Faustus gives to thee his soul." Ah, there it stay'd.
Why shouldst thou not? Is not thy soul thine own?
Then write again, "Faustus gives to thee his soul."

Re-enter Mephistophilis *with a chafer of coals.*

Meph. Here's fire. Come, Faustus, set it[13] on.
Faust. So; now the blood begins to clear again;

[2] Add. Q 1616, before l. 15.
[3] Q_2 adds *of*.
[4] Then a great port.
[5] Reckon up.
[6] Add. Q 1616.
[7] Q 1616; earlier eds. *I liue.*
[8] Provided that.
[9] Add. Q 1616.
[10] *I.e.*, misery loves company.
[11] Add. Q 1616.
[12] Add. Q 1616.
[13] The dish of blood.

Now will I make an end immediately. [*Writes.*]

MEPH. [*aside*] O, what will not I do to obtain his soul?

FAUST. *Consummatum est:* this bill is ended,
And Faustus hath bequeath'd his soul to Lucifer.
But what is this inscription on mine arm?
Homo, fuge! Whither should I fly?
If unto God, he'll throw thee down to hell.
My senses are deceiv'd; here's nothing writ!—
I see it plain; here in this place is writ
Homo, fuge! Yet shall not Faustus fly.

MEPH. [*aside*] I'll fetch him somewhat to delight his mind. *Exit.*

Re-enter [MEPHISTOPHILIS] *with* Devils, *giving crowns and rich apparel to* FAUSTUS, *and dance, and then depart.*

FAUST. Speak, Mephistophilis; what means this show?

MEPH. Nothing, Faustus, but to delight thy mind withal,
And to show thee what magic can perform.

FAUST. But may I raise up spirits when I please?

MEPH. Ay, Faustus, and do greater things than these.

FAUST. Then there's enough for a thousand souls.
Here, Mephistophilis, receive this scroll,
A deed of gift of body and of soul;
But yet conditionally that thou perform
All articles prescrib'd between us both.

MEPH. Faustus, I swear by hell and Lucifer
To effect all promises between us made.

FAUST. Then hear me read them: "On these conditions following. First, that Faustus may be a spirit in form and substance. Secondly, that Mephistophilis shall be his servant, and at his command. Thirdly, that Mephistophilis shall do for him and bring him whatsoever. Fourthly, that he shall be in his chamber or house invisible. Lastly, that he shall appear to the said John Faustus, at all times, in what form or shape soever he please. I, John Faustus, of Wittenberg, Doctor, by these presents do give both body and soul to Lucifer, Prince of the East, and his minister, Mephistophilis; and furthermore grant unto them, that four-and-twenty years being expired, the articles above written inviolate, full power to fetch or carry the said John Faustus, body and soul, flesh, blood, or goods, into their habitation wheresoever. By me, John Faustus."

MEPH. Speak, Faustus; do you deliver this as your deed?

FAUST. Ay, take it, and the Devil give thee good on 't.

MEPH. Now, Faustus, ask what thou wilt.

FAUST. First will I question with thee about hell.
Tell me, where is the place that men call hell?

MEPH. Under the Heavens.

FAUST. Ay, [so are all things else;] [14] but whereabout?

MEPH. Within the bowels of these elements,
Where we are tortur'd and remain for ever;
Hell has no limits, nor is circumscrib'd
In one self place; for where we are is hell,
And where hell is [there] [14] must we ever be;
And, to conclude, when all the world dissolves,
And every creature shall be purified,
All places shall be hell that is not Heaven.

FAUST. Come, I think hell's a fable.

MEPH. Ay, think so still, till experience change thy mind.

FAUST. Why, think'st thou then that Faustus shall be damn'd?

MEPH. Ay, of necessity; for here's the scroll
Wherein thou hast given thy soul to Lucifer.

FAUST. Ay, and body too; but what of that?
Think'st thou that Faustus is so fond [15] to imagine
That after this life there is any pain?
Tush! these are trifles, and mere old wives' tales!

MEPH. But, Faustus, I am an instance to prove the contrary,
For I am damn'd, and am now in hell.

FAUST. How! now in hell!
Nay, an this be hell, I'll willingly be damn'd here;
What,[16] walking, disputing, etc?
But, leaving off this, let me have a wife,
The fairest maid in Germany;
For I am wanton and lascivious,
And cannot live without a wife.

MEPH. How! a wife?
I prithee, Faustus, talk not of a wife.

FAUST. Nay, sweet Mephistophilis, fetch me one, for I will have one.

MEPH. Well, thou wilt have one. Sit there till I come;
I'll fetch thee a wife in the Devil's name.

[*Exit.*]

[14] Add. Q 1616. [15] Foolish.
[16] Q 1616 adds *sleeping, eating.*

Re-enter [Mephistophilis] *with a* Devil *dress'd like a woman, with fireworks.*

Meph. Tell, Faustus, how dost thou like thy wife?

Faust. A plague on her for a hot whore!

Meph. Tut, Faustus,
Marriage is but a ceremonial toy;
If thou lovest me, think [no] [17] more of it.
I'll cull thee out the fairest courtesans
And bring them ev'ry morning to thy bed;
She whom thine eye shall like, thy heart shall have,
Be she as chaste as was Penelope,
As wise as Saba,[18] or as beautiful
As was bright Lucifer before his fall.
Hold, take this book; peruse it thoroughly:
The iterating of these lines brings gold;
The framing of this circle on the ground
Brings whirlwinds, tempests, thunder and lightning;
Pronounce this thrice devoutly to thyself,
And men in armor shall appear to thee,
Ready to execute what thou desir'st.

Faust. Thanks, Mephistophilis; yet fain would I have a book wherein I might behold all spells and incantations, that I might raise up spirits when I please.

Meph. Here they are, in this book. *There turn to them.*

Faust. Now would I have a book where I might see all characters and planets of the Heavens, that I might know their motions and dispositions.

Meph. Here they are too. *Turn to them.*

Faust. Nay, let me have one book more — and then I have done — wherein I might see all plants, herbs, and trees that grow upon the earth.

Meph. Here they be.

Faust. O, thou art deceived.

Meph. Tut, I warrant thee. *Turn to them.* [*Exeunt.*]

[Scene II] [19]

[*Enter* Faustus *in his study, and* Mephistophilis.] [20]

Faust. When I behold the Heavens, then I repent,
And curse thee, wicked Mephistophilis,
Because thou hast depriv'd me of those joys.

Meph. Why, Faustus,
Think'st thou Heaven is such a glorious thing?
I tell thee 't is not half so fair as thou,
Or any man that breathes on earth.

Faust. How provest thou that?

Meph. It was made for man; therefore is man more excellent.

Faust. If it were made for man, 't was made for me!
I will renounce this magic and repent.

Enter Good Angel *and* Evil Angel.

G. Ang. Faustus, repent; yet God will pity thee.

E. Ang. Thou art a spirit; God cannot pity thee.

Faust. Who buzzeth in mine ears I am a spirit?
Be I a devil, yet God may pity me;
Ay, God will pity me if I repent.

E. Ang. Ay, but Faustus never shall repent. *Exeunt* [Angels].

Faust. My heart's so hard'ned I cannot repent.
Scarce can I name salvation, faith, or Heaven,
But fearful echoes thunder in mine ears
"Faustus, thou art damn'd!" Then swords and knives,
Poison, guns, halters, and envenom'd steel
Are laid before me to despatch myself;
And long ere this I should have slain myself,
Had not sweet pleasure conquer'd deep despair.
Have I not made blind Homer sing to me
Of Alexander's [21] love and Œnon's death?
And hath not he that built the walls of Thebes
With ravishing sound of his melodious harp
Made music with my Mephistophilis?
Why should I die then, or basely despair?
I am resolv'd; Faustus shall ne'er repent.
Come, Mephistophilis, let us dispute again,
And argue of divine astrology.
Tell me, are there many heavens above the moon?
Are all celestial bodies but one globe,
As is the substance of this centric earth?

Meph. As are the elements, such are the spheres
Mutually folded in each other's orb,
And, Faustus,
All jointly move upon one axletree,
Whose terminine is term'd the world's wide pole;

[17] Add. Q_2.
[18] The Queen of Sheba.
[19] The same.
[20] Add. Q 1616, which prefaces the entrance with a short version of Wagner's speech at the opening of Act III. Q_1 has no break. Evidently the end of Sc. i was tampered with before 1604; it may originally have been followed by a comic scene.
[21] Paris's.

Nor are the names of Saturn, Mars, or Jupiter
Feign'd, but are erring stars.

FAUST. But tell me, have they all one motion, both *situ et tempore?*[22]

MEPH. All jointly move from east to west in four-and-twenty hours upon the poles of the world, but differ in their motion upon the poles of the zodiac.

FAUST. Tush! These slender trifles Wagner can decide.
Hath Mephistophilis no greater skill?
Who knows not the double motion of the planets?
The first is finish'd in a natural day;
The second thus: as Saturn in thirty years; Jupiter in twelve; Mars in four; the Sun, Venus, and Mercury in a year; the moon in twenty-eight days. Tush, these are freshmen's suppositions. But tell me, hath every sphere a dominion or *intelligenti*[a]?

MEPH. Ay.

FAUST. How many heavens, or spheres, are there?

MEPH. Nine: the seven planets, the firmament, and the empyreal heaven.

FAUST. Well, resolve me in this question: Why have we not conjunctions, oppositions, aspects, eclipses, all at one time, but in some years we have more, in some less?

MEPH. *Per inæqualem motum respectu totius.*[23]

FAUST. Well, I am answered. Tell me who made the world.

MEPH. I will not.

FAUST. Sweet Mephistophilis, tell me.

MEPH. Move me not, for I will not tell thee.

FAUST. Villain, have I not bound thee to tell me anything?

MEPH. Ay, that is not against our kingdom; but this is.
Think thou on hell, Faustus, for thou art damn'd.

FAUST. Think, Faustus, upon God that made the world.

MEPH. Remember this. *Exit.*

FAUST. Ay, go, accursed spirit, to ugly hell;
'T is thou hast damn'd distressed Faustus' soul.
Is 't not too late?

Re-enter Good Angel *and* Evil [Angel].

E. ANG. Too late.

G. ANG. Never too late, if Faustus can repent.

E. ANG. If thou repent, devils shall tear thee in pieces.

G. ANG. Repent, and they shall never raze thy skin.

Exeunt [Angels].

FAUST. Ah, Christ, my Savior,
Seek to save distressed Faustus' soul.

Enter LUCIFER, BELZEBUB, *and* MEPHISTOPHILIS.

LUC. Christ cannot save thy soul, for he is just;
There 's none but I have int'rest in the same.

FAUST. O, who art thou, that look'st so terrible?

LUC. I am Lucifer,
And this is my companion prince in hell.

FAUST. O Faustus, they are come to fetch away thy soul!

LUC. We come to tell thee thou dost injure us;
Thou talk'st of Christ, contrary to thy promise;
Thou shouldst not think of God: think of the Devil,
And of his dam, too.[24]

FAUST. Nor will I henceforth; pardon me in this,
And Faustus vows never to look to Heaven,
Never to name God, or to pray to Him,
To burn his Scriptures, slay his ministers,
And make my spirits pull his churches down.

LUC. Do so, and we will highly gratify thee. Faustus, we are come from hell to show thee some pastime. Sit down, and thou shalt see all the Seven Deadly Sins appear in their proper shapes.

FAUST. That sight will be pleasing unto me
As Paradise was to Adam the first day
Of his creation.

LUC. Talk not of Paradise nor creation, but mark this show; talk of the Devil, and nothing else. — Come away!

Enter the Seven Deadly Sins.

Now, Faustus, examine them of their several names and dispositions.

FAUST. What art thou — the first?

PRIDE. I am Pride. I disdain to have any

[22] In both the direction and the duration of their revolutions.

[23] On account of their unequal motion in relation to the whole. — After l. 65 Q 1616 adds:
Faust. But is there not *Cœlum igneum, & Cristalinum?*
Meph. No Faustus they be but Fables.

[24] Evidently an actor's gag.

parents. I am like to Ovid's flea[25]: I can creep into every corner of a wench; sometimes, like a periwig, I sit upon her brow;[26] or like a fan of feathers, I kiss her lips;[27] indeed I do — what do I not? But, fie, what a scent is here! I'll not speak another word, except the ground were perfum'd, and covered with cloth of arras.

FAUST. What art thou — the second?

COVET. I am Covetousness, begotten of an old churl in an old leathern bag; and might I have my wish, I would desire that this house and all the people in it were turn'd to gold, that I might lock you up in my good chest. O, my sweet gold!

FAUST. What art thou — the third?

WRATH. I am Wrath. I had neither father nor mother: I leap'd out of a lion's mouth when I was scarce half an hour old; and ever since I have run up and down the world with this case[28] of rapiers, wounding myself when I had nobody to fight withal. I was born in hell; and look to it, for some of you shall be[29] my father.

FAUST. What art thou — the fourth?

ENVY. I am Envy, begotten of a chimney sweeper and an oyster-wife. I cannot read, and therefore wish all books were burnt. I am lean with seeing others eat. O, that there would come a famine through all the world, that all might die, and I live alone! Then thou shouldst see how fat I would be. But must thou sit and I stand? Come down with a vengeance!

FAUST. Away, envious rascal! — What art thou — the fifth?

GLUT. Who, I, sir? I am Gluttony. My parents are all dead, and the devil a penny they have left me, but a bare pension, and that is thirty meals a day and ten bevers[30] — a small trifle to suffice nature. O, I come of a royal parentage! My grandfather was a gammon of bacon, my grandmother a hogshead of claret wine; my godfathers were these: Peter Pickleherring and Martin Martlemas-beef.[31] O, but my godmother, she was a jolly gentlewoman, and well beloved in every good town and city; her name was Mistress Margery March-beer. Now, Faustus, thou hast heard all my progeny,[32] wilt thou bid me to supper?

FAUST. No, I'll see thee hanged; thou wilt eat up all my victuals.

GLUT. Then the Devil choke thee!

FAUST. Choke thyself, glutton! — Who art thou — the sixth?

SLOTH. I am Sloth. I was begotten on a sunny bank, where I have lain ever since; and you have done me great injury to bring me from thence. Let me be carried thither again by Gluttony and Lechery. I'll not speak another word for a king's ransom.

FAUST. What are you, Mistress Minx, — the seventh and last?

LECH. Who, I, sir? I am one that loves an inch of raw mutton[33] better than an ell of fried stockfish;[34] and the first letter of my name begins with Lechery.

LUC. Away! to hell, to hell!

Exeunt the Sins.

— Now, Faustus, how dost thou like this?

FAUST. O, this feeds my soul!

LUC. Tut, Faustus, in hell is all manner of delight.

FAUST. O might I see hell, and return again,
How happy were I then!

LUC. Thou shalt; I will send for thee at midnight.
In meantime take this book; peruse it throughly,
And thou shalt turn thyself into what shape thou wilt.

FAUST. Great thanks, mighty Lucifer!
This will I keep as chary as my life.

LUC. Farewell, Faustus, and think on the Devil.

FAUST. Farewell, great Lucifer! — Come, Mephistophilis.

Exeunt omnes.

[SCENE III][35]

Enter ROBIN *the Ostler with a book in his hand.*

ROBIN. O, this is admirable! Here I ha' stol'n one of Dr. Faustus' conjuring books,

[25] The *Carmen de Pulice*, probably of medieval origin, was attributed to Ovid. (Boas.)

[26] Q 1616 adds *next, like a Necke-lace I hang about her Necke.*

[27] In place of the next seven words Q 1616 reads *And then turning my selfe to a wrought Smocke do what I list.*

[28] Pair.

[29] One of you devils is doubtless.

[30] Between-meal refreshments.

[31] The feast of St. Martin (Nov. 11) "was the customary time for hanging up [salted] provisions." (Nares.)

[32] Lineage.

[33] Punning on "mutton" = wench, harlot.

[34] Salted or dried fish.

[35] An inn-yard. Q_1 places this scene, erroneously, after the chorus which opens Act IV, and immediately before the comic scene, III, ii. Q 1616

and i' faith I mean to search some circles[36] for my own use! Now will I make all the maidens in our parish dance at my pleasure, stark naked before me; and so by that means I shall see more than e'er I felt or saw yet.

Enter RALPH[37] *calling* ROBIN.

RALPH. Robin, prithee come away; there's a gentleman tarries to have his horse, and he would have his things rubb'd and made clean. He keeps such a chafing with my mistress about it; and she has sent me to look thee out. Prithee come away.

ROBIN. Keep out, keep out, or else you are blown up, you are dismemb'red, Ralph; keep out, for I am about a roaring piece of work.

RALPH. Come, what doest thou with that same book? Thou canst not read.

ROBIN. Yes, my master and mistress shall find that I can read, he for his forehead,[38] she for her private study; she's born to bear with me, or else my art fails.

RALPH. Why, Robin, what book is that?

ROBIN. What book! Why, the most intolerable book for conjuring that e'er was invented by any brimstone devil.

RALPH. Canst thou conjure with it?

ROBIN. I can do all these things easily with it: first, I can make thee drunk with ippocras[39] at any ta[v]ern in Europe for nothing; that's one of my conjuring works.

RALPH. Our Master Parson says that's nothing.

ROBIN. True, Ralph; and more, Ralph, if thou hast any mind to Nan Spit, our kitchen-maid, then turn her and wind her to thy own use, as often as thou wilt, and at midnight.

RALPH. O brave, Robin, shall I have Nan Spit, and to mine own use? On that condition I'll feed thy devil with horsebread as long as he lives, of free cost.

ROBIN. No more, sweet Ralph; let's go and make clean our boots, which lie foul upon our hands, and then to our conjuring in the Devil's name. *Exeunt.*

correctly places II, iii, though in an altered version; Ralph becomes Dick, a hostler, and Robin seems to be the clown of I, iv. Brooke suggests that the appearance of II, iii, and III, iii, consecutively in Q_1 "is presumably due to the fact that they were not in the original MS, but formed a supplement on separate sheets."

36 Common with a double meaning in these plays.

37 Old eds. *Rafe*, throughout.

38 Innumerable jests in these plays allude to the horns which were supposed to grow in the brows of a deceived husband.

39 A drink made of wine, sugared and spiced.

[ACT III]

Enter WAGNER, *solus* [*as* Chorus].[1]

WAGNER. Learned Faustus, to know the secrets of astronomy
Graven in the book of Jove's high firmament,
Did mount himself to scale Olympus' top,
Being seated in a chariot burning bright,
Drawn by the strength of yoky dragons'[2] necks.
[He views the clouds, the planets, and the stars,
The tropic zones, and quarters of the sky,
From the bright circle of the horned moon
Even to the height of *Primum Mobile;*[3]
And, whirling round with this circumference,
Within the concave compass of the pole,
From east to west his dragons swiftly glide
And in eight days did bring him home again.
Not long he stayed within his quiet house,
To rest his bones after his weary toil;
But new exploits do hale him out again,
And, mounted then upon a dragon's back,
That with his wings did part the subtle air,]
He now is gone to prove cosmography,
[That measures coasts and kingdoms of the earth:]
And, as I guess, will first arrive at Rome,
To see the Pope and manner of his court,
And take some part of holy Peter's feast,
That to this day is highly solemniz'd.
Exit WAGNER.

[SCENE I][4]

Enter FAUSTUS *and* MEPHISTOPHILIS.

FAUST. Having now, my good Mephistophilis,
Pass'd with delight the stately town of Trier,[5]
Environ'd round with airy mountain-tops,
With walls of flint, and deep entrenched lakes,
Not to be won by any conquering prince;
From Paris next, coasting the realm of France,
We saw the river Maine fall into Rhine,

1 In Q_1 this speech, assigned to Wagner, and cut for the stage, comes between II, ii, and III, i. In Q 1616 it appears, incorrectly, between II, i and ii, and again (assigned to Chorus) to open Act III, with the addition of the bracketed lines.

2 Among properties for this play Henslowe lists a dragon. Wagner suggests that Faustus may have alighted from it at the opening of III, i. But see, also, on S. D. following I, iii, 25.

3 "The axle of the heavens, that moveth the whole firmament." (English Faust Book.)

4 Rome. The Pope's privy-chamber.

5 Treves.

Whose banks are set with groves of fruitful vines;
Then up to Naples, rich Campania,[6]
Whose buildings fair and gorgeous to the eye,
The streets straight forth, and pav'd with finest brick,
Quarters the town in four equivalents.
There saw we learned Maro's [7] golden tomb,
The way he cut, an English mile in length,
Thorough a rock of stone in one night's space;
From thence to Venice, Padua, and the rest,
In midst of which a sumptuous temple stands;[8]
That threats the stars with her aspiring top,
[Whose frame is paved with sundry-colored stones
And roof'd aloft with curious work in gold.]
Thus hitherto hath Faustus spent his time:
But tell me, now, what resting-place is this?
Hast thou, as erst I did command,
Conducted me within the walls of Rome?

MEPH. [I have, my Faustus; and, for proof thereof,
This is the goodly palace of the Pope;
And 'cause we are no common guests,
I choose his privy-chamber for our use.][9]

FAUST. I hope his Holiness will bid us welcome.

MEPH. [All's one, for we'll be bold with his ven'son.]
And now, my Faustus, that thou mayst perceive
What Rome containeth to delight thee with,
Know that this city stands upon seven hills
That underprops the groundwork of the same.
[Just through the midst runs flowing Tiber's stream,
With winding banks that cut it in two parts,][10]
Over the which four stately bridges lean,
That makes safe passage to each part of Rome.
Upon the bridge call'd Ponto Angelo
Erected is a castle passing strong,
Within whose walls such store of ordnance are,
And double cannons, fram'd of carved brass,
As match the days within one complete year;
Besides the gates and high pyramides,
Which Julius Cæsar brought from Africa.

FAUST. Now by the kingdoms of infernal rule,
Of Styx, Acheron, and the fiery lake
Of ever-burning Phlegethon, I swear
That I do long to see the monuments
And situation of bright-splendent Rome:
Come, therefore; let's away.

MEPH. Nay, Faustus, stay; I know you'd fain see the Pope,
And take some part of holy Peter's feast,
[11] Where thou shalt see a troop of bald-pate friars,
Whose *summum bonum* is in belly-cheer.

FAUST. Well, I am content to compass, then, some sport,
And by their folly make us merriment.
Then charm me, that I may be invisible, to do what I please,
Unseen of any whilst I stay in Rome.
[MEPHISTOPHILIS *charms him.*]

MEPH. So, Faustus; now
Do what thou wilt, thou shalt not be discerned.

Sound a sennet.[12] *Enter the* POPE *and the* CARDINAL *of* LORRAINE *to the banquet, with* Friars *attending.*

POPE. My Lord of Lorraine, wilt please you draw near?

FAUST. Fall to, and the Devil choke you an [13] you spare!

POPE. How now! Who's that which spake? — Friars, look about.

[1] FRIAR. Here's nobody, if it like your Holiness.

POPE. My Lord, here is a dainty dish was sent me from the Bishop of Milan.

FAUST. I thank you, sir. *Snatch it.*

POPE. How now! Who's that which snatch'd the meat from me? Will no man look? — My Lord, this dish was sent me from the Cardinal of Florence.

[6] The English Faust Book reads "to Campania [*i.e.*, the province] in the Kingdom of Naples." Brooke observes that Marlowe evidently took "Campania" as another name for the *city* of Naples.

[7] Virgil's. A tunnel near it was supposed to be the work of his magic.

[8] St. Mark's, at Venice; not, as Brooke suggests, a "composite structure in a nameless city." Though in the Faust Book Padua is visited and St. Anthony's there is admired, "sumptuous" occurs in the E. F. B.'s description of St. Mark's, and any great church may be said to be lofty. For "and the rest", Q 1616 misunderstandingly reads "and the East", and for "in *midst* of which" it despairingly reads "in *one* of which," another indication of its inferiority. Padua is here taken as a Venetian possession; "the rest" are the other territories of Venice. Ll. 19, 20, unquestionably genuine, are added (*i.e.*, preserved) by Q 1616.

[9] This speech, and the next line of Mephistophilis, are from Q 1616; earlier eds. replace them by actors' garbled prose.

[10] Add. Q 1616.

[11] The next seven lines are replaced in Q 1616 by an addition of 205 ll., probably by Rowley, in which Faust and Mephistophilis, disguised as cardinals, play a part in the Pope's disposition of a rival, the "Saxon Bruno."

[12] Fanfare of trumpets.

[13] If.

FAUST. You say true; I'll ha't.

[*Snatches it.*]

POPE. What, again? — My Lord, I'll drink to your Grace.

FAUST. I'll pledge your Grace.

[*Snatches the cup.*]

C. of LOR. My Lord, it may be some ghost newly crept out of purgatory, come to beg a pardon of your Holiness.

POPE. It may be so. — Friars, prepare a dirge to lay the fury of this ghost. — Once again, my Lord, fall to.

The POPE *crosseth himself.*

FAUST. What, are you crossing of yourself? Well, use that trick no more, I would advise you. — (*Cross again.*) Well, there's the second time. Aware the third, I give you fair warning.

Cross again, and FAUSTUS *hits him a box of the ear; and they all run away.*

Come on, Mephistophilis, what shall we do?

MEPH. Nay, I know not. We shall be curs'd with bell, book, and candle.

FAUST. How! bell, book, and candle, —
candle, book, and bell,
Forward and backward to curse Faustus to hell!
Anon you shall hear a hog grunt, a calf bleat, and an ass bray,
Because it is Saint Peter's holiday.

Re-enter all the Friars *to sing the dirge.*

[1] FRIAR. Come, brethren, let's about our business with good devotion.

Sing this:

Cursed be he that stole away his Holiness' meat from the table! *Maledicat Dominus!*[14]

Cursed be he that struck his Holiness a blow on the face! *Maledicat Dominus!*

Cursed be he that took Friar Sandelo a blow on the pate! *Maledicat Dominus!*

Cursed be he that disturbeth our holy dirge! *Maledicat Dominus!*

Cursed be he that took away his Holiness' wine! *Maledicat Dominus! Et omnes sancti!*[15] *Amen!*

[MEPHISTOPHILIS *and* FAUSTUS] *beat the* Friars, *and fling fireworks among them, and so exeunt.*

[14] May the Lord curse him.
[15] And all the Saints.

[SCENE II][16]

Enter ROBIN *and* RALPH[17] *with a silver goblet.*

ROBIN. Come, Ralph, did not I tell thee we were for ever made by this Doctor Faustus book? *Ecce signum*, here's a simple purchase[18] for horsekeepers; our horses shall eat no hay as long as this lasts.

Enter the Vintner.

RALPH. But, Robin, here comes the vintner.

ROBIN. Hush! I'll gull him supernaturally. — Drawer, I hope all is paid; God be with you. — Come, Ralph.

VINT. Soft, sir; a word with you. I must yet have a goblet paid from you, ere you go.

ROBIN. I, a goblet, Ralph; I, a goblet! I scorn you, and you are but a &c.[19] I, a goblet! Search me.

VINT. I mean so, sir, with your favor.

[*Searches him.*]

ROBIN. How say you now?

VINT. I must say somewhat to your fellow. You, sir!

RALPH. Me, sir! me, sir! Search your fill. [Vintner *searches him.*] Now, sir, you may be ashamed to burden honest men with a matter of truth.[20]

VINT. Well, t' one of you hath this goblet about you.

ROBIN. [*aside*] You lie, drawer; 't is afore me. — Sirrah you, I'll teach ye to impeach honest men; stand by; I'll scour you for a goblet! Stand aside you had best, I charge you in the name of Belzebub. — [*aside to* RALPH] Look to the goblet, Ralph.

VINT. What mean you, sirrah?

ROBIN. I'll tell you what I mean. (*He reads* [*from the book.*]) *Sanctobulorum, Periphrasticon* — Nay, I'll tickle you, vintner. — [*aside to* RALPH] Look to the goblet, Ralph. — [*Reads.*] *Polypragmos Belseborams framanto pacostiphos tostu, Mephistophilis, etc.*

Enter MEPHISTOPHILIS, *sets squibs at their backs,* [*and then exit*].[21] *They run about.*

[16] An inn. In Q 1616 this scene, as here, follows III, i. In Q_1 the order is III, i; chorus to IV; II, iii; III, ii. The scene in Q 1616 differs widely.
[17] Old eds. *Rafe* throughout.
[18] Piece of loot.
[19] The low comedian was expected to supply a string of racy invectives.
[20] A question of honesty.
[21] Add. Dyce, in view of Mephistophilis's reentry. The double entrance indicates textual corruption. The squibs were "an afterthought." (Simpson.)

VINT. *O nomine Domine!* [22] what mean'st thou, Robin? Thou hast no goblet.

RALPH. *Peccatum peccatorum!* [23] Here's thy goblet, good vintner.

ROBIN. *Misericordia pro nobis!* [24] What shall I do? Good Devil, forgive me now, and I'll never rob thy library more.

Re-enter to them MEPHISTOPHILIS.

MEPH. Vanish, villains!
Th' one like an ape, another like a bear, the third an ass, for doing this enterprise. — [25]
[*Exit* Vintner.]
Monarch of hell, under whose black survey
Great potentates do kneel with awful fear,
Upon whose altars thousand souls do lie,
How am I vexed with these villains' charms!
From Constantinople am I hither come
Only for pleasure of these damned slaves.

ROBIN. How? from Constantinople? You have had a great journey. Will you take sixpence in your purse to pay for your supper, and be gone?

MEPH. Well, villains, for your presumption, I transform thee into an ape, and thee into a dog; and so, begone! *Exit.*

ROBIN. How, into an ape? That's brave! I'll have fine sport with the boys. I'll get nuts and apples enow.

RALPH. And I must be a dog.

ROBIN. I' faith thy head will never be out of the pottage pot. *Exeunt.*

[ACT IV]

Enter Chorus.[26]

CHORUS. When Faustus had with pleasure ta'en the view
Of rarest things and royal courts of kings,
He stay'd his course and so returned home;
Where such as bear his absence but with grief,
I mean his friends and near'st companions,
Did gratulate his safety with kind words,
And in their conference of what befell,
Touching his journey through the world and air,
They put forth questions of astrology,
Which Faustus answer'd with such learned skill
As they admir'd and wond'red at his wit.
Now is his fame spread forth in every land;
Amongst the rest the Emperor is one;
Carolus the Fifth, at whose palace now
Faustus is feasted 'mongst his noblemen.
What there he did in trial of his art,
I leave untold — your eyes shall see perform'd.
Exit.

[SCENE I] [27]

Enter EMPEROR, FAUSTUS, [MEPHISTOPHILIS,] *and a* Knight, *with attendants.*

EMP. Master Doctor Faustus, I have heard strange report of thy knowledge in the black art, how that none in my empire nor in the whole world can compare with thee for the rare effects of magic; they say thou hast a familiar spirit, by whom thou canst accomplish what thou list. This, therefore, is my request, that thou let me see some proof of thy skill, that mine eyes may be witnesses to confirm what mine ears have heard reported; and here I swear to thee, by the honor of mine imperial crown, that, whatever thou doest, thou shalt be no ways prejudiced or endamaged.

KNIGHT. (*aside*) I' faith he looks much like a conjuror.

FAUST. My gracious Sovereign, though I must confess myself far inferior to the report men have published, and nothing answerable [28] to the honor of your imperial Majesty, yet for that love and duty binds me thereunto, I am content to do whatsoever your Majesty shall command me.

EMP. Then, Doctor Faustus, mark what I shall say.
As I was sometime solitary set
Within my closet, sundry thoughts arose
About the honor of mine ancestors,
How they had won by prowess such exploits,
Got such riches, subdued so many kingdoms,
As we that do succeed, or they that shall
Hereafter possess our throne, shall
(I fear me) ne'er attain to that degree
Of high renown and great authority;
Amongst which kings is Alexander the Great,
Chief spectacle of the world's preëminence,

[22] The Vintner's imperfect Latin for "in the name of the Lord."
[23] Sin of sins.
[24] Mercy on us.
[25] Mod. eds. omit this speech; it may be an alternative ending for the scene. The double transformation indicates corruption.
[26] Q 1616 om. this speech; in Q_1 it appears, misplaced, after III, i.
[27] A room in the imperial palace (at Innsbruck). Q 1616 rewrites and expands this scene, which it prefaces with another at the Emperor's court.
[28] In no respect adequate.

The bright shining of whose glorious acts
Lightens the world with his[29] reflecting beams,
As, when I heard but motion[30] made of him,
It grieves my soul I never saw the man.
If, therefore, thou by cunning of thine art
Canst raise this man from hollow vaults below,
Where lies entomb'd this famous conqueror,
And bring with him his beauteous paramour,
Both in their right shapes, gesture, and attire
They us'd to wear during their time of life,
Thou shalt both satisfy my just desire
And give me cause to praise thee whilst I live.

FAUST. My gracious Lord, I am ready to accomplish your request so far forth as by art, and power of my spirit, I am able to perform.

KNIGHT. (*aside*) I' faith that 's just nothing at all.

FAUST. But, if it like your Grace, it is not in my ability to present before your eyes the true substantial bodies of those two deceased princes, which long since are consumed to dust.

KNIGHT. (*aside*) Ay, marry, Master Doctor, now there 's a sign of grace in you, when you will confess the truth.

FAUST. But such spirits as can lively resemble Alexander and his paramour shall appear before your Grace in that manner that they best liv'd in, in their most flourishing estate; which I doubt not shall sufficiently content your imperial Majesty.

EMP. Go to, Master Doctor; let me see them presently.[31]

KNIGHT. Do you hear, Master Doctor? You bring Alexander and his paramour before the Emperor!

FAUST. How then, sir?

KNIGHT. I' faith that 's as true as Diana turn'd me to a stag!

FAUST. No, sir, but when Actæon died, he left the horns for you. Mephistophilis, begone. *Exit* MEPHISTOPHILIS.

KNIGHT. Nay, an you go to conjuring, I 'll be gone. *Exit* Knight.

FAUST. I'll meet with you anon for interrupting me so. — Here they are, my gracious Lord.

Re-enter MEPHISTOPHILIS *with* [Spirits *in the shapes of*] ALEXANDER *and his* Paramour.

EMP. Master Doctor, I heard this lady while she liv'd had a wart or mole in her neck. How shall I know whether it be so or no?

FAUST. Your Highness may boldly go and see. [*Exeunt* Spirits.]

EMP. Sure these are no spirits, but the true substantial bodies of those two deceased princes.

FAUST. Will 't please your Highness now to send for the knight that was so pleasant with me here of late?

EMP. One of you call him forth. [*Exit* Attendant.]

Re-enter the Knight *with a pair of horns on his head.*

How now, Sir Knight! Why I had thought thou hadst been a bachelor; but now I see thou hast a wife, that not only gives thee horns, but makes thee wear them. Feel on thy head.

KNIGHT. Thou damned wretch and execrable dog,
Bred in the concave of some monstrous rock,
How dar'st thou thus abuse a gentleman?
Villain, I say, undo what thou hast done!

FAUST. O, not so fast, sir; there 's no haste; but, good, are you rememb'red how you crossed me in my conference with the Emperor? I think I have met with you for it.

EMP. Good Master Doctor, at my entreaty release him; he hath done penance sufficient.

FAUST. My gracious Lord, not so much for the injury he off'red me here in your presence, as to delight you with some mirth, hath Faustus worthily requited this injurious knight; which being all I desire, I am content to release him of his horns; and, Sir Knight, hereafter speak well of scholars. — Mephistophilis, transform him straight. [MEPHISTOPHILIS *removes the horns.*] Now, my good Lord, having done my duty I humbly take my leave.

EMP. Farewell, Master Doctor; yet, ere you go,
Expect from me a bounteous reward. [*Exeunt.*]

[SCENE II][32]

[*Enter* FAUSTUS *and* MEPHISTOPHILIS.]

FAUST. Now, Mephistophilis, the restless course
That Time doth run with calm and silent foot,
Short'ning my days and thread of vital life,
Calls for the payment of my latest years;

[29] Its. [30] Mention. [31] At once.

[32] A green; afterwards Faustus's house. The wreckage of several scenes probably confronts us here; most of this is rubbish, but note the Marlovian column still standing in ll. 45–50. Two additional scenes precede this in Q 1616, which reduces our Sc. ii.

Therefore, sweet Mephistophilis, let us
Make haste to Wittenberg.

MEPH. What, will you go on horseback or on foot?

FAUST. Nay, till I am past this fair and pleasant green,
I'll walk on foot.

Enter a Horse-Courser.

HORSE-C. I have been all this day seeking one Master Fustian; mass, see where he is! — God save you, Master Doctor!

FAUST. What, horse-courser! You are well met.

HORSE-C. Do you hear, sir? I have brought you forty dollars for your horse.

FAUST. I cannot sell him so; if thou lik'st him for fifty, take him.

HORSE-C. Alas, sir, I have no more. — I pray you speak for me.

MEPH. I pray you let him have him; he is an honest fellow, and he has a great charge, neither wife nor child.

FAUST. Well, come, give me your money. [Horse-Courser *gives* FAUSTUS *the money*.] My boy will deliver him to you. But I must tell you one thing before you have him: ride him not into the water at any hand.

HORSE-C. Why, sir, will he not drink of all waters?

FAUST. O yes, he will drink of all waters, but ride him not into the water; ride him over hedge or ditch, or where thou wilt, but not into the water.

HORSE-C. Well, sir. — [*aside*] Now am I made man for ever. I'll not leave my horse for forty.[33] If he had but the quality of hey ding ding, hey ding ding, I'd make a brave living on him; he has a buttock as slick as an eel. — Well, God buy, sir; your boy will deliver him me. But hark ye, sir; if my horse be sick or ill at ease, if I bring his water to you, you'll tell me what it is?

Exit Horse-Courser.

FAUST. Away, you villain; what, dost think I am a horse-doctor? —
What art thou, Faustus, but a man condemn'd to die?
Thy fatal time doth draw to final end;
Despair doth drive distrust unto my thoughts.
Confound these passions with a quiet sleep.
Tush, Christ did call the thief upon the cross;
Then rest thee, Faustus, quiet in conceit.

Sleep in his chair.

[33] *I.e.*, any number of others. (Boas.)

Re-enter Horse-Courser, *all wet, crying.*

HORSE-C. Alas, alas! Doctor Fustian, quotha? Mass, Doctor Lopus[34] was never such a doctor. Has given me a purgation has purg'd me of forty dollars; I shall never see them more. But yet, like an ass as I was, I would not be ruled by him, for he bade me I should ride him into no water. Now I, thinking my horse had had some rare quality that he would not have had me known of, I, like a vent'rous youth, rid him into the deep pond at the town's end. I was no sooner in the middle of the pond, but my horse vanish'd away, and I sat upon a bottle[35] of hay, never so near drowning in my life. But I'll seek out my Doctor, and have my forty dollars again, or I'll make it the dearest horse — O, yonder is his snipper-snapper.[36] — Do you hear? You hey-pass,[37] where's your master?

MEPH. Why, sir, what would you? You cannot speak with him.

HORSE-C. But I will speak with him.

MEPH. Why, he's fast asleep. Come some other time.

HORSE-C. I'll speak with him now, or I'll break his glass windows about his ears.

MEPH. I tell thee he has not slept this eight nights.

HORSE-C. An he have not slept this eight weeks, I'll speak with him.

MEPH. See where he is, fast asleep.

HORSE-C. Ay, this is he. — God save ye, Master Doctor! Master Doctor, Master Doctor Fustian! — Forty dollars, forty dollars for a bottle of hay!

MEPH. Why, thou seest he hears thee not.

HORSE-C. So ho, ho! — so ho, ho! (*Holla in his ear.*) No, will you not wake? I'll make you wake ere I go. (*Pull him by the leg, and pull it away.*) Alas, I am undone! What shall I do?

FAUST. O my leg, my leg! Help, Mephistophilis! Call the officers. My leg, my leg!

MEPH. Come, villain, to the constable.

HORSE-C. O Lord, sir, let me go, and I'll give you forty dollars more.

MEPH. Where be they?

HORSE-C. I have none about me. Come to my ostry[38] and I'll give them you.

[34] Queen Elizabeth's physician, Roderigo Lopez, a Spanish Jew, charged with conspiring to poison her and executed in 1594 — nearly a year after Marlowe's death!

[35] Truss.

[36] Whippersnapper.

[37] Juggler, since this was his cry. (Dyce, Ward.)

[38] Hostelry, inn.

MEPH. Begone quickly.

Horse-Courser *runs away.*

FAUST. What, is he gone? Farewell he! Faustus has his leg again, and the horse-courser, I take it, a bottle of hay for his labor. Well, this trick shall cost him forty dollars more.

Enter WAGNER.

How now, Wagner, what's the news with thee?

WAG. Sir, the Duke of Vanholt doth earnestly entreat your company.

FAUST. The Duke of Vanholt! an honorable gentleman, to whom I must be no niggard of my cunning. Come, Mephistophilis, let's away to him. *Exeunt.*

[SCENE III] [39]

Enter [40] *the* DUKE [*of* VANHOLT], *the* DUCHESS, [FAUSTUS, *and* MEPHISTOPHILIS.]

DUKE. Believe me, Master Doctor, this merriment hath much pleased me.

FAUST. My gracious Lord, I am glad it contents you so well. — But it may be, madam, you take no delight in this. I have heard that great-bellied women do long for some dainties or other. What is it, madam? Tell me, and you shall have it.

DUCHESS. Thanks, good Master Doctor; and for I see your courteous intent to pleasure me, I will not hide from you the thing my heart desires; and were it now summer, as it is January and the dead time of the winter, I would desire no better meat than a dish of ripe grapes.

FAUST. Alas, madam, that's nothing. Mephistophilis, begone. (*Exit* MEPHISTOPHILIS.) Were it a greater thing than this, so it would content you, you should have it.

Re-enter MEPHISTOPHILIS *with the grapes.*

Here they be, madam; wilt please you taste on them?

DUKE. Believe me, Master Doctor, this makes me wonder above the rest, that being in the dead time of winter and in the month of January, how you should come by these grapes.

FAUST. If it like your Grace, the year is divided into two circles over the whole world, that, when it is here winter with us, in the contrary circle it is summer with them, as in India, Saba,[41] and farther countries in the East; and by means of a swift spirit that I have, I had them brought hither, as ye see. — How do you like them, madam; be they good?

DUCHESS. Believe me, Master Doctor, they be the best grapes that e'er I tasted in my life before.

FAUST. I am glad they content you so, madam.

DUKE. Come, madam, let us in, where you must well reward this learned man for the great kindness he hath show'd to you.

DUCHESS. And so I will, my Lord; and, whilst I live, rest beholding for this courtesy.

FAUST. I humbly thank your Grace.

DUKE. Come, Master Doctor, follow us and receive your reward. *Exeunt.*

[ACT V — SCENE I] [1]

Enter WAGNER, *solus.*

WAG. I think my master means to die shortly,
For he hath given to me all his goods;
And yet, methinks if that death were near,
He would not banquet and carouse and swill
Amongst the students, as even now he doth,
Who are at supper with such belly-cheer
As Wagner ne'er beheld in all his life.
See where they come! Belike the feast is ended. [*Exit.*]

Enter FAUSTUS, *with two or three* Scholars [*and* MEPHISTOPHILIS].

1 SCHOL. Master Doctor Faustus, since our conference about fair ladies, which was the beautiful'st in all the world,[2] we have determined with ourselves that Helen of Greece was the admirablest lady that ever lived. Therefore, Master Doctor, if you will do us that favor, as to let us see that peerless dame of Greece, whom all the world admires for majesty, we should think ourselves much beholding unto you.

FAUST. Gentlemen,
For that I know your friendship is unfeigned,
And Faustus' custom is not to deny

[39] A residence of the Duke of "Vanholt." In Q 1616 another comic scene, with the horse-courser, precedes this. Sc. iii is expanded in Q 1616.

[40] Q_1 adds *to them*, indicating corruption, since Faust and Mephistophilis have just left the stage.

[41] Sheba.

[1] Wittenberg. A room in Faustus's house.

[2] Simpson notes the survival of a Marlovian line, beginning "which", indicating that this prose is an adapter's work.

The just requests of those that wish him well,
You shall behold that peerless dame of Greece,
No otherways for pomp and majesty
Than when Sir Paris cross'd the seas with her
And brought the spoils to rich Dardania.
Be silent, then; for danger is in words.

Music sounds, and HELEN *passeth over the stage.*

2 SCHOL. Too simple is my wit to tell her praise,
Whom all the world admires for majesty.

3 SCHOL. No marvel though the angry Greeks pursu'd
With ten years' war the rape[3] of such a queen,
Whose heavenly beauty passeth all compare.

1 SCHOL. Since we have seen the pride of Nature's works
And only paragon of excellence,
Let us depart; and for this glorious deed
Happy and blest be Faustus evermore.

FAUSTUS. Gentlemen, farewell; the same I wish to you.

Exeunt Scholars.

Enter an Old Man.

OLD MAN. Ah, Doctor Faustus, that I might prevail
To guide thy steps unto the way of life,
By which sweet path thou mayst attain the goal
That shall conduct thee to celestial rest!
Break heart, drop blood, and mingle it with tears,
Tears falling from repentant heaviness
Of thy most vild and loathsome filthiness,
The stench whereof corrupts the inward soul
With such flagitious crimes of heinous sins
As no commiseration may expel,
But mercy, Faustus, of thy Savior sweet,
Whose blood alone must wash away thy guilt.

FAUST. Where art thou, Faustus? Wretch, what hast thou done?
Damn'd art thou, Faustus, damn'd; despair and die!
Hell calls for right, and with a roaring voice
Says "Faustus, come; thine hour is [almost][4] come!"
And Faustus [now][4] will come to do thee right.

MEPHISTOPHILIS *gives him a dagger.*

OLD MAN. Ah, stay, good Faustus, stay thy desperate steps!
I see an angel hovers o'er thy head,
And, with a vial full of precious grace,
Offers to pour the same into thy soul;
Then call for mercy, and avoid despair.

FAUST. Ah, my sweet friend, I feel
Thy words do comfort my distressed soul.
Leave me awhile to ponder on my sins.

OLD MAN. I go, sweet Faustus, but with heavy cheer,
Fearing the ruin of thy hopeless soul. [*Exit.*]

FAUST. Accursed Faustus, where is mercy now?
I do repent, and yet I do despair;
Hell strives with grace for conquest in my breast.
What shall I do to shun the snares of death?

MEPH. Thou traitor, Faustus, I arrest thy soul
For disobedience to my sovereign lord;
Revolt, or I'll in piecemeal tear thy flesh.

FAUST. [I do repent I e'er offended him;][5]
Sweet Mephistophilis, entreat thy lord
To pardon my unjust presumption,
And with my blood again I will confirm
My former vow I made to Lucifer.

MEPH. Do it now then quickly, with unfeigned heart,
Lest danger do attend thy drift.

FAUST. Torment, sweet friend, that base and crooked age[6]
That durst dissuade me from my Lucifer,
With greatest torments that our hell affords.

MEPH. His faith is great; I cannot touch his soul;
But what I may afflict his body with
I will attempt, which is but little worth.

FAUST. One thing, good servant, let me crave of thee,
To glut the longing of my heart's desire,
That I might have unto my paramour
That heavenly Helen, which I saw of late,
Whose sweet embracings may extinguish clean
These thoughts that do dissuade me from my vow,
And keep mine oath I made to Lucifer.

MEPH. Faustus, this or what else thou shalt desire
Shall be perform'd in twinkling of an eye.

Re-enter HELEN.

FAUST. Was this the face that launch'd a thousand ships,
And burnt the topless[7] towers of Ilium?

[3] Capture.
[4] Add. Q 1616.
[5] Add. Q 1616.
[6] Old man.
[7] Incomparably lofty.

Sweet Helen, make me immortal with a kiss.—
Her lips sucks forth my soul; see where it flies!—
Come, Helen, come, give me my soul again.
Here will I dwell, for Heaven be in these lips,
And all is dross that is not Helena.
I will be Paris, and for love of thee,
Instead of Troy shall Wittenberg be sack'd;
And I will combat with weak Menelaus,
And wear thy colors on my plumed crest;
Yea, I will wound Achilles in the heel,
And then return to Helen for a kiss.
O, thou art fairer than the evening air
Clad in the beauty of a thousand stars;
Brighter art thou than flaming Jupiter
When he appear'd to hapless Semele;
More lovely than the monarch of the sky
In wanton Arethusa's azur'd arms;[8]
And none but thou shalt be my paramour.

Re-enter Old Man.[9] *Exeunt* [*the others*].

Old Man. Accursed Faustus, miserable man,
That from thy soul exclud'st the grace of Heaven,
And fliest the throne of his tribunal seat!

Enter the Devils.

Satan begins to sift[10] me with his pride.[11]
As in this furnace God shall try my faith,
My faith, vile hell, shall triumph over thee.
Ambitious fiends, see how the Heavens smiles
At your repulse, and laughs your state to scorn!
Hence, hell! for hence I fly unto my God.

Exeunt.

[Scene II][12]

Enter Faustus *with the* Scholars.

Faust. Ah, gentlemen!

1 Schol. What ails Faustus?

Faust. Ah, my sweet chamber-fellow, had I lived with thee, then had I lived still! but now I die eternally. Look, comes he not? comes he not?

2 Schol. What means Faustus?

3 Schol. Belike he is grown into some sickness by being oversolitary.

1 Schol. If it be so, we'll have physicians to cure him.—'T is but a surfeit; never fear, man.

Faust. A surfeit of deadly sin that hath damn'd both body and soul.

2 Schol. Yet, Faustus, look up to Heaven; remember God's mercies are infinite.

Faust. But Faustus' offence can ne'er be pardoned; the serpent that tempted Eve may be sav'd, but not Faustus. Ah, gentlemen, hear me with patience, and tremble not at my speeches. Though my heart pants and quivers to remember that I have been a student here these thirty years, oh, would I had never seen Wittenberg, never read book! And what wonders I have done, all Germany can witness, yea, all the world; for which Faustus hath lost both Germany and the world, yea, Heaven itself, Heaven, the seat of God, the throne of the blessed, the kingdom of joy; and must remain in hell for ever, hell, ah, hell, for ever! Sweet friends, what shall become of Faustus, being in hell for ever?

3 Schol. Yet, Faustus, call on God.

Faust. On God, whom Faustus hath abjur'd! on God, whom Faustus hath blasphemed! Ah, my God, I would weep, but the Devil draws in my tears. Gush forth blood instead of tears! Yea, life and soul—Oh, he stays my tongue! I would lift up my hands, but see, they hold them, they hold them!

All. Who, Faustus?

Faust. Lucifer and Mephistophilis.[13] Ah, gentlemen! I gave them my soul for my cunning.[14]

All. God forbid!

Faust. God forbade it indeed; but Faustus hath done it. For vain pleasure of four-and-twenty years hath Faustus lost eternal joy and felicity. I writ them a bill with mine own blood; the date is expired, the time will come, and he will fetch me.

1 Schol. Why did not Faustus tell us of this before, that divines might have prayed for thee?

Faust. Oft have I thought to have done so; but the Devil threat'ned to tear me in pieces if I nam'd God; to fetch both body and soul if I once gave ear to divinity; and

[8] No such episode is known to classical mythology. (Boas.) Brooke suggests that *Arethusa* may be a slip (or possibly an intentional alteration) for Leucothoe, beloved by Apollo. (See Ovid's *Metamorphoses*, IV, 230, ff.)
[9] Om. Q 1616; in Q_1 placed before l. 101.
[10] Cf. *Luke*, xxii, 31.
[11] Display (of power).
[12] The same.

[13] In Q 1616 Lucifer, Belzebub, and Mephistophilis open the scene, and the last speaks twice in an interpolation of 48 ll., which comes after l. 77.
[14] Knowledge.

now 't is too late. Gentlemen, away! lest you perish with me.

2 SCHOL. Oh, what shall we do to [save] [15] Faustus?

FAUST. Talk not of me, but save yourselves, and depart.

3 SCHOL. God will strengthen me. I will stay with Faustus.

1 SCHOL. Tempt not God, sweet friend; but let us into the next room, and there pray for him.

FAUST. Ay, pray for me, pray for me! and what noise soever ye hear come not unto me, for nothing can rescue me.

2 SCHOL. Pray thou, and we will pray that God may have mercy upon thee.

FAUST. Gentlemen, farewell. If I live till morning I 'll visit you; if not, Faustus is gone to hell.

ALL. Faustus, farewell!

Exeunt Scholars. *The clock strikes eleven.*

FAUST. Ah, Faustus,
Now hast thou but one bare hour to live,
And then thou must be damn'd perpetually!
Stand still, you ever-moving spheres of Heaven,
That time may cease, and midnight never come;
Fair Nature's eye, rise, rise again and make
Perpetual day; or let this hour be but
A year, a month, a week, a natural day,
That Faustus may repent and save his soul!
O lente, lente, currite noctis equi! [16]
The stars move still,[17] time runs, the clock will strike,
The Devil will come, and Faustus must be damn'd.
O, I 'll leap up to my God! Who pulls me down?
See, see where Christ's blood streams in the firmament!
One drop would save my soul — half a drop! ah, my Christ! —
Ah, rend not my heart for naming of my Christ! —
Yet will I call on him! — O, spare me, Lucifer! —
Where is it now? 'T is gone; and see where God
Stretcheth out his arm, and bends his ireful brows! —
Mountain and hills, come, come and fall on me,
And hide me from the heavy wrath of God!
No! no! —
Then will I headlong run into the earth! —
Earth, gape! — O no, it will not harbor me! —
You stars that reign'd at my nativity,
Whose influence hath allotted death and hell,
Now draw up Faustus like a foggy mist
Into the entrails of yon lab'ring cloud,
That when you vomit forth into the air,
My limbs may issue from their smoky mouths,[18]
So [19] that my soul may but ascend to Heaven.

The watch strikes.

Ah, half the hour is past! 'T will all be past anon!
O God,
If thou wilt not have mercy on my soul,
Yet for Christ's sake, whose blood hath ransom'd me,
Impose some end to my incessant pain;
Let Faustus live in hell a thousand years,
A hundred thousand, and at last be sav'd! —
O, no end is limited to damned souls!
Why wert thou not a creature wanting soul?
Or why is this immortal that thou hast?
Ah, Pythagoras' metempsychosis! were that true,
This soul should fly from me, and I be chang'd
Unto some brutish beast! All beasts are happy,
For, when they die,
Their souls are soon dissolv'd in elements;
But mine must live, still to be plagu'd in hell.
Curs'd be the parents that engend'red me!
No, Faustus, curse thyself, curse Lucifer,
That hath depriv'd thee of the joys of Heaven.

The clock striketh twelve.

O, it strikes, it strikes! Now, body, turn to air,
Or Lucifer will bear thee quick to hell!

Thunder and lightning.

O soul, be chang'd into little water-drops,
And fall into the ocean — ne'er be found! —
My God, my God, look not so fierce on me!

[15] Add. Q 1616.
[16] Run slowly, slowly, steeds of the night. (Ovid, *Amores*, I, xiii, 40.)
[17] Unceasingly.
[18] Brooke, calling attention to the censor's mutilation of this soliloquy in Q 1616, and to the actors' unmetrical insertions in Q 1, suggests that ll. 106, 107, may have stood in place of the "doubtless histrionic" l. 99. "Their dislocation may have been occasioned by the fact that originally each movement of the invocation ended [with l. 108]."
[19] Provided that.

Enter Devils.

Adders and serpents, let me breathe awhile ! —
Ugly hell, gape not ! — Come not, Lucifer ! —
I 'll burn my books ! — Ah, Mephistophilis ! [20]
Exeunt [Devils] *with him.*

Enter Chorus.

CHO. Cut is the branch that might have grown full straight,
And burned is Apollo's laurel bough,

[20] Q 1616 adds 18 lines, in which the scholars discover Faustus's dismembered body.

That sometime [21] grew within this learned man.
Faustus is gone ; regard his hellish fall,
Whose fiendful fortune may exhort the wise
Only to wonder at unlawful things,
Whose deepness doth entice such forward wits
To practise more than heavenly power permits.
[*Exit.*]

Terminat hora diem ; terminat author opus.[22]

[21] Formerly.
[22] The hour ends the day ; the author ends his work.

The Famous

TRAGEDY

OF

THE RICH IEVV OF *MALTA*.

AS IT VVAS PLAYD BEFORE THE KING AND QVEENE, IN HIS MAJESTIES Theatre at *White-Hall*, by her Majesties Servants at the *Cock-pit*.

Written by CHRISTOPHER MARLO.

LONDON;

Printed by *I. B.* for *Nicholas Vavasour*, and are to be sold at his Shop in the Inner-Temple, neere the Church. 1633.

INTRODUCTORY NOTE

As in the case of *Faustus*, so long a period intervened between the production of *The Jew of Malta* (c. 1590) and the appearance of the first (known) edition (1633) that our text is very corrupt. Again we must try to reconstruct a splendid edifice which has fallen into partial ruin and been put to base uses. Yet here the initial collapse seems due to the author, who evidently began a tragedy and failed to sustain it. Barabas, like Faustus and Tamburlaine, is a child of the Renaissance; though he is not like them a hero, but a hero-villain. The play is a melodrama rather than a tragedy, or, as has been seriously suggested, a farce. Barabas is the crafty (to the Elizabethans, Machiavellian) scoundrel who, clever as he is, finally overreaches himself. The audience doubtless laughed derisively at his villainous asides and hugely enjoyed his fall. The conclusion is irresistible that, whatever his original intention, Marlowe turned his efforts into capitalizing anti-Semitic prejudice.

He certainly succeeded. The great puzzle is the flagging, toward the end of Act II, of the undeniable power and grandeur of the opening. Various theories have been proposed to account for it; but, unless indeed the second half of the play is largely a reconstruction, Professor Brooke's seems most reasonable. The thread of the plot is throughout probably Marlowe's, but in the first two acts the central character is humanized. In the rest of the play we have the bare plot, possibly with interpolations and alterations, but certainly stripped of the humanizing touches with which Shakespeare manages to keep Shylock invested even after the game goes against him. In both cases the Elizabethans gloated over the villain's ruin. But Shakespeare's Jew, execrated though he be, is always a fellow-creature. Shakespeare's original conception was less bold than Marlowe's. Perhaps it was easier to sustain.

No source for the play has been found. Eminent sixteenth-century Jews resident in Constantinople and powerful politically and commercially have been suggested as possible inspirations by Professors Kellner and Brooke (see introduction to Bennett's edition for references and summaries). Marlowe may have learned about them through his diplomatic connections (he was for a time an agent of the Privy Council), or from London Jews.

Henslowe records that Lord Strange's company was acting *The Jew of Malta* in 1592–93, and that it was not then a new play. It was apparently the most popular of Marlowe's dramas. In 1594 several companies performed it; but it finally rested in the possession of the Admiral's Men, who acted it at least till 1596, with Edward Alleyn in the title rôle. There was a revival in 1601, and another probably not long prior to the publication of Q 1633. On the latter occasion it was acted at the Cockpit and also at court, with prologues and epilogues by Thomas Heywood, who may have revised it. And there may have been an earlier revision in 1601.

The Jew of Malta was edited for the Case Marlowe by H. S. Bennett (1931). Though an entry was made in the Stationers' Register in 1594, the first surviving edition is that of 1633, in quarto, on which the present text is based.

THE JEW OF MALTA

BY

CHRISTOPHER MARLOWE

[DRAMATIS PERSONAE

FERNEZE, Governor of Malta.
LODOWICK, his son.
SELIM CALYMATH, son to the Grand Seignior.
MARTIN DEL BOSCO, Vice-Admiral of Spain.
MATHIAS, a gentleman.
BARABAS, a wealthy Jew.
ITHAMORE, his slave.
JACOMO, } friars.
BARNARDINE, }
PILIA-BORZA, a bully.
Two Merchants.

Three Jews.
Knights, Bassoes, Officers, Reader, Guard, Messenger, Slaves, and Carpenters.

KATHERINE, mother to Mathias.
ABIGAIL, daughter to Barabas.
BELLAMIRA, a courtesan.
Abbess.
A Nun.

MACHIAVEL, speaker of the prologue.

THE SCENE — *Malta*.]

[THE PROLOGUE]

[*Enter*] MACHIAVEL.

ALBEIT the world think Machiavel is dead,
Yet was his soul but flown beyond the Alps,
And, now the Guise[1] is dead, is come from France
To view this land and frolic with his friends.
To some, perhaps, my name is odious,
But such as love me guard me from their tongues;
And let them know that I am Machiavel,
And weigh not men, and therefore not men's words.
Admir'd I am of those that hate me most.
Though some speak openly against my books,[2]
Yet will they read me, and thereby attain
To Peter's chair; and when they cast me off,
Are poison'd by my climbing followers.
I count religion but a childish toy,
And hold there is no sin but ignorance.
Birds of the air will tell of murders past —
I am asham'd to hear such fooleries.
Many will talk of title to a crown:
What right had Cæsar to the empery?[3]
Might first made kings, and laws were then most sure
When, like the Draco's,[4] they were writ in blood.
Hence comes it that a strong-built citadel
Commands much more than letters can import;
Which maxim had Phalaris observ'd,
H' had never bellowed, in a brazen bull,
Of great ones' envy. O' the poor petty wits[5]
Let me be envi'd and not pitied!
But whither am I bound? I come not, I,
To read a lecture here in Britainy,[6]
But to present the tragedy of a Jew,
Who smiles to see how full his bags are cramm'd,
Which money was not got without my means.
I crave but this: grace him as he deserves,
And let him not be entertain'd the worse
Because he favors me. [*Exit.*]

[1] Assassinated in 1588; he organized the Massacre of St. Bartholomew in 1572. See Marlowe's play on that subject.
[2] *The Prince*, and others.
[3] Q *Empire*.
[4] Q *Drancus*.
[5] So Brereton; mod. eds. *wights;* Q *wites*.
[6] So Bullen; Q *Britaine*.

[ACT I — SCENE I]

Enter[7] BARABAS *in his countinghouse, with heaps of gold before him.*

BAR. So that of thus much that return was made;
And of the third part of the Persian ships,
There was the venture summ'd and satisfied.
As for those [Scaenites],[8] and the men of Uz,
That bought my Spanish oils and wines of Greece,
Here have I purs'd their paltry silver[l]ings.[9]
Fie, what a trouble 't is to count this trash!
Well fare the Arabians, who so richly pay
The things they traffic for with wedge of gold,
Whereof a man may easily in a day
Tell[10] that which may maintain him all his life.
The needy groom, that never fing'red groat,
Would make a miracle of thus much coin;
But he whose steel-barr'd coffers are cramm'd full,
And all his lifetime hath been tired,[11]
Wearying his fingers' ends with telling it,
Would in his age be loath to labor so,
And for a pound to sweat himself to death.
Give me the merchants of the Indian mines,
That trade in metal of the purest mold;
The wealthy Moor, that in the eastern rocks
Without control can pick his riches up,
And in his house heap pearl like pebble-stones,
Receive them free, and sell them by the weight;
Bags of fiery opals, sapphires, amethysts,
Jacinths, hard topaz, grass-green emeralds,
Beauteous rubies, sparkling diamonds,
And seld-seen costly stones of so great price
As one of them, indifferently rated,[12]
And of a carat of this quantity,
May serve in peril of calamity
To ransome great kings from captivity.
This is the ware wherein consists my wealth;
And thus methinks should men of judgment frame
Their means of traffic from[13] the vulgar trade,
And as their wealth increaseth, so inclose
Infinite riches in a little room.
But now how stands the wind?
Into what corner peers my halcyon's bill?[14]
Ha! to the east? Yes. See, how stands the vanes?
East and by south; why, then, I hope my ships
I sent for Egypt and the bordering isles
Are gotten up by Nilus' winding banks;
Mine argosy[15] from Alexandria,
Loaden with spice and silks, now under sail,
Are smoothly gliding down by Candy[16] shore
To Malta, through our Mediterranean sea.
But who comes here? How now?

Enter a Merchant.

MERCH. Barabas, thy ships are safe,
Riding in Malta road, and all the merchants
With other merchandise are safe arriv'd,
And have sent me to know whether yourself
Will come and custom[17] them.

BAR. The ships are safe thou say'st, and richly fraught?

MERCH. They are.

BAR. Why then go bid them come ashore,
And bring with them their bills of entry.[11]
I hope our credit in the customhouse
Will serve as well as I were present there.
Go send 'em threescore camels, thirty mules,
And twenty wagons to bring up the ware.
But art thou master in a ship of mine,
And is thy credit not enough for that?

MERCH. The very custom barely comes to more
Than many merchants of the town are worth,
And therefore far exceeds my credit, sir.

BAR. Go tell 'em the Jew of Malta sent thee, man:
Tush! who amongst 'em knows not Barabas?

MERCH. I go.

BAR. So, then; there 's somewhat come.
Sirrah, which of my ships art thou master of?

MERCH. Of the Speranza, sir.

BAR. And saw'st thou not
Mine argosy at Alexandria?
Thou couldst not come from Egypt, or by Caire,
But at the entry there into the sea,
Where Nilus pays his tribute to the main,
Thou needs must sail by Alexandria.

[7] He was actually "discovered" in the inner stage.
[8] Arab nomads mentioned by the cosmographers. Conj. Miss Seaton (*Review of English Studies*, V, 398). Q *Samintes*.
[9] Shekels.
[10] Count.
[11] Trisyllabic.
[12] Impartially valued.
[13] Away from.
[14] One of the "vulgar errors" mentioned by Sir Thomas Browne is "that a kingfisher, hanged by the bill, showeth in what quarter the wind is."
[15] Large merchantmen.
[16] Cretan.
[17] Pay the customs.

MERCH. I neither saw them, nor inquir'd of them;
But this we heard some of our seamen say,
They wond'red how you durst with so much wealth
Trust such a crazed vessel, and so far.

BAR. Tush, they are wise! I know her and her strength.
[But][18] go, go thou thy ways, discharge thy ship,
And bid my factor bring his loading in.
[*Exit* Merchant.]
And yet I wonder at this argosy.

Enter a second Merchant.

2 MERCH. Thine argosy from Alexandria,
Know, Barabas, doth ride in Malta road,
Laden with riches and exceeding store
Of Persian silks, of gold, and orient[19] pearl.

BAR. How chance you came not with those other ships
That sail'd by Egypt?

2 MERCH. Sir, we saw 'em not.

BAR. Belike they coasted round by Candy shore
About their oils, or other businesses.
But 't was ill done of you to come so far
Without the aid or conduct of their ships.

2 MERCH. Sir, we were wafted by a Spanish fleet,
That never left us till within a league,
That had the galleys of the Turk in chase.

BAR. O! they were going up to Sicily.
Well, go,
And bid the merchants and my men despatch
And come ashore, and see the fraught dischar'd.

2 MERCH. I go. *Exit.*

BAR. Thus trolls our fortune in by land and sea,
And thus are we on every side enrich'd.
These are blessings promis'd to the Jews,
And herein was old Abram's happiness.
What more may Heaven do for earthly man
Than thus to pour out plenty in their laps,
Ripping the bowels of the earth for them,
Making the sea their servants, and the winds
To drive their substance with successful blasts?
Who hateth me but for my happiness?
Or who is honor'd now but for his wealth?
Rather had I, a Jew, be hated thus,
Than pitied in a Christian poverty;
For I can see no fruits in all their faith,
But malice, falsehood, and excessive pride,
Which, methinks, fits not their profession.
Haply some hapless man hath conscience,
And for his conscience lives in beggary.
They say we are a scatter'd nation;
I cannot tell, but we have scambled[20] up
More wealth by far than those that brag of faith.
There's Kirriah Jairim, the great Jew of Greece,
Obed in Bairseth, Nones in Portugal,
Myself in Malta, some in Italy,
Many in France, and wealthy every one;
Ay, wealthier far than any Christian.
I must confess we come not to be kings;
That's not our fault: alas, our number's few,
And crowns come either by succession,
Or urg'd by force; and nothing violent,
Oft have I heard tell, can be permanent.
Give us a peaceful rule, make Christians kings,
That thirst so much for principality.
I have no charge, nor many children,
But one sole daughter, whom I hold as dear
As Agamemnon did his Iphigen;
And all I have is hers. But who comes here?

Enter three Jews.[21]

1 JEW. Tush, tell not me; 't was done of policy.

2 JEW. Come, therefore, let us go to Barabas,
For he can counsel best in these affairs;
And here he comes.

BAR. Why, how now, countrymen!
Why flock you thus to me in multitudes?[22]
What accident's betided to the Jews?

1 JEW. A fleet of warlike galleys, Barabas,
Are come from Turkey, and lie in our road;
And they this day sit in the council-house
To entertain them and their embassy.

BAR. Why, let 'em come, so they come not to war;
Or let 'em war, so we be conquerors: —
(*aside*) Nay, let 'em combat, conquer, and kill all,
So they spare me, my daughter, and my wealth.

[18] Emend. Dyce; Q *By*.
[19] Lustrous.
[20] Scrambled.
[21] The outer stage now being the street before Barabas's house.
[22] Here and in Scene ii, the three Jews stand for a multitude; like the "three or four most vile and ragged foils" Shakespeare asks us to consider an army in *Henry V*.

1 JEW. Were it for confirmation of a league,
They would not come in warlike manner thus.

2 JEW. I fear their coming will afflict us all.

BAR. Fond[23] men! what dream you of their multitudes?
What need they treat of peace that are in league?
The Turks and those of Malta are in league.
Tut, tut, there is some other matter in 't.

1 JEW. Why, Barabas, they come for peace or war.

BAR. Happily for neither, but to pass along
Towards Venice by the Adriatic Sea;
With[24] whom they have attempted many times,
But never could effect their stratagem.

3 JEW. And very wisely said. It may be so.

2 JEW. But there 's a meeting in the senate-house,
And all the Jews in Malta must be there.

BAR. Hum; all the Jews in Malta must be there?
Ay, like enough. Why, then, let every man
Provide him, and be there for fashion sake.[25]
If anything shall there concern our state,
Assure yourselves I 'll look — (*aside*) unto myself.

1 JEW. I know you will. Well, brethren, let us go.

2 JEW. Let 's take our leaves. Farewell, good Barabas.

BAR. Do so. Farewell, Zaareth; farewell, Temainte. [*Exeunt the three* Jews.]
And, Barabas, now search this secret out;
Summon thy senses, call thy wits together;
These silly men mistake the matter clean.
Long to the Turk did Malta contribute;
Which tribute, all in policy, I fear,
The Turks have let increase to such a sum
As all the wealth of Malta cannot pay;
And now by that advantage thinks, belike,
To seize upon the town; ay, that he seeks.
Howe'er the world go, I 'll make sure for one,
And seek in time to intercept the worst,
Warily guarding that which I ha' got.
Ego mihimet sum semper proximus.[26]
Why, let 'em enter, let 'em take the town.
[*Exit.*]

[23] Foolish.
[24] Against.
[25] As a formality.
[26] Misquoted from Terence, *Andria*, IV, i, 12: *Proximus sum egomet mihi*: *i.e.*, number one comes first.

[SCENE II] [27]

Enter [FERNEZE, *governor*] [28] *of Malta*, Knights, [*and* Officers;] *met by* CALYMATH [*and*] Bassoes *of the Turk*.

FERN. Now, Bassoes, what demand you at our hands?

[1] BAS. Know, Knights of Malta, that we came from Rhodes,
From Cyprus, Candy, and those other isles
That lie betwixt the Mediterranean seas.

FERN. What 's Cyprus, Candy, and those other isles
To us or Malta? What at our hands demand ye?

CAL. The ten years' tribute that remains unpaid.

FERN. Alas! my Lord, the sum is overgreat;
I hope your Highness will consider us.

CAL. I wish, grave [Governor,][29] 't were in my power
To favor you; but 't is my father's cause,
Wherein I may not, nay, I dare not dally.

FERN. Then give us leave, great Selim Calymath.

CAL. Stand all aside, and let the Knights determine,
And send to keep our galleys under sail,
For happily[30] we shall not tarry here. —
Now, Governor, how are you resolv'd?

FERN. Thus: since your hard conditions are such
That you will needs have ten years' tribute past,
We may have time to make collection
Amongst the inhabitants of Malta for 't.

[1] BAS. That 's more than is in our commission.

CAL. What, Callapine! a little courtesy.
Let 's know their time, perhaps it is not long;
And 't is more kingly to obtain by peace
Than to enforce conditions by constraint.
What respite ask you, Governor?

FERN. But a month.

CAL. We grant a month, but see you keep your promise.
Now launch our galleys back again to sea,
Where we 'll attend the respite you have ta'en,

[27] The Senate-house; afterwards, a street between it and Barabas's house.
[28] Q *Gouernors*. Ferneze's first speech is tagged *Gouer*. and thereafter *Gov*. throughout.
[29] Q *Gouernor*; also in ll. 17, 27, 32, 129.
[30] Haply.

And for the money send our messenger.
Farewell, great Governor and brave Knights
of Malta.
Exeunt [CALYMATH *and* Bassoes].

FERN. And all good fortune wait on Calymath!
Go one and call those Jews of Malta hither.
Were they not summon'd to appear to-day?

OFF. They were, my Lord, and here they come.

Enter BARABAS *and three* Jews.

1 KNIGHT. Have you determined what to say to them?

FERN. Yes, give me leave; — and, Hebrews, now come near.
From the Emperor of Turkey is arriv'd
Great Selim Calymath, his Highness' son,
To levy of us ten years' tribute past;
Now then, here know that it concerneth us —

BAR. Then, good my Lord, to keep your quiet still,
Your Lordship shall do well to let them have it.

FERN. Soft, Barabas, there's more 'longs to 't than so.
To what this ten years' tribute will amount,
That we have cast,[31] but cannot compass it
By reason of the wars that robb'd our store;
And therefore are we to request your aid.

BAR. Alas, my Lord, we are no soldiers;
And what's our aid against so great a prince?

1 KNIGHT. Tut, Jew, we know thou art no soldier;
Thou art a merchant and a moneyed man,
And 't is thy money, Barabas, we seek.

BAR. How, my Lord! my money?

FERN. Thine and the rest.
For, to be short, amongst you 't must be had.

1 JEW. Alas, my Lord, the most of us are poor.

FERN. Then let the rich increase your portions.

BAR. Are strangers[32] with your tribute to be tax'd?

2 KNIGHT. Have strangers leave with us to get their wealth?
Then let them with us contribute.

BAR. How? equally?

FERN. No, Jew, like infidels.
For through our sufferance of your hateful lives,
Who stand accursed in the sight of Heaven,
These taxes and afflictions are befall'n,
And therefore thus we are determined. —
Read there the articles of our decrees.

READER. "First, the tribute-money of the Turks shall all be levied amongst the Jews, and each of them to pay one-half of his estate."

BAR. [*aside*] How, half his estate? I hope you mean not mine.

FERN. Read on.

READER. "Secondly, he that denies to pay shall straight become a Christian."

BAR. [*aside*] How, a Christian? Hum, what's here to do?

READER. "Lastly, he that denies this shall absolutely lose all he has."

ALL THREE JEWS. O my Lord, we will give half.

BAR. O[33] earth-mettl'd villains, and no Hebrews born!
And will you basely thus submit yourselves
To leave your goods to their arbitrament?

FERN. Why, Barabas, wilt thou be christ'ned?

BAR. No, Governor, I will be no convertite.[34]

FERN. Then pay thy half.

BAR. Why, know you what you did by this device?
Half of my substance is a city's wealth.
Governor, it was not got so easily;
Nor will I part so slightly therewithal.

FERN. Sir, half is the penalty of our decree,
Either pay that, or we will seize on all.

BAR. *Corpo di Dio!* stay! you shall have half;
Let me be us'd but as my brethren are.

FERN. No, Jew; thou hast denied the articles,
And now it cannot be recall'd.
[*Exeunt* Officers, *on a sign from* FERNEZE.]

BAR. Will you then steal my goods?
Is theft the ground of your religion?

FERN. No, Jew; we take particularly thine
To save the ruin of a multitude;
And better one want for a common good
Than many perish for a private man.
Yet, Barabas, we will not banish thee;
But here in Malta, where thou gott'st thy wealth,
Live still, and, if thou canst, get more.

BAR. Christians, what or how can I multiply?
Of naught is nothing made.

[31] Computed. [32] Foreigners.

[33] A hypermetrical monosyllable often begins a line of Elizabethan blank verse.
[34] Convert.

1 KNIGHT. From naught at first thou cam'st to little wealth,
From little unto more, from more to most.
If your first curse fall heavy on thy head,
And make thee poor and scorn'd of all the world,
'T is not our fault, but thy inherent sin.

BAR. What, bring you Scripture to confirm your wrongs?
Preach me not out of my possessions.
Some Jews are wicked, as all Christians are;
But say the tribe that I descended of
Were all in general cast away for sin,
Shall I be tried by their transgression?
The man that dealeth righteously shall live;
And which of you can charge me otherwise?

FERN. Out, wretched Barabas!
Sham'st thou not thus to justify thyself,
As if we knew not thy profession?
If thou rely upon thy righteousness,
Be patient and thy riches will increase.
Excess of wealth is cause of covetousness;
And covetousness, O, 't is a monstrous sin.

BAR. Ay, but theft is worse. Tush! take not from me then,
For that is theft; and if you rob me thus,
I must be forc'd to steal and compass more.

1 KNIGHT. Grave Governor, list not to his exclaims.
Convert his mansion to a nunnery;

Re-enter Officers.

His house will harbor many holy nuns.

FERN. It shall be so. Now, officers, have you done?

OFF. Ay, my Lord, we have seiz'd upon the goods
And wares of Barabas, which being valued,
Amount to more than all the wealth in Malta.
And of the other we have seized half.

[FERN.][35] Then we'll take order for the residue.[36]

BAR. Well then, my Lord, say, are you satisfied?
You have my goods, my money, and my wealth,
My ships, my store, and all that I enjoy'd;
And, having all, you can request no more,
Unless your unrelenting, flinty hearts
Suppress all pity in your stony breasts,
And now shall move you to bereave my life.

[35] Om. Q. Sup. Robinson.

[36] We'll make arrangements for the rest of this business.

FERN. No, Barabas, to stain our hands with blood
Is far from us and our profession.

BAR. Why, I esteem the injury far less
To take the lives of miserable men
Than be the causers of their misery.
You have my wealth, the labor of my life,
The comfort of mine age, my children's hope,
And therefore ne'er distinguish of the wrong.[37]

FERN. Content thee, Barabas, thou hast naught but right.

BAR. Your extreme right does me exceeding wrong;
But take it to you, i' the Devil's name.

FERN. Come, let us in, and gather of these goods
The money for this tribute of the Turk.

1 KNIGHT. 'T is necessary that be look'd unto;
For if we break our day, we break the league,
And that will prove but simple policy.

Exeunt [*all but* BARABAS *and the* Jews].[38]

BAR. Ay, policy! that's their profession,
And not simplicity, as they suggest.
The plagues of Egypt, and the curse of Heaven,
Earth's barrenness, and all men's hatred[39]
Inflict upon them, thou great *Primus Motor!*[40]
And here upon my knees, striking the earth,
I ban their souls to everlasting pains
And extreme tortures of the fiery deep,
That thus have dealt with me in my distress.

1 JEW. O yet be patient, gentle Barabas.

BAR. O silly brethren, born to see this day,
Why stand you thus unmov'd with my laments?
Why weep you not to think upon my wrongs?
Why pine not I, and die in this distress?

1 JEW. Why, Barabas, as hardly can we brook
The cruel handling of ourselves in this;
Thou seest they have taken half our goods.

BAR. Why did you yield to their extortion?
You were a multitude, and I but one;
And of me only have they taken all.

1 JEW. Yet, Brother Barabas, remember Job.

BAR. What tell you me of Job? I wot his wealth
Was written thus: he had seven thousand sheep,

[37] *I.e.*, make a distinction between the two injuries.

[38] The outer stage now represents the street.

[39] Trisyllabic.

[40] God, First Cause of motion.

Three thousand camels, and two hundred yoke
Of laboring oxen, and five hundred
She-asses; but for every one of those,
Had they been valued at indifferent rate,
I had at home, and in mine argosy,
And other ships that came from Egypt last,
As much as would have bought his beasts and him,
And yet have kept enough to live upon;
So that not he, but I, may curse the day,
Thy fatal birthday, forlorn Barabas,
And henceforth wish for an eternal night,
That clouds of darkness may inclose my flesh,
And hide these extreme sorrows from mine eyes:
For only I have toil'd to inherit here
The months of vanity and loss of time,
And painful nights, have been appointed me.[41]

2 Jew. Good Barabas, be patient.[42]

Bar. Ay, ay;
Pray, leave me in my patience. You that
Were ne'er possess'd of wealth, are pleas'd with want;
But give him liberty at least to mourn,
That in a field amidst his enemies
Doth see his soldiers slain, himself disarm'd,
And knows no means of his recovery.
Ay, let me sorrow for this sudden chance;
'T is in the trouble of my spirit I speak;
Great injuries are not so soon forgot.

1 Jew. Come, let us leave him; in his ireful mood
Our words will but increase his ecstasy.[43]

2 Jew. On, then; but trust me 't is a misery
To see a man in such affliction. —
Farewell, Barabas! *Exeunt* [*the three* Jews].

Bar. Ay, fare you well.
See the simplicity of these base slaves,
Who, for the villains have no wit themselves,
Think me to be a senseless lump of clay
That will with every water wash to dirt.
No, Barabas is born to better chance,
And fram'd of finer mold than common men,
That measure naught but by the present time.
A reaching thought will search his deepest wits,
And cast[44] with cunning for the time to come;
For evils are apt to happen every day. —
But whither wends my beauteous Abigail?

Enter Abigail, *the Jew's daughter*.

O, what has made my lovely daughter sad?
What, woman! moan not for a little loss;
Thy father has enough in store for thee.

Abig. Not for myself, but aged Barabas;
Father, for thee lamenteth Abigail.
But I will learn to leave these fruitless tears,
And, urg'd thereto with my afflictions,
With fierce exclaims run to the senate-house,
And in the senate reprehend them all,
And rent[45] their hearts with tearing of my hair,
Till they reduce[46] the wrongs done to my father.

Bar. No, Abigail, things past recovery
Are hardly cur'd with exclamations.
Be silent, Daughter; sufferance breeds ease,
And time may yield us an occasion
Which on the sudden cannot serve the turn.
Besides, my girl, think me not all so fond
As negligently to forego so much
Without provision for thyself and me.
Ten thousand portagues,[47] besides great pearls,
Rich costly jewels, and stones infinite,
Fearing the worst of this before it fell,
I closely hid.

Abig. Where, father?

Bar. In my house, my girl.

Abig. Then shall they ne'er be seen of Barabas,
For they have seiz'd upon thy house and wares.

Bar. But they will give me leave once more, I trow,
To go into my house.

Abig. That may they not;
For there I left the Governor placing nuns,
Displacing me; and of thy house they mean
To make a nunnery, where none but their own sect[48]
Must enter in, men generally barr'd.

Bar. My gold, my gold, and all my wealth is gone!
You partial heavens, have I deserv'd this plague?
What, will you thus oppose me, luckless stars,
To make me desperate in my poverty?
And knowing me impatient in distress,
Think me so mad as I will hang myself,
That I may vanish o'er the earth in air,
And leave no memory that e'er I was?
No, I will live; nor loathe I this my life;
And, since you leave me in the ocean thus

[41] Cf. *Job*, iii, 1, ff. "Which" is understood before "have."
[42] Trisyllabic. [43] Fit of emotion. [44] Plan.
[45] Rend.
[46] Restore, redress.
[47] Gold coins of Portugal, formerly worth about $20.
[48] Sex.

To sink or swim, and put me to my shifts,
I 'll rouse my senses and awake myself.
Daughter, I have it! Thou perceiv'st the plight
Wherein these Christians have oppressed me.
Be rul'd by me, for in extremity
We ought to make bar of no policy.

ABIG. Father, whate'er it be to injure them
That have so manifestly wronged us,
What will not Abigail attempt?

BAR. Why, so;
Then thus: thou told'st me they have turn'd my house
Into a nunnery, and some nuns are there.

ABIG. I did.

BAR. Then, Abigail, there must my girl
Entreat the abbess to be entertain'd.

ABIG. How, as a nun?

BAR. Ay, Daughter, for religion
Hides many mischiefs from suspicion.

ABIG. Ay, but, Father, they will suspect me there.

BAR. Let 'em suspect; but be thou so precise[49]
As they may think it done of holiness.
Entreat 'em fair, and give them friendly speech,
And seem to them as if thy sins were great,
Till thou has gotten to be entertain'd.

ABIG. Thus, Father, shall I much dissemble.

BAR. Tush!
As good dissemble that thou never mean'st,
As first mean truth and then dissemble it.
A counterfeit profession is better
Than unseen hypocrisy.

ABIG. Well, Father, say I be entertain'd,
What then shall follow?

BAR. This shall follow then:
There have I hid, close underneath the plank
That runs along the upper-chamber floor,
The gold and jewels which I kept for thee.
But here they come; be cunning, Abigail.

ABIG. Then, Father, go with me.

BAR. No, Abigail, in this
It is not necessary I be seen;
For I will seem offended with thee for't.
Be close,[50] my girl, for this must fetch my gold.

[*They retire.*]

Enter Friars [JACOMO *and* BARNARDINE, *an* Abbess, *and a* Nun.] [51]

[F. JAC.] Sisters,
We now are almost at the new-made nunnery.

[ABB.] [52] The better; for we love not to be seen.
'T is thirty winters long since some of us
Did stray so far amongst the multitude.

F. JAC. But, madam, this house
And waters of this new-made nunnery [53]
Will much delight you.

[ABB.] It may be so; but who comes here?

[ABIGAIL *comes forward.*]

ABIG. Grave abbess, and you, happy virgins' guide,
Pity the state of a distressed maid.

ABB. What art thou, daughter?

ABIG. The hopeless daughter of a hapless Jew,
The Jew of Malta, wretched Barabas;
Sometimes [54] the owner of a goodly house,
Which they have now turn'd to a nunnery.

ABB. Well, daughter, say, what is thy suit with us?

ABIG. Fearing the afflictions which my father feels
Proceed from sin, or want of faith in us,
I 'd pass away my life in penitence,
And be a novice in your nunnery,
To make atonement for my laboring soul.

F. JAC. No doubt, brother, but this proceedeth of the spirit.

F. BARN. Ay, and a moving spirit too, brother; but come,
Let us entreat she may be entertain'd.

ABB. Well, daughter, we admit you for a nun.

ABIG. First let me as a novice learn to frame
My solitary life to your strait laws,
And let me lodge where I was wont to lie.
I do not doubt, by your divine precepts
And mine own industry, but to profit much.

BAR. [*aside*] As much, I hope, as all I hid is worth.

ABB. Come, daughter, follow us.

BAR. [*coming forward*] Why, how now, Abigail, what mak'st [55] thou
Amongst these hateful Christians?

F. JAC. Hinder her not, thou man of little faith,
For she has mortified herself.[56]

BAR. How! mortified?

F. JAC. And is admitted to the sisterhood.

[49] Pious, puritanical.
[50] Secret.
[51] Q *Enter three Fryars and two Nuns.* They are not named in speech tags, throughout.
[52] Q *1Nun,* and for her next speech *Nun.*
[53] This repetition, and the metrical irregularities of the passage, indicate corruption, probably due to the omission of part of the original text.
[54] Formerly.
[55] Dost.
[56] Rendered herself dead to the world.

BAR. Child of perdition, and thy father's shame,
What wilt thou do among these hateful fiends?
I charge thee on my blessing that thou leave
These devils, and their damned heresy.

ABIG. Father, give [57] me —

BAR. (*whispers to her.*) Nay, back, Abigail,
And think upon the jewels and the gold;
The board is marked thus that covers it. —
Away, accursed, from thy father's sight.

F. JAC. Barabas, although thou art in misbelief,
And wilt not see thine own afflictions,
Yet let thy daughter be no longer blind.

BAR. Blind friar, I reck not thy persuasions, — [*aside to* ABIGAIL]
The board is marked thus + that covers it. —
For I had rather die than see her thus.
Wilt thou forsake me too in my distress,
Seduced daughter? — (*aside to her*) Go; forget n[o]t! —
Becomes it Jews to be so credulous? —
(*aside to her*) To-morrow early I'll be at the door. —
No, come not at me; if thou wilt be damn'd,
Forget me, see me not, and so begone. —
(*aside to her*) Farewell, remember to-morrow morning. —
Out, out, thou wretch!

[*Exeunt, on one side* BARABAS, *on the other side* Friars, Abbess, Nun, *and* ABIGAIL.]

Enter MATHIAS.

MATH. Who's this? Fair Abigail, the rich Jew's daughter,
Become a nun? Her father's sudden fall
Has humbled her and brought her down to this.
Tut, she were fitter for a tale of love,
Than to be tired out with orisons;
And better would she far become a bed,
Embraced in a friendly lover's arms,
Than rise at midnight to a solemn mass.

Enter LODOWICK.

LOD. Why, how now, Don Mathias, in a dump?

MATH. Believe me, noble Lodowick, I have seen
The strangest sight, in my opinion,
That ever I beheld.

LOD. What was 't, I prithee?

MATH. A fair young maid, scarce fourteen years of age,
The sweetest flower in Cytherea's field,
Cropp'd from the pleasures of the fruitful earth,
And strangely metamorph[o]s'd nun.

LOD. But say, what was she?

MATH. Why, the rich Jew's daughter.

LOD. What, Barabas, whose goods were lately seiz'd?
Is she so fair?

MATH. And matchless beautiful,
As, had you seen her, 't would have mov'd your heart,
Though [countermur'd] [58] with walls of brass, to love,
Or at the least to pity.

LOD. An if she be so fair as you report,
'T were time well spent to go and visit her.
How say you, shall we?

MATH. I must and will, sir; there's no remedy.

LOD. And so will I, too, or it shall go hard.
Farewell, Mathias.

MATH. Farewell, Lodowick.

Exeunt.

ACT II — [SCENE I] [1]

Enter BARABAS *with a light.*

BAR. Thus, like the sad presaging raven, that tolls
The sick man's passport in her hollow beak,
And in the shadow of the silent night
Doth shake contagion from her sable wings,
Vex'd and tormented runs poor Barabas
With fatal curses towards these Christians.
The incertain pleasures of swift-footed Time
Have ta'en their flight, and left me in despair;
And of my former riches rests no more
But bare remembrance, like a soldier's scar,
That has no further comfort for his maim.
O Thou that with a fiery pillar ledd'st
The sons of Israel through the dismal shades,
Light Abraham's offspring, and direct the hand
Of Abigail this night; or let the day
Turn to eternal darkness after this!
No sleep can fasten on my watchful eyes,
Nor quiet enter my distemper'd thoughts,
Till I have answer of my Abigail.

[57] Emend. Dyce, *forgive.* But probably Abigail is about to request a paternal blessing.

[58] Conj. Deighton; Q *countermin'd.* Cf. *Spanish Tragedy,* III, vii, 16.

[1] Before Barabas's house.

Enter ABIGAIL *above.*

ABIG. Now have I happily espi'd a time
To search the plank my father did appoint;
And here behold, unseen, where I have found
The gold, the pearls, and jewels, which he hid.

BAR. Now I remember those old women's words,
Who in my wealth would tell me winter's tales,
And speak of spirits and ghosts that glide by night
About the place where treasure hath been hid;
And now methinks that I am one of those,
For whilst I live here lives my soul's sole hope,
And, when I die, here shall my spirit walk.

ABIG. Now that my father's fortune were so good
As but to be about this happy place.
'T is not so happy; yet, when we parted last,
He said he would attend me in the morn.
Then, gentle sleep, where'er his body rests,
Give charge to Morpheus that he may dream
A golden dream, and of the sudden walk,
Come, and receive the treasure I have found.

BAR. *Bueno para todos mi ganado no era.*[2]
As good go on as sit so sadly thus.
But stay, what star shines yonder in the east?
The loadstar of my life, if Abigail.
Who 's there?

ABIG. Who 's that?

BAR. Peace, Abigail, 't is I.

ABIG. Then, Father, here receive thy happiness.

BAR. Hast thou 't?

[She] throws down bags.

ABIG. Here, hast thou 't? There 's more, and more, and more.

BAR. O my girl, my gold, my fortune, my felicity!
Strength to my soul, death to mine enemy,
Welcome, the first beginner of my bliss!
O A[b]igail, Abigail, that I had thee here too;
Then my desires were fully satisfied.
But I will practise[3] thy enlargement thence.
O girl, O gold, O beauty, O my bliss!

Hugs his bags.

ABIG. Father, it draweth towards midnight now,
And 'bout this time the nuns begin to wake;
To shun suspicion, therefore, let us part.

BAR. Farewell, my joy, and by my fingers take
A kiss from him that sends it from his soul.
Now Phœbus ope the eyelids of the day,
And, for the raven, wake the morning lark,
That I may hover with her in the air,
Singing o'er these, as she does o'er her young,
Hermoso [placer de los dineros.][4] *Exeunt.*

[SCENE II][5]

Enter Governor [FERNEZE], MARTIN DEL BOSCO, [*and*] *the* Knights.

FERN. Now, captain, tell us whither thou art bound?
Whence is thy ship that anchors in our road?
And why thou cam'st ashore without our leave?

BOSC. Governor of Malta, hither am I bound;
My ship, the Flying Dragon, is of Spain,
And so am I; Del Bosco is my name,
Vice-admiral unto the Catholic King.

1 KNIGHT. 'T is true, my Lord; therefore entreat[6] him well.

BOSC. Our fraught is Grecians, Turks, and Afric Moors.
For late upon the coast of Corsica,
Because we vail'd[7] not to the [Turkish][8] fleet,
Their creeping galleys had us in the chase.
But suddenly the wind began to rise,
And then we [luff'd and tack'd][9] and fought at ease.
Some have we fir'd, and many have we sunk;
But one amongst the rest became our prize.
The captain 's slain; the rest remain our slaves,
Of whom we would make sale in Malta here.

FERN. Martin del Bosco, I have heard of thee;
Welcome to Malta, and to all of us.
But to admit a sale of these thy Turks
We may not, nay, we dare not give consent,
By reason of a tributary league.

1 KNIGHT. Del Bosco, as thou lovest and honor'st us,
Persuade our governor against the Turk;
This truce we have is but in hope of gold,
And with that sum he craves might we wage war.

BOSC. Will Knights of Malta be in league with Turks,
And buy it basely, too, for sums of gold?

[2] My flock was not good for all. Emend. Dyce; Q (garbling the Spanish): *Birn para todos, my ganada no er. I.e.*, my wealth does not avail me in every emergency.

[3] Plot.

[4] Beautiful pleasure of money. Emend. Dyce; Q *Hermoso Piarer, de les Dinirch.*

[5] Unlocated; presumably the senate-house.

[6] Treat.

[7] Struck topsails or dipped flags in deference.

[8] Emend. Gilchrist; Q *Spanish.*

[9] Emend. Dyce; Q *left and tooke.*

My Lord, remember that, to Europe's shame,
The Christian Isle of Rhodes, from whence you came,
Was lately lost, and you were stated[10] here
To be at deadly enmity with Turks.

FERN. Captain, we know it; but our force is small.

BOSC. What is the sum that Calymath requires?

FERN. A hundred thousand crowns.

BOSC. My lord and king hath title to this isle,
And he means quickly to expel you hence;
Therefore be rul'd by me, and keep the gold.
I'll write unto his Majesty for aid,
And not depart until I see you free.

FERN. On this condition shall thy Turks be sold.
Go, officers, and set them straight in show.

[*Exeunt* Officers.]

Bosco, thou shalt be Malta's general;
We and our warlike knights will follow thee
Against these barbarous, misbelieving Turks.

BOSC. So shall you imitate those you succeed;
For when their hideous force environ'd Rhodes,
Small though the number was that kept the town,
They fought it out, and not a man surviv'd
To bring the hapless news to Christendom.[11]

FERN. So will we fight it out. Come, let's away!
Proud, daring Calymath, instead of gold,
We'll send the[e] bullets wrapp'd in smoke and fire.
Claim tribute where thou wilt, we are resolv'd;
Honor is bought with blood and not with gold. *Exeunt.*

[SCENE III][12]

Enter Officers *with* [ITHAMORE *and other*] Slaves.

1 OFF. This is the market-place, here let 'em stand;
Fear not their sale, for they'll be quickly bought.

2 OFF. Every one's price is written on his back,
And so much must they yield or not be sold.

1 OFF. Here comes the Jew; had not his goods been seiz'd,
He'd give us present money for them all.

Enter BARABAS.

BAR. In spite of these swine-eating Christians, —
Unchosen nation, never circumcis'd,
Such as, poor villains, were ne'er thought upon
Till Titus and Vespasian conquer'd us —
Am I become as wealthy as I was.
They hop'd my daughter would ha' been a nun;
But she's at home, and I have bought a house
As great and fair as is the Governor's.
And there in spite of Malta will I dwell,
Having Ferneze's hand,[13] whose heart I'll have;
Ay, and his son's too, or it shall go hard.
I am not of the tribe of Levi, I,
That can so soon forget an injury.
We Jews can fawn like spaniels when we please;
And when we grin we bite, yet are our looks
As innocent and harmless as a lamb's.
I learn'd in Florence[14] how to kiss my hand,
Heave up my shoulders when they call me dog,
And duck as low as any barefoot friar;
Hoping to see them starve upon a stall,[15]
Or else be gather'd for in our synagogue,
That, when the offering-basin comes to me,
Even for charity I may spit into 't.
Here comes Don Lodowick, the Governor's son,
One that I love for his good father's sake.

Enter LODOWICK.

LOD. I hear the wealthy Jew walked this way.
I'll seek him out, and so insinuate
That I may have a sight of Abigail;
For Don Mathias tells me she is fair.

BAR. [*aside*] Now will I show myself
To have more of the serpent than the dove;
That is, more knave than fool.

LOD. Yond' walks the Jew; now for fair Abigail.

BAR. [*aside*] Ay, ay, no doubt but she's at your command.

[10] Stationed. The Knights of St. John of Jerusalem were expelled from Rhodes by the Turks in 1522; Charles V granted Malta to them in 1529.

[11] On the contrary, the Knights made excellent terms.

[12] The market-place, ll. 1–6, 98–168; a street, ll. 7–98; the street before Barabas's new house, l. 169 to end.

[13] Probably a promise of safety, in writing.

[14] The home of Machiavelli; the reiteration of *policy* in this play is also referable to the Elizabethan notion of his theories.

[15] Assigned quarters (in an almshouse). (*N.E.D.*)

LOD. Barabas, thou know'st I am the Governor's son.

BAR. I would you were his father, too, sir;
That's all the harm I wish you. — [*aside*] The slave[16] looks
Like a hog's cheek new sing'd.

LOD. Whither walk'st thou, Barabas?

BAR. No further; 't is a custom held with us,
That when we speak with Gentiles like to you,
We turn into the air to purge ourselves;
For unto us the promise doth belong.

LOD. Well, Barabas, canst help me to a diamond?

BAR. O, sir, your father had my diamonds.
Yet I have one left that will serve your turn. —
[*aside*] I mean my daughter; but ere he shall have her
I'll sacrifice her on a pile of wood.
I ha' the poison of the city[17] for him,
And the white leprosy.

LOD. What sparkle does it give without a foil?[18]

BAR. The diamond that I talk of ne'er was foil'd. —
[*aside*] But when he touches it, it will be foil'd.[19] —
Lord Lodowick, it sparkles bright and fair.

LOD. Is it square or pointed, pray let me know.

BAR. Pointed[20] it is, good sir — (*aside*) but not for you.

LOD. I like it much the better.

BAR. So do I too.

LOD. How shows it by night?

BAR. Outshines Cynthia's rays:
— (*aside*) You'll like it better far a-nights than days.

LOD. And what's the price?

BAR. [*aside*] Your life an if you have it. —
O my Lord,
We will not jar about the price; come to my house
And I will give 't your Honor — (*aside*) with a vengeance.

LOD. No, Barabas, I will deserve it first.

BAR. Good sir,
Your father has deserv'd it at my hands,
Who, of mere charity and Christian ruth,
To bring me to religious purity,
And as it were in catechising sort,
To make me mindful of my mortal sins,
Against my will, and whether I would or no,
Seiz'd all I had, and thrust me out a' doors,
And made my house a place for nuns most chaste.

LOD. No doubt your soul shall reap the fruit of it.

BAR. Ay, but, my Lord, the harvest is far off.
And yet I know the prayers of those nuns
And holy friars, having money for their pains,
Are wondrous; — (*aside*) and indeed do no man good —
And seeing they are not idle, but still doing,
'T is likely they in time may reap some fruit —
I mean in fullness of perfection.

LOD. Good Barabas, glance not at[21] our holy nuns.

BAR. No, but I do it through a burning zeal, —
(*aside*) Hoping ere long to set the house afire;
For though they do a while increase and multiply,
I'll have a saying[22] to that nunnery. —
As for the diamond, sir, I told you of,
Come home and there's no price shall make us part,
Even for your honorable father's sake. —
(*aside*) It shall go hard but I will see your death. —
But now I must be gone to buy a slave.

LOD. And, Barabas, I'll bear thee company.

BAR. Come, then; — here's the market-place.
What's the price of this slave? Two hundred crowns!
Do the Turk[s] weigh so much?

1 OFF. Sir, that's his price.

BAR. What, can he steal, that you demand so much?
Belike he has some new trick for a purse;
And if he has, he is worth three hundred plates,[23]
So that, being bought, the town seal might be got
To keep him for his lifetime from the gallows.
The sessions day is critical to thieves,
And few or none 'scape but by being purg'd.

LOD. Ratest thou this Moor but at two hundred plates?

1 OFF. No more, my Lord.

[16] His neatly shaved face.
[17] Possibly a misprint. (Dyce.)
[18] Metal leaf placed under a gem to increase its brilliance.
[19] Defiled.
[20] Punning on "pointed" and "appointed."
[21] Cast no reflections on.
[22] Something to say.
[23] Silver coins.

BAR. Why should this Turk be dearer than that Moor?

1 OFF. Because he is young and has more qualities.

BAR. What, hast thou the philosopher's stone?[24] An thou hast, break my head with it; I'll forgive thee.

[SLAVE.][25] No, sir; I can cut and shave.

BAR. Let me see, sirrah, are you not an old shaver?

[SLAVE.] Alas, sir! I am a very youth.

BAR. A youth? I'll buy you, and marry you to Lady Vanity,[26] if you do well.

[SLAVE.] I will serve you, sir.

BAR. Some wicked trick or other. It may be, under color of shaving, thou'lt cut my throat for my goods. Tell me, hast thou thy health well?

[SLAVE.] Ay, passing well.

BAR. So much the worse; I must have one that's sickly, [an 't][27] be but for sparing victuals. 'T is not a stone of beef a day will maintain you in these chops;[28] let me see one that's somewhat leaner.

1 OFF. Here's a leaner; how like you him?

BAR. Where was thou born?

ITHA. In Thrace; brought up in Arabia.

BAR. So much the better; thou art for my turn.
An hundred crowns? I'll have him; there's the coin.

1 OFF. Then mark him, sir, and take him hence.

BAR. [*aside*] Ay, mark him, you were best; for this is he
That by my help shall do much villainy. —
My Lord, farewell. — Come, sirrah, you are mine. —
As for the diamond, it shall be yours;
I pray, sir, be no stranger at my house;
All that I have shall be at your command.

Enter MATHIAS [*and his* Mother, KATHERINE].

MATH. [*aside*] What makes the Jew and Lodowick so private?
I fear me 't is about fair Abigail.

BAR. Yonder comes Don Mathias; let us stay;[29]
He loves my daughter, and she holds him dear:
But I have sworn to frustrate both their hopes,
And be reveng'd upon the — [*aside*] Governor!

[*Exit* LODOWICK.]

[KATH.][30] This Moor is comeliest, is he not? Speak, Son.

MATH. No, this is the better, Mother; view this well.

BAR. [*aside to* MATHIAS] Seem not to know me here before your mother,
Lest she mistrust the match that is in hand.
When you have brought her home, come to my house;
Think of me as thy father; Son, farewell.

MATH. [*aside to* BARABAS] But wherefore talk'd Don Lodowick with you?

BAR. [*aside to* MATHIAS] Tush, man! we talk'd of diamonds, not of Abigail.

KATH. Tell me, Mathias, is not that the Jew?

BAR. As for the comment on the Maccabees,
I have it, sir, and 't is at your command.

MATH. Yes, madam, and my talk with him was
About the borrowing of a book or two.

KATH. Converse not with him; he is cast off from Heaven. —
Thou hast thy crowns, fellow. — Come, let's away.

MATH. Sirrah, Jew, remember the book.

BAR. Marry will I, sir.

Exeunt [MATHIAS *and his* Mother].

OFF. Come, I have made
A reasonable market; let's away.

[*Exeunt* Officers *with* Slaves.]

BAR. Now let me know thy name, and therewithal
Thy birth, condition, and profession.

ITHA. Faith, sir, my birth is but mean; my name's Ithamore; my profession what you please.

BAR. Hast thou no trade? Then listen to my words,
And I will teach [thee][31] that shall stick by thee.
First be thou void of these affections:
Compassion, love, vain hope, and heartless fear;
Be mov'd at nothing, see thou pity none,
But to thyself smile when the Christians moan.

ITHA. O, brave! Master, I worship your nose[32] for this.

[24] Sought by alchemists, to turn other metals into gold.
[25] Q assigns to Ithamore, throughout.
[26] A character in the Morality plays.
[27] Q *and.*
[28] Jaws; *i.e.*, your fat face.
[29] Stop talking.

[30] Q *Mater*, throughout.
[31] Add. Reed.
[32] Barabas was played with a false nose.

BAR. As for myself, I walk abroad a-nights
And kill sick people groaning under walls;
Sometimes I go about and poison wells;
And now and then, to cherish Christian thieves,
I am content to lose some of my crowns,
That I may, walking in my gallery,[33]
See 'em go pinion'd along by my door.
Being young, I studied physic, and began
To practise first upon the Italian;
There I enrich'd the priests with burials,
And always kept the sextons' arms in ure [34]
With digging graves and ringing dead men's knells.
And after that was I an engineer,
And in the wars 'twixt France and Germany,
Under pretence of helping Charles the Fifth,
Slew friend and enemy with my stratagems.
Then after that was I an usurer,
And with extorting, cozening,[35] forfeiting,
And tricks belonging unto brokery,
I fill'd the jails with bankrouts in a year,
And with young orphans planted hospitals,
And every moon made some or other mad,
And now and then one hang himself for grief,
Pinning upon his breast a long great scroll
How I with interest tormented him.
But mark how I am blest for plaguing them:
I have as much coin as will buy the town.
But tell me now, how hast thou spent thy time?

ITHA. Faith, master,
In setting Christian villages on fire,
Chaining of eunuchs, binding galley-slaves.
One time I was an ostler in an inn,
And in the nighttime secretly would I steal
To travellers' chambers, and there cut their throats.
Once at Jerusalem, where the pilgrims kneel'd,
I strowed powder on the marble stones,
And therewithal their knees would rankle so,
That I have laugh'd a-good [36] to see the cripples
Go limping home to Christendom on stilts.[37]

BAR. Why this is something. Make account of me
As of thy fellow; we are villains both,
Both circumcised, we hate Christians both.
Be true and secret, thou shalt want no gold.
But stand aside; here comes Don Lodowick.

Re-enter LODOWICK.

LOD. O, Barabas, well met;
Where is the diamond you told me of?

BAR. I have it for you, sir; please you walk in with me.
What ho, Abigail! open the door, I say.

Enter ABIGAIL

ABIG. In good time, father; here are letters come
From Ormus, and the post [38] stays here within.

BAR. Give me the letters. — (*aside*) Daughter, do you hear,
Entertain Lodowick, the Governor's son,
With all the courtesy you can afford,
Provided that you keep your maidenhead.
Use him as if he were a Philistine;
Dissemble, swear, protest, vow to love him;
He is not of the seed of Abraham. —
I am a little busy, sir, pray pardon me.
Abigail, bid him welcome for my sake.

ABIG. For your sake and his own he's welcome hither.

BAR. Daughter, a word more; — [*aside*] kiss him, speak him fair,
And like a cunning Jew so cast about
That ye be both made sure [39] ere you come out.

ABIG. [*aside*] O father! Don Mathias is my love.

BAR. [*aside*] I know it; yet I say, make love to him;
Do, it is requisite it should be so. —
Nay, on my life, it is my factor's hand;
But go you in, I'll think upon the account.

[*Exeunt* ABIGAIL *and* LODOWICK *into the house.*]

The account is made, for Lodowick dies.
My factor sends me word a merchant's fled
That owes me for a hundred tun of wine.
I weigh it thus much [*snapping his fingers*]; I have wealth enough.
For now by this has he kiss'd Abigail;
And she vows love to him, and he to her.
As sure as Heaven rain'd manna for the Jews,
So sure shall he and Don Mathias die:
His father was [40] my chiefest enemy.

Re-enter MATHIAS.

Whither goes Don Mathias? Stay awhile.

MATH. Whither but to my fair love, Abigail?

BAR. Thou know'st, and Heaven can witness it is true,
That I intend my daughter shall be thine.

MATH. Ay, Barabas, or else thou wrong'st me much.

[33] Balcony.
[34] Use, practice.
[35] Cheating, befooling.
[36] Heartily, in earnest.
[37] Crutches.
[38] Messenger.
[39] Betrothed.
[40] *I.e.*, in the late proceedings.

BAR. O, Heaven forbid I should have such a thought.
Pardon me though I weep; the Governor's son
Will, whether I will or no, have Abigail:
He sends her letters, bracelets, jewels, rings.
MATH. Does she receive them?
BAR. She? No, Mathias, no, but sends them back;
And when he comes, she locks herself up fast;
Yet through the keyhole will he talk to her,
While she runs to the window looking out
When you should come and hale him from the door.
MATH. O treacherous Lodowick!
BAR. Even now, as I came home, he slipp'd me in;
And I am sure he is with Abigail.
MATH. I'll rouse him thence.
BAR. Not for all Malta; therefore sheathe your sword.
If you love me, no quarrels in my house;
But steal you in, and seem to see him not.
I'll give him such a warning ere he goes
As he shall have small hopes of Abigail.
Away, for here they come.

Re-enter LODOWICK [*and*] ABIGAIL.

MATH. What, hand in hand! I cannot suffer this.
BAR. Mathias, as thou lov'st me, not a word.
MATH. Well, let it pass; another time shall serve. *Exit.*
LOD. Barabas, is not that the widow's son?
BAR. Ay, and take heed, for he hath sworn your death.
LOD. My death? What, is the baseborn peasant mad?
BAR. No, no; but happily[41] he stands in fear
Of that which you, I think, ne'er dream upon,
My daughter here, a paltry silly girl.
LOD. Why, loves she Don Mathias?
BAR. Doth she not with her smiling answer you?
ABIG. [*aside*] He has my heart; I smile against my will.
LOD. Barabas, thou know'st I have lov'd thy daughter long.
BAR. And so has she done you, even from a child.
LOD. And now I can no longer hold my mind.
BAR. Nor I the affection that I bear to you.
LOD. This is thy diamond; tell me shall I have it?
BAR. Win it, and wear it; it is yet [unfoil'd].[42]
O, but I know your Lordship would disdain
To marry with the daughter of a Jew;
And yet I'll give her many a golden cross,[43]
With Christian posies[44] round about the ring.
LOD. 'T is not thy wealth, but her that I esteem.
Yet crave I thy consent.
BAR. And mine you have, yet let me talk to her. —
(*Aside*) This offspring of Cain, this Jebusite,
That never tasted of the Passover
Nor e'er shall see the land of Canaan
Nor our Messias that is yet to come,
This gentle[45] maggot, Lodowick, I mean,
Must be deluded. Let him have thy hand,
But keep thy heart till Don Mathias comes.
ABIG. [*aside*] What, shall I be betroth'd to Lodowick?
BAR. [*aside*] It's no sin to deceive a Christian,
For they themselves hold it a principle
Faith is not to be held with heretics;
But all are heretics that are not Jews;
This follows well, and therefore, Daughter, fear not. —
I have entreated her, and she will grant.
LOD. Then, gentle Abigail, plight thy faith to me.
ABIG. I cannot choose, seeing my father bids.
Nothing but death shall part my love and me.
LOD. Now have I that for which my soul hath long'd.
BAR. (*aside.*) So have not I, but yet I hope I shall.
ABIG. [*aside*] O wretched Abigail, what hast [thou][46] done?
LOD. Why on the sudden is your color chang'd?
ABIG. I know not, but farewell; I must be gone.
BAR. Stay her, but let her not speak one word more.
LOD. Mute a' the sudden! Here's a sudden change.
BAR. O, muse not at it, 't is the Hebrews' guise,

[41] Haply.

[42] Emend. Collier; Q *vnsoyl'd*.
[43] Coin with a cross on one side.
[44] Mottoes; *i.e.*, the inscriptions.
[45] Punning on "gentile."
[46] Q *thee*.

That maidens new betroth'd should weep awhile.
Trouble her not ; sweet Lodowick, depart ;
She is thy wife, and thou shalt be mine heir.

LOD. O, is 't the custom ? Then I am resolv'd ;[47]
But rathe[r] let the brightsome heavens be dim
And nature's beauty choke with stifling clouds,
Than my fair Abigail should frown on me. —
There comes the villain ; now I 'll be reveng'd.

Re-enter MATHIAS.

BAR. Be quiet, Lodowick ; it is enough
That I have made thee sure to Abigail.

LOD. Well, let him go. *Exit.*

BAR. Well, but for me, as you went in at doors
You had been stabb'd ; but not a word on 't now ;
Here must no speeches pass nor swords be drawn.

MATH. Suffer me, Barabas, but to follow him.

BAR. No ; so shall I, if any hurt be done,
Be made an accessary of your deeds.
Revenge it on him when you meet him next.

MATH. For this I 'll have his heart.

BAR. Do so ; lo, here I give thee Abigail.

MATH. What greater gift can poor Mathias have ?
Shall Lodowick rob me of so fair a love ?
My life is not so dear as Abigail.

BAR. My heart misgives me that, to cross your love,
He 's with your mother ; therefore after him.

MATH. What, is he gone unto my mother ?

BAR. Nay, if you will, stay till she comes herself.

MATH. I cannot stay ; for if my mother come,
She 'll die with grief. *Exit.*

ABIG. I cannot take my leave of him for tears.
Father, why have you thus incens'd them both ?

BAR. What 's that to thee ?

ABIG. I 'll make 'em friends again.

BAR. You 'll make 'em friends ! Are there not Jews enow
In Malta, but thou must dote upon a Christian ?

ABIG. I will have Don Mathias ; he is my love.

BAR. Yes, you shall have him. — Go, put her in.

ITHA. Ay, I 'll put her in.

[*Puts* ABIGAIL *in.*]

BAR. Now tell me, Ithamore, how lik'st thou this ?

ITHA. Faith, master, I think by this
You purchase both their lives ; is it not so ?

BAR. True ; and it shall be cunningly perform'd.

ITHA. O master, that I might have a hand in this.

BAR. Ay, so thou shalt ; 't is thou must do the deed.
Take this, and bear it to Mathias straight,
[*Gives a letter.*]
And tell him that it comes from Lodowick.

ITHA. 'T is poison'd, is it not ?

BAR. No, no ; and yet it might be done that way.
It is a challenge feign'd from Lodowick.

ITHA. Fear not ; I 'll so set his heart afire
That he shall verily think it comes from him.

BAR. I cannot choose but like thy readiness ;
Yet be not rash, but do it cunningly.

ITHA. As I behave myself in this, employ me hereafter.

BAR. Away then. *Exit* [ITHAMORE].
So ; now will I go in to Lodowick
And, like a cunning spirit, feign some lie,
Till I have set 'em both at enmity. *Exit.*

ACT III — [SCENE I][1]

Enter [BELLAMIRA,] *a courtesan.*

BELL. Since this town was besieg'd, my gain grows cold.
The time has been that, but for one bare night,
A hundred ducats have been freely given ;
But now against my will I must be chaste,
And yet I know my beauty doth not fail.
From Venice merchants and from Padua
Were wont to come rare-witted gentlemen,
Scholars, I mean, learned and liberal ;
And now, save Pilia-Borza, comes there none,
And he is very seldom from my house ;
And here he comes.

[47] Satisfied.

[1] A street near Bellamira's house.

Enter PILIA-BORZA.

PILIA. Hold thee, wench; there's something for thee to spend. [*Shows a bag of silver.*]

BELL. 'T is silver; I disdain it.

PILIA. Ay, but the Jew has gold,
And I will have it, or it shall go hard.

COURT. Tell me, how cam'st thou by this?

PILIA. Faith, walking the back lanes, through the gardens, I chanc'd to cast mine eye up to the Jew's countinghouse, where I saw some bags of money, and in the night I clamber'd up with my hooks, and, as I was taking my choice, I heard a rumbling in the house; so I took only this, and run my way. But here's the Jew's man.

Enter ITHAMORE.

BELL. Hide the bag.

PILIA. Look not towards him; let's away. Zoons, what a looking thou keep'st; thou 'lt betray 's anon.

[*Exeunt* BELLAMIRA *and* PILIA-BORZA.]

ITHA. O the sweetest face that ever I beheld! I know she is a courtesan by her attire. Now would I give a hundred of the Jew's crowns that I had such a concubine.
Well, I have deliver'd the challenge in such sort
As meet they will, and fighting die — brave sport! *Exit.*

[SCENE II][2]

Enter MATHIAS.

MATH. This is the place; now Abigail shall see
Whether Mathias holds her dear or no.

Enter LODOWICK, *reading.*[3]

MATH. What, dares the villain write in such base terms?

LOD. I did it; and revenge it if thou dar'st. [*They*] *fight.*

Enter BARABAS, *above.*

BAR. O, bravely fought; and yet they thrust not home.
Now, Lodowick! now, Mathias! — So! [*Both fall.*]
So now they have show'd themselves to be tall[4] fellows.

[*Cries*] *within.* Part 'em, part 'em.

BAR. Ay, part 'em now they are dead. Farewell, farewell. *Exit.*

Enter FERNEZE, KATHERINE [*and* Attendants].

FERN. What sight is this? — my Lodowick slain!
These arms of mine shall be thy sepulchre.

KATH. Who is this? My son Mathias slain!

FERN. O Lodowick! hadst thou perish'd by the Turk,
Wretched Ferneze might have veng'd thy death.

KATH. Thy son slew mine, and I'll revenge his death.

FERN. Look, Katherine, look; thy son gave mine these wounds.

KATH. O, leave to grieve me; I am griev'd enough.

FERN. O, that my sighs could turn to lively breath,
And these my tears to blood, that he might live.

KATH. Who made them enemies?

FERN. I know not, and that grieves me most of all.

KATH. My son lov'd thine.

FERN. And so did Lodowick him.

KATH. Lend me that weapon that did kill my son,
And it shall murder me.

FERN. Nay, madam, stay; that weapon was my son's,
And on that rather should Ferneze die.

KATH. Hold; let's inquire the causers of their deaths,
That we may venge their blood upon their heads.

FERN. Then take them up, and let them be interr'd
Within one sacred monument of stone;
Upon which altar I will offer up
My daily sacrifice of sighs and tears,
And with my prayers pierce impartial Heavens,
Till they [reveal][5] the causers of our smarts,
Which forc'd their hands divide united hearts.
Come, Katherina, our losses equal are;
Then of true grief let us take equal share.

Exeunt [*with the bodies*].

[2] Before the house of Barabas.
[3] Cf. III, iii, 20–22.
[4] Valiant.

[5] Conj. Dyce; om. Q.

[Scene III] [6]

Enter Ithamore.

Itha. Why, was there ever seen such villainy,
So neatly plotted, and so well perform'd?
Both held in hand,[7] and flatly both beguil'd?

Enter Abigail.

Abig. Why, how now, Ithamore, why laugh'st thou so?

Itha. O mistress, ha! ha! ha!

Abig. Why, what ail'st thou?

Itha. O my master!

Abig. Ha!

Itha. O mistress! I have the bravest,[8] gravest, secret, subtle, bottle-nos'd knave to my master, that ever gentleman had.

Abig. Say, knave, why rail'st upon my father thus?

Itha. O, my master has the bravest policy.

Abig. Wherein?

Itha. Why, know you not?

Abig. Why, no.

Itha. Know you not of Mathias' and Don Lodowick's disaster?

Abig. No; what was it?

Itha. Why, the Devil invented a challenge, my master writ it, and I carried it, first to Lodowick, and *imprimis* to Mathias.
And then they met, [and,] [9] as the story says,
In doleful wise they ended both their days.

Abig. And was my father furtherer of their deaths?

Itha. Am I Ithamore?

Abig. Yes.

Itha. So sure did your father write, and I carry the challenge.

Abig. Well, Ithamore, let me request thee this:
Go to the new-made nunnery, and inquire
For any of the friars of Saint [Jacques,] [10]
And say I pray them come and speak with me.

Itha. I pray, mistress, will you answer me to one question? [11]

Abig. Well, sirrah, what is 't?

Itha. A very feeling one: have not the nuns fine sport with the friars now and then?

Abig. Go to, sirrah sauce; is this your question? Get ye gone.

Itha. I will, forsooth, mistress. *Exit.*

Abig. Hard-hearted father, unkind Barabas!
Was this the pursuit of thy policy?
To make me show them favor severally,
That by my favor they should both be slain?
Admit thou lov'dst not Lodowick for his [sire],[12]
Yet Don Mathias ne'er offended thee;
But thou wert set upon extreme revenge,
Because the [sire] [13] dispossess'd thee once,
And couldst not venge it, but upon his son,
Nor on his son, but by Mathias' means,
Nor on Mathias, but by murdering me.
But I perceive there is no love on earth,
Pity in Jews, nor piety in Turks.
But here comes cursed Ithamore, with the friar.

Enter Ithamore [*and*] Friar [Jacomo].

F. Jac. *Virgo, salve.*

Itha. When! duck you? [14]

Abig. Welcome, grave friar; Ithamore, begone. *Exit* [Ithamore].
Know, holy sir, I am bold to solicit thee.

F. Jac. Wherein?

Abig. To get me be admitted for a nun.

F. Jac. Why, Abigail, it is not yet long since
That I did labor thy admission,
And then thou didst not like that holy life.

Abig. Then were my thoughts so frail and unconfirm'd,
And I was chain'd to follies of the world;
But now experience, purchased with grief,
Has made me see the difference of things.
My sinful soul, alas, hath pac'd too long
The fatal labyrinth of misbelief,
Far from the Son [15] that gives eternal life.

F. Jac. Who taught thee this?

Abig. The abbess of the house,
Whose zealous admonition I embrace.
Oh, therefore, Jacom[o], let me be one,
Although unworthy, of that sisterhood.

F. Jac. Abigail, I will; but see thou change no more.
For that will be most heavy to thy soul.

Abig. That was my father's fault.

F. Jac. Thy father's! how?

Abig. Nay, you shall pardon me. — [*aside*] O Barabas,

[6] Unlocated; presumably a room in Barabas's house.
[7] Led on and deluded.
[8] Finest.
[9] Add. Robinson.
[10] "Jacobins," *i.e.*, Dominicans. Cor. Collier; Q *Iaynes*.
[11] An interpolated piece of clowning? (Bennett, on ll. 34–41.)
[12] Emend. Dyce; Q *sinne*.
[13] Conj. Brooke; Q *Pryor*.
[14] The Friars were given to bobs and curtsies. "When" is an exclamation of impatience.
[15] With a pun on *sun*.

Though thou deservest hardly at my hands,
Yet never shall these lips bewray thy life.

F. JAC. Come, shall we go?

ABIG. My duty waits on you.

Exeunt.

[SCENE IV] [16]

Enter BARABAS, *reading a letter.*

BAR. What, Abigail become a nun again!
False and unkind; [17] what, hast thou lost thy father?
And all unknown, and unconstrain'd of me,
Art thou again got to the nunnery?
Now here she writes, and wills me to repent.
Repentance! *Spurca!* [18] what pretendeth [19] this?
I fear she knows — 't is so — of my device
In Don Mathias' and Lodovico's deaths.
If so, 't is time that it be seen into;
For she that varies from me in belief
Gives great presumption that she loves me not;
Or, loving, doth dislike of something done.
But who comes here?

[*Enter* ITHAMORE.]

O Ithamore, come near;
Come near, my love; come near, thy master's life;
My trusty servant, nay, my second [self]: [20]
For I have now no hope but even in thee,
And on that hope my happiness is built.
When saw'st thou Abigail?

ITHA. To-day.

BAR. With whom?

ITHA. A friar.

BAR. A friar! false villain, he hath done the deed.

ITHA. How, sir?

BAR. Why, made mine Abigail a nun.

ITHA. That 's no lie, for she sent me for him.

BAR. O unhappy day!
False, credulous, inconstant Abigail!
But let 'em go; and, Ithamore, from hence
Ne'er shall she grieve me more with her disgrace;
Ne'er shall she live to inherit aught of mine,
Be bless'd of me, nor come within my gates,
But perish underneath my bitter curse,
Like Cain by Adam for his brother's death.

ITHA. O master!

BAR. Ithamore, entreat not for her, I am mov'd,
And she is hateful to my soul and me;
And ['less] [21] thou yield to this that I entreat,
I cannot think but that thou hat'st my life.

ITHA. Who, I, master? Why, I'll run to some rock
And throw myself headlong into the sea;
Why, I'll do anything for your sweet sake.

BAR. O trusty Ithamore, no servant, but my friend,
I here adopt thee for mine only heir;
All that I have is thine when I am dead,
And whilst I live use half; spend as myself.
Here take my keys, — I'll give 'em thee anon.
Go buy thee garments; but thou shalt not want.
Only know this, that thus thou art to do;
But first go fetch me in the pot of rice
That for our supper stands upon the fire.

ITHA. [*aside*] I hold [22] my head my master's hungry. — I go, sir. *Exit.*

BAR. Thus every villain ambles after wealth,
Although he ne'er be richer than in hope.
But, hush 't!

Re-enter ITHAMORE *with the pot.*

ITHA. Here 't is, master.

BAR. Well said, [23] Ithamore.
What, hast thou brought the ladle with thee too?

ITHA. Yes, sir; the proverb says he that eats with the Devil had need of a long spoon. I have brought you a ladle.

BAR. Very well, Ithamore; then now be secret;
And for thy sake, whom I so dearly love,
Now shalt thou see the death of Abigail,
That thou mayst freely live to be my heir.

ITHA. Why, master, will you poison her with a mess of rice porridge? That will preserve life, make her round and plump, and batten more than you are aware.

BAR. Ay, but, Ithamore, seest thou this?
It is a precious powder that I bought
Of an Italian in Ancona once,
Whose operation is to bind, infect,
And poison deeply, yet not appear
In forty hours after it is ta'en.

ITHA. How, master?

BAR. Thus, Ithamore.
This even they use in Malta here — 't is called

[16] A room in Barabas's house.
[17] Unnatural.
[18] An opprobrious exclamation. (Lat. *spurcus.*)
[19] Portendeth.
[20] Conj. Dyce; Q *life.*

[21] Conj. Collier; Q *least.*
[22] Bet.
[23] Well done.

Saint Jacques' Even, — and then, I say, they use
To send their alms unto the nunneries.
Among the rest bear this, and set it there;
There's a dark entry where they take it in,
Where they must neither see the messenger,
Nor make inquiry who hath sent it them.

ITHA. How so?

BAR. Belike there is some ceremony in 't.
There, Ithamore, must thou go place this [pot]![24]
Stay, let me spice it first.

ITHA. Pray do, and let me help you, master.
Pray let me taste first.

BAR. Prithee do. — What say'st thou now?

ITHA. Troth, master, I'm loath such a pot of pottage should be spoil'd.

BAR. Peace, Ithamore; 't is better so than spar'd.
Assure thyself thou shalt have broth by the eye:[25]
My purse, my coffer, and myself is thine.

ITHA. Well, master, I go.

BAR. Stay, first let me stir it, Ithamore.
As fatal be it to her as the draught
Of which great Alexander drunk and died;
And with her let it work like Borgia's wine,
Whereof his sire, the Pope, was poisoned.
In few,[26] the blood of Hydra, Lerna's bane,
The juice of hebon,[27] and Cocytus' breath,
And all the poisons of the Stygian pool
Break from the fiery kingdom, and in this
Vomit your venom and envenom her
That like a fiend hath left her father thus.

ITHA. [*aside*] What a blessing has he giv'n 't!
Was ever pot of rice porridge so sauc'd? —
What shall I do with it?

BAR. O, my sweet Ithamore, go set it down,
And come again so soon as thou hast done,
For I have other business for thee.

ITHA. Here's a drench to poison a whole stable of Flanders mares. I'll carry 't to the nuns with a powder.[28]

BAR. And the horse pestilence to boot; away!

ITHA. I am gone.
Pay me my wages, for my work is done. *Exit.*

BAR. I'll pay thee with a vengeance, Ithamore. *Exit.*

[24] Cor. Reed; Q *plot*. [25] In abundance.
[26] In short.
[27] A poison; perhaps henbane, perhaps yew. — Lerna, a marshy district near Argos, was the place where Hercules killed the Hydra. The river Cocytus, a tributary of the Acheron, was one of the rivers of Hades. So was the Styx.
[28] In haste. With an obvious pun.

[SCENE V][29]

Enter FERNEZE, DEL BOSCO, Knights, [*and a*] Bashaw.

FERN. Welcome, great [Bashaw][30]; how fares Calymath?
What wind drives you thus into Malta road?

BAS. The wind that bloweth all the world besides —
Desire of gold.

FERN. Desire of gold, great sir?
That's to be gotten in the Western Ind;
In Malta are no golden minerals.

BAS. To you of Malta thus saith Calymath:
The time you took for respite is at hand,
For the performance of your promise pass'd;
And for the tribute money I am sent.

FERN. Bashaw, in brief, shalt have no tribute here,
Nor shall the heathens live upon our spoil.
First will we raze the city walls ourselves,
Lay waste the island, hew the temples down,
And, shipping off[31] our goods to Sicily,
Open an entrance for the wasteful sea,
Whose billows, beating the resistless banks,
Shall overflow it with their refluence.

BAS. Well, Governor, since thou hast broke the league
By flat denial of the promis'd tribute,
Talk not of razing down your city walls.
You shall not need trouble yourselves so far,
For Selim Calymath shall come himself,
And with brass bullets batter down your towers
And turn proud Malta to a wilderness
For these intolerable wrongs of yours;
And so, farewell.

FERN. Farewell. — [*Exit* Basso.]
And now, you men of Malta, look about,
And let's provide to welcome Calymath.
Close your portcullis, charge your basilisks,[32]
And as you profitably take up arms,
So now courageously encounter them;
For by this answer, broken is the league,
And naught is to be look'd for now but wars;
And naught to us more welcome is than wars.
Exeunt.

[SCENE VI][33]

Enter [*the*] *two* Friars [JACOMO *and* BARNARDINE].

F. JAC. O, brother, brother, all the nuns are sick,

[29] Unlocated; perhaps the senate-house.
[30] Q *Bashaws*. [31] Q *of*. [32] Large cannon.
[33] The courtyard of the nunnery.

And physic will not help them ; they must die.

F. BARN. The Abbess sent for me to be confess'd ;
O, what a sad confession will there be !

F. JAC. And so did fair Maria send for me.
I'll to her lodging ; hereabouts she lies. *Exit.*

Enter ABIGAIL.

F. BARN. What, all dead, save only Abigail?

ABIG. And I shall die too, for I feel death coming.
Where is the friar that convers'd with me?

F. BARN. O, he is gone to see the other nuns.

ABIG. I sent for him, but seeing you are come,
Be you my ghostly father ; and first know
That in this house I liv'd religiously,
Chaste, and devout, much sorrowing for my sins ;
But ere I came ——

F. BARN. What then?

ABIG. I did offend high Heaven so grievously
As I am almost desperate for my sins ;
And one offence torments me more than all.
You knew Mathias and Don Lodowick?

F. BARN. Yes, what of them?

ABIG. My father did contract me to 'em both :
First to Don Lodowick ; him I never lov'd ;
Mathias was the man that I held dear ;
And for his sake did I become a nun.

F. BARN. So, say how was their end?

ABIG. Both jealous of my love, envied[34] each other,
And by my father's practice,[35] which is there
Set down at large, the gallants were both slain.
[*Gives a paper.*]

F. BARN. O monstrous villainy !

ABIG. To work my peace, this I confess to thee ;
Reveal it not, for then my father dies.

F. BARN. Know that confession must not be reveal'd ;
The canon law forbids it, and the priest
That makes it known, being degraded first,
Shall be condemn'd and then sent to the fire.

ABIG. So I have heard ; pray, therefore, keep it close.[36]
Death seizeth on my heart ; ah, gentle friar,
Convert my father, that he may be sav'd,
And witness that I die a Christian. [*Dies.*]

F. BARN. Ay, and a virgin too ; that grieves me most.
But I must to the Jew and exclaim on[37] him,
And make him stand in fear of me.

Re-enter Friar [JACOMO].

F. JAC. O brother, all the nuns are dead ; let's bury them.

F. BARN. First help to bury this ; then go with me
And help me to exclaim against the Jew.

F. JAC. Why, what has he done?

F. BARN. A thing that makes me tremble to unfold.

F. JAC. What, has he crucified a child?

F. BARN. No, but a worse thing ; 't was told me in shrift ;
Thou know'st 't is death an if it be reveal'd.
Come, let 's away. *Exeunt.*

[34] Entertained a grudge against.
[35] Plot.
[36] Secret.
[37] Accuse.

ACT IV — [SCENE I][1]

Enter BARABAS [*and*] ITHAMORE. *Bells within.*

BAR. There is no music to[2] a Christian's knell :
How sweet the bells ring now the nuns are dead,
That sound at other times like tinkers' pans !
I was afraid the poison had not wrought ;
Or, though it wrought, it would have done no good,
For every year they swell, and yet they live.
Now all are dead ; not one remains alive.

ITHA. That 's brave, master ; but think you it will not be known?

BAR. How can it, if we two be secret?

ITHA. For my part fear you not.

BAR. I 'd cut thy throat if I did.

ITHA. And reason too.
But here 's a royal monastery hard by ;
Good master, let me poison all the monks.

BAR. Thou shalt not need, for now the nuns are dead
They 'll die with grief.

ITHA. Do you not sorrow for your daughter's death?

BAR. No, but I grieve because she liv'd so long.

[1] The street before Barabas's house.
[2] Comparable to.

An Hebrew born, and would become a Christian!
[Catso],[3] *diabol[o]*!

Enter the two Friars [Jacomo *and* Barnardine].

Itha. Look, look, master; here come two religious caterpillars.

Bar. I smelt 'em ere they came.

Itha. God-a-mercy, nose! Come, let 's be gone.

F. Barn. Stay, wicked Jew; repent, I say, and stay.

F. Jac. Thou hast offended, therefore must be damn'd.

Bar. [*aside to* Ithamore] I fear they know we sent the poison'd broth.

Itha. [*aside*] And so do I, master; therefore speak 'em fair.

F. Barn. Barabas, thou hast ——

F. Jac. Ay, that thou hast ——

Bar. True, I have money, what though I have?

F. Barn. Thou art a ——

F. Jac. Ay, that thou art, a —

Bar. What needs all this? I know I am a Jew.

F. Barn. Thy daughter ——

F. Jac. Ay, thy daughter ——

Bar. O speak not of her! then I die with grief.

F. Barn. Remember that ——

F. Jac. Ay, remember that ——

Bar. I must needs say that I have been a great usurer.

F. Barn. Thou hast committed ——

Bar. Fornication — but that was in another country; and besides, the wench is dead.

F. Barn. Ay, but, Barabas,
Remember Mathias and Don Lodowick.

Bar. Why, what of them?

F. Barn. I will not say that by a forged challenge they met.

Bar. (*aside*) She has confess'd, and we are both undone —
My bosom inmates[4]! but I must dissemble. —
O holy friars, the burden of my sins
Lie heavy on my soul; then pray you tell me,
Is't not too late now to turn Christian?
I have been zealous in the Jewish faith,
Hard-hearted to the poor, a covetous wretch,
That would for lucre's sake have sold my soul.
A hundred for a hundred I have ta'en;
And now for store of wealth may I compare
With all the Jews of Malta; but what is wealth?
I am a Jew, and therefore am I lost.
Would penance serve for this my sin,
I could afford to whip myself to death, —

Itha. And so could I; but penance will not serve.

Bar. To fast, to pray, and wear a shirt of hair,
And on my knees creep to Jerusalem.
Cellars of wine, and sollars[5] full of wheat,
Warehouses stuff'd with spices and with drugs,
Whole chests of gold, in bullion and in coin,
Besides I know not how much weight in pearl,
Orient[6] and round, have I within my house;
At Alexandria, merchandise unsold.
But yesterday two ships went from this town;
Their voyage will be worth ten thousand crowns.
In Florence, Venice, Antwerp, London, Seville,
Frankfort, Lübeck, Moscow, and where not,
Have I debts owing; and, in most of these,
Great sums of money lying in the banco;
All this I'll give to some religious house
So[7] I may be baptiz'd and live therein.

F. Jac. O good Barabas, come to our house.

F. Barn. O no, good Barabas, come to our house;
And, Barabas, you know ——

Bar. I know that I have highly sinn'd.
You shall convert me, you shall have all my wealth.

F. Jac. O Barabas, their laws are strict.

Bar. I know they are, and I will be with you.

F. Barn. They wear no shirts, and they go barefoot too.

Bar. Then 't is not for me; and I am resolv'd
You shall confess me, and have all my goods.

F. Jac. Good Barabas, come to me.

Bar. [*aside to* F. Jac.] You see I answer him, and yet he stays;
Rid him away, and go you home with me.

F. Jac. I'll be with you to-night.

Bar. Come to my house at one a'clock this night.

F. Jac. You hear your answer, and you may be gone.

F. Barn. Why, go; get you away.

F. Jac. I will not go for thee.

[3] Cor. Dyce; Q *Catho*, for *cazzo*, an obscene (Italian) exclamation.

[4] *I.e.*, the friars are now in my secrets; though possibly the plural is erroneous and the reference is to Abigail.

[5] Lofts. [6] Lustrous. [7] Provided that.

F. Barn. Not? then I'll make thee go!
F. Jac. How, dost call me rogue?[8] *Fight.*
Itha. Part 'em, master, part 'em.
Bar. This is mere frailty, brethren; be content.
Friar Barnadine, go you with Ithamore. —
[*aside*] You know my mind; let me alone with him.[9]
[F. Jac.] Why does he go to thy house? Let him be gone.
Bar. I'll give him something and so stop his mouth.

Exit [Ithamore *with* Friar Barnardine].

I never heard of any man but he
Malign'd the order of the Jacobins.
But do you think that I believe his words?
Why, brother, you converted Abigail;
And I am bound in charity to requite it,
And so I will. O Jacom[o], fail not, but come.
F. Jac. But, Barabas, who shall be your godfathers?
For presently you shall be shriv'd.
Bar. Marry, the Turk[10] shall be one of my godfathers;
But not a word to any of your covent.[11]
F. Jac. I warrant thee, Barabas. *Exit.*
Bar. So; now the fear is past, and I am safe;
For he that shriv'd her is within my house.
What if I murder'd him ere Jacom[o] comes?
Now I have such a plot for both their lives
As never Jew nor Christian knew the like.
One turn'd my daughter, therefore he shall die;
The other knows enough to have my life,
Therefore 't is not requisite he should live.
But are not both these wise men to suppose
That I will leave my house, my goods, and all,
To fast and be well whipp'd? I'll none of that.
Now, Friar Barnardine, I come to you;
I'll feast you, lodge you, give you fair words,
And after that, I and my trusty Turk —
No more, but so; it must and shall be done.

[Scene II][12]

Enter Ithamore [*to* Barabas].

Bar. Ithamore, tell me, is the friar asleep?
Itha. Yes; and I know not what the reason is,
Do what I can he will not strip himself,
Nor go to bed, but sleeps in his own clothes.
I fear me he mistrusts what we intend.
Bar. No, 't is an order which the friars use.
Yet, if he knew our meanings, could he scape?
Itha. No, none can hear him, cry he ne'er so loud.
Bar. Why, true; therefore did I place him there.
The other chambers open towards the street.
Itha. You loiter, master; wherefore stay we thus?
O how I long to see him shake his heels.
Bar. Come on, sirrah.
Off with your girdle; make a handsome noose. —
Friar, awake!

[*They put the noose round the* Friar's *neck.*]

F. Barn. What, do you mean to strangle me?
Itha. Yes, 'cause you use to confess.
Bar. Blame not us but the proverb, "Confess and be hang'd." Pull hard!
F. Barn. What, will you [have][13] my life?
Bar. Pull hard, I say. — You would have had my goods.
Itha. Ay, and our lives too; therefore pull amain. — [*They strangle him.*]
'T is neatly done, sir; here's no print at all.
Bar. Then is it as it should be; take him up.
Itha. Nay, master; be rul'd by me a little.
[*Stands the body against the wall with a staff in its hand.*] So; let him lean upon his staff.
Excellent! he stands as if he were begging of bacon.
Bar. Who would not think but that this friar liv'd?
What time o' night is 't now, sweet Ithamore?
Itha. Towards one.
Bar. Then will not Jacom[o] be long from hence. [*Exeunt.*]

[Scene III][14]

Enter [Friar] Jacom[o].

F. Jac. This is the hour wherein I shall proceed;[15]
O happy hour, wherein I shall convert
An infidel and bring his gold into our treasury!
But soft, is not this Barnardine? It is;
And, understanding I should come this way,

[8] Misunderstanding "go."
[9] Leave me to deal with him. (Q assigns this line and the next to Ithamore.)
[10] Ithamore. [11] Convent.
[12] The stage now represents a room in Barabas's house; Friar Barnardine is asleep behind the curtains of the inner stage. After l. 24 the outer stage represents the street before the house.
[13] Emend. Reed; Q *saue.*
[14] The same. [15] Get on, succeed.

Stands here a'purpose, meaning me some wrong
And intercept my going to the Jew. —
Barnardine!
Wilt thou not speak? Thou think'st I see thee not;
Away, I'd wish thee, and let me go by.
No, wilt thou not? Nay, then, I'll force my way;
And see, a staff stands ready for the purpose.
As thou lik'st that, stop me another time.

Strike him; he falls.

Enter BARABAS [*and* ITHAMORE].

BAR. Why, how now, Jacom[o]; what hast thou done?

F. JAC. Why, stricken him that would have struck at me.

BAR. Who is it? Barnardine! Now out, alas, he is slain!

ITHA. Ay, master, he's slain; look how his brains drop out on's nose.

F. JAC. Good sirs, I have done't; but nobody knows it but you two; I may escape.

BAR. So might my man and I hang with you for company.

ITHA. No, let us bear him to the magistrates.

F. JAC. Good Barabas, let me go.

BAR. No, pardon me; the law must have its course.
I must be forc'd to give in evidence
That, being importun'd by this Barnardine
To be a Christian, I shut him out
And there he sat. Now I, to keep my word,
And give my goods and substance to your house,
Was up thus early, with intent to go
Unto your friary, because you stay'd.

ITHA. Fie upon 'em, master; will you turn Christian when holy friars turn devils and murder one another?

BAR. No, for this example I'll remain a Jew.
Heaven bless me! What, a friar a murderer!
When shall you see a Jew commit the like?

ITHA. Why, a Turk could ha' done no more.

BAR. To-morrow is the sessions; you shall to it.
Come, Ithamore, let's help to take him hence.

F. JAC. Villains, I am a sacred person; touch me not.

BAR. The law shall touch you; we'll but lead you, we.
'Las, I could weep at your calamity!
Take in the staff, too, for that must be shown;
Law wills that each particular be known.

Exeunt.

[SCENE IV] [16]

Enter Courtesan [BELLAMIRA] *and* PILIA-BORZA.

[BELL.] [17] Pilia-Borza, didst thou meet with Ithamore?

PILIA. I did.

BELL. And didst thou deliver my letter?

PILIA. I did.

BELL. And what think'st thou? Will he come?

PILIA. I think so, and yet I cannot tell; for at the reading of the letter he look'd like a man of another world.

BELL. Why so?

PILIA. That such a base slave as he should be saluted by such a tall [18] man as I am, from such a beautiful dame as you.

BELL. And what said he?

PILIA. Not a wise word; only gave me a nod, as who should say, "Is it even so?" and so I left him, being driven to a non-plus at the critical aspect of my terrible countenance.

BELL. And where didst meet him?

PILIA. Upon mine own freehold, within forty foot of the gallows, conning his neck-verse, I take it, looking of a friar's execution, whom I saluted with an old hempen proverb, *Hodie tibi, cras mihi*, and so I left him to the mercy of the hangman; but, the exercise [19] being done, see where he comes.

Enter ITHAMORE.

ITHA. I never knew a man take his death so patiently as this friar. He was ready to leap off ere the halter was about his neck; and when the hangman had put on his hempen tippet, he made such haste to his prayers as if he had had another cure to serve. Well, go whither he will, I'll be none of his followers in haste; and, now I think on't, going to the execution, a fellow met me with a muschatoes [20] like a raven's wing, and a dagger with a hilt like a warming pan, and he gave me a letter from one Madam Bellamira, saluting me in such sort as if he had meant to make clean my boots with his lips; the effect was that I should come

[16] The street before Bellamira's house; after l. 100, the curtains of the inner stage doubtless being opened, a room in the house.

[17] Q. *Curt.*, throughout.

[18] Valiant.

[19] Ceremony, service.

[20] Moustache.

to her house. I wonder what the reason is; it may be she sees more in me than I can find in myself, for she writes further that she loves me ever since she saw me; and who would not requite such love? Here 's her house, and here she comes, and now would I were gone; I am not worthy to look upon her.

PILIA. This is the gentleman you writ to.

ITHA. [*aside*] Gentleman! he flouts me; what gentry can be in a poor Turk of tenpence? I'll be gone.

BELL. Is 't not a sweet-fac'd youth, Pilia?

ITHA. [*aside*] Again, "sweet youth!" — Did not you, sir, bring the sweet youth a letter?

PILIA. I did, sir, and from this gentlewoman, who, as myself, and the rest of the family, stand or fall at your service.

BELL. Though woman's modesty should hale me back,
I can withhold no longer; welcome, sweet love.

ITHA. [*aside*] Now am I clean, or rather foully, out of the way.

BELL. Whither so soon?

ITHA. [*aside*] I'll go steal some money from my master to make me handsome. — Pray pardon me, I must go and see a ship discharg'd.

BELL. Canst thou be so unkind to leave me thus?

PILIA. An ye did but know how she loves you, sir.

ITHA. Nay, I care not how much she loves me. — Sweet Bellamira, would I had my master's wealth for thy sake.

PILIA. And you can have it, sir, an if you please.

ITHA. If 't were above ground, I could and would have it; but he hides and buries it up, as partridges do their eggs, under the earth.

PILIA. And is 't not possible to find it out?

ITHA. By no means possible.

BELL. [*aside to* PILIA-BORZA] What shall we do with this base villain then?

PILIA. [*aside to her*] Let me alone; do but you speak him fair. —
But you know some secrets of the Jew,
Which if they were reveal'd would do him harm.

ITHA. Ay, and such as — go to, no more! I'll make him send me half he has, and glad he scapes so, too. Pen and ink! I'll write unto him; we'll have money straight.

PILIA. Send for a hundred crowns at least.

[ITHAMORE] *writes.*

ITHA. Ten hundred thousand crowns. "Master Barabas."

PILIA. Write not so submissively, but threat'ning him.

ITHA. [*writing*] "Sirrah Barabas, send me a hundred crowns."

PILIA. Put in two hundred at least.

ITHA. [*writing*] "I charge thee send me three hundred by this bearer, and this shall be your warrant: if you do not — no more, but so."

PILIA. Tell him you will confess.

ITHA. [*writing*] "Otherwise I'll confess all." — Vanish, and return in a twinkle.

PILIA. Let me alone; I'll use him in his kind.[21]

[*Exit* PILIA-BORZA.]

ITHA. Hang him, Jew!

BELL. Now, gentle Ithamore, lie in my lap. —
Where are my maids? Provide a running[22] banquet.
Send to the merchant; bid him bring me silks.
Shall Ithamore, my love, go in such rags?

ITHA. And bid the jeweller come hither, too.

BELL. I have no husband, sweet; I'll marry thee.

ITHA. Content; but we will leave this paltry land,
And sail from hence to Greece, to lovely Greece.
I'll be thy Jason, thou my golden fleece;
Where painted carpets o'er the meads are hurl'd,
And Bacchus' vineyards o'erspread the world,
Where woods and forests go in goodly green,
I'll be Adonis, thou shalt be Love's Queen.
The meads, the orchards, and the primrose lanes,
Instead of sedge and reed, bear sugar canes;
Thou in those groves, by Dis above,
Shalt live with me and be my love.

BELL. Whither will I not go with gentle Ithamore?

Re-enter PILIA-BORZA.

ITHA. How now! hast thou the gold?

PILIA. Yes.

ITHA. But came it freely? Did the cow give down her milk freely?

PILIA. At reading of the letter, he star'd and stamp'd and turn'd aside. I took him by the [beard],[23] and look'd upon him thus;

[21] According to his nature.
[22] Hasty.
[23] Cor. Reed; Q *sterd.*

told him he were best to send it; then he hugg'd and embrac'd me.

ITHA. Rather for fear than love.

PILIA. Then, like a Jew, he laugh'd and jeer'd, and told me he lov'd me for your sake, and said what a faithful servant you had been.

ITHA. The more villain he to keep me thus. Here's goodly 'parel, is there not?

PILIA. To conclude, he gave me ten crowns.[24]

ITHA. But ten? I'll not leave him worth a gray groat. Give me a ream [25] of paper; we'll have a kingdom of gold for 't.

PILIA. Write for five hundred crowns.

ITHA. [*writing*] "Sirrah Jew, as you love your life send me five hundred crowns, and give the bearer one hundred." Tell him I must have 't.

PILIA. I warrant your Worship shall have 't.

ITHA. And if he ask why I demand so much, tell him I scorn to write a line under a hundred crowns.

PILIA. You'd make a rich poet, sir. I am gone. *Exit.*

ITHA. Take thou the money; spend it for my sake.

BELL. 'T is not thy money, but thyself I weigh;
Thus Bellamira esteems of gold. [*Throws it aside.*] But thus of thee. *Kiss him.*

ITHA. That kiss again! she runs division [26] of my lips.
What an eye she casts on me! It twinkles like a star.

BELL. Come, my dear love, let's in and sleep together.

ITHA. O, that ten thousand nights were put in one,
That we might sleep seven years together afore we wake!

BELL. Come, amorous wag, first banquet and then sleep. *Exeunt.*

[SCENE V] [27]

Enter BARABAS, *reading a letter.*

BAR. "Barabas, send me three hundred crowns." —
Plain Barabas! O, that wicked courtesan!
He was not wont to call me Barabas.
"Or else I will confess;" ay, there it goes;
But, if I get him, *coupe de gorge* for that.
He sent a shaggy totter'd,[28] staring slave,
That when he speaks draws out his grisly beard,
And winds it twice or thrice about his ear;
Whose face has been a grindstone for men's swords;
His hands are hack'd, some fingers cut quite off;
Who, when he speaks, grunts like a hog, and looks
Like one that is employ'd in catzerie [29]
And crossbiting,[30] — such a rogue
As is the husband to a hundred whores;
And I by him must send three hundred crowns!
Well, my hope is he will not stay there still;
And when he comes — O, that he were but here!

Enter PILIA-BORZA.

PILIA. Jew, I must ha' more gold.

BAR. Why, want'st thou any of thy tale? [31]

PILIA. No; but three hundred will not serve his turn.

BAR. Not serve his turn, sir?

PILIA. No, sir; and therefore I must have five hundred more.

BAR. I'll rather —

PILIA. O good words, sir, and send it you were best! See, there's his letter.

BAR. Might he not as well come as send? Pray bid him come and fetch it; what he writes for you, ye shall have straight.

PILIA. Ay, and the rest too, or else —

BAR. (*aside*) I must make this villain away. — Please you dine with me, sir; — and you shall be most heartily poison'd.

PILIA. No, God-a-mercy. Shall I have these crowns?

BAR. I cannot do it; I have lost my keys.

PILIA. O, if that be all, I can pick ope your locks.

BAR. Or climb up to my countinghouse window — you know my meaning.

PILIA. I know enough, and therefore talk not to me of your countinghouse. The gold! or know, Jew, it is in my power to hang thee.

BAR. [*aside*] I am betray'd. —
'T is not five hundred crowns that I esteem;

[24] *I.e.*, as a tip, besides the three hundred.

[25] Punning on *realm*, often spelled without the "l."

[26] Executes "a rapid melodic passage." (*N. E. D.*) A musical term.

[27] Unlocated; presumably a room in Barabas's house, despite l. 59.

[28] Tattered.

[29] Nares derives from *catso* (see on IV, i, 19). It evidently means rascality of some sort.

[30] Swindling. The next line alludes to the practice of blackmailing a man by decoying him into a compromising situation with a prostitute and then confronting him with a confederate who poses as her husband.

[31] Reckoning.

I am not mov'd at that : this angers me,
That he, who knows I love him as myself,
Should write in this imperious vein. Why, sir,
You know I have no child, and unto whom
Should I leave all but unto Ithamore?
PILIA. Here 's many words, but no crowns.
The crowns!
BAR. Commend me to him, sir, most humbly,[32]
And unto your good mistress, as unknown.[33]
PILIA. Speak, shall I have 'em, sir?
BAR. Sir, here they are. —
O, that I should part with so much gold! —
Here, take 'em, fellow, with as good a will —
[*aside*] As I would see thee hang'd. — O, love stops my breath;
Never lov'd man servant as I do Ithamore.
PILIA. I know it, sir.
BAR. Pray, when, sir, shall I see you at my house?
PILIA. Soon enough, to your cost, sir. Fare you well. *Exit.*
BAR. Nay, to thine own cost, villain, if thou com'st. —
Was ever Jew tormented as I am?
To have a shag-rag knave to come [34] —
Three hundred crowns — and then five hundred crowns!
Well, I must seek a means to rid 'em all,
And presently [35]; for in his villainy
He will tell all he knows, and I shall die for 't. —
I have it!
I will in some disguise go see the slave,
And how the villain revels with my gold. *Exit.*

[SCENE VI] [36]

Enter Courtesan [BELLAMIRA,] ITHAMORE, [*and*] PILIA-BORZA.

BELL. I'll pledge thee, love, and therefore drink it off.
ITHA. Say'st thou me so? Have at it; and do you hear? [*Whispers.*]
BELL. Go to, it shall be so.
ITHA. Of that condition I will drink it up.
Here 's to thee!
[BELL.] Nay, I'll have all or none.
ITHA. There, if thou lov'st me, do not leave a drop.
BELL. Love thee! Fill me three glasses.
ITHA. Three-and-fifty dozen, I'll pledge thee.
PILIA. Knavely spoke, and like a knight at arms.
ITHA. Hey, *Rivo Castiliano!* [37] A man 's a man!
BELL. Now to the Jew.
ITHA. Ha! to the Jew, and send me money you [38] were best.
PILIA. What wouldst thou do if he should send thee none?
ITHA. Do nothing; but I know what I know; he 's a murderer.
BELL. I had not thought he had been so brave a man.
ITHA. You knew Mathias and the Governor's son; he and I kill'd 'em both, and yet never touch'd 'em.
PILIA. O, bravely done.
ITHA. I carried the broth that poison'd the nuns; and he and I — snickle! hand to! fast! [39] — strangled a friar.
BELL. You two alone?
ITHA. We two; and 't was never known, nor never shall be for me.
PILIA. [*aside to* BELLAMIRA] This shall with me unto the Governor.
BELL. [*aside to* PILIA-BORZA] And fit it should; but first let 's ha' more gold. —
Come, gentle Ithamore, lie in my lap.
ITHA. Love me little, love me long. Let music rumble
Whilst I in thy incony [40] lap do tumble.

Enter BARABAS, *with a lute, disguis'd.*

BELL. A French musician! Come, let 's hear your skill.
BAR. Must tuna my lute for sound, twang, twang, first.
ITHA. Wilt drink, Frenchman? Here 's to thee with a —— pox on this drunken hiccup!
BAR. *Gramercy, mounsier.*
BELL. Prithee, Pilia-Borza, bid the fiddler give me the posy in his hat there.

[32] Trisyllabic.
[33] As yet unknown to me.
[34] A word has perhaps been omitted.
[35] At once.
[36] Inside Bellamira's house, and also, apparently, the street before it.

[37] A bacchanalian exclamation of uncertain origin. "Rivo" may = "stream" (Ital.). On "Castiliano" see [London] *Times Lit. Sup.*, May 4, 1933, p. 312. It may = *Castiglione*, which seems to have been a name for the Italian wine usually called *Lacrimae Christi*.
[38] There is no need to emend *he*. It is more dramatic for the drunken Turk to shake his fist at the absent Jew.
[39] Q *snicle hand too fast*. Punctuated and explained by Kittredge, = Snare him! lay your hand to it! firmly now! (With appropriate gestures.)
[40] Dainty. Cor. Reed; Q *incoomy*.

PILIA. Sirrah, you must give my mistress your posy.

BAR. *A voustre commandement, madam.*

BELL. How sweet, my Ithamore, the flowers smell.

ITHA. Like thy breath, sweetheart; no violet like 'em.

PILIA. Foh! methinks they stink like a hollyhock.

BAR. [*aside*] So, now I am reveng'd upon 'em all.
The scent thereof was death; I poison'd it.

ITHA. Play, fiddler, or I'll cut your cat's guts into chitterlings.

BAR. *Pardona moy;* be no in tune yet; so now, now all be in.

ITHA. Give him a crown, and fill me out more wine.

PILIA. There's two crowns for thee; play.

BAR. (*aside*) How liberally the villain gives me mine own gold! [*Plays.*]

PILIA. Methinks he fingers very well.

BAR. (*aside*) So did you when you stole my gold.

PILIA. How swift he runs!

BAR. (*aside*) You run swifter when you threw my gold out of my window.

BELL. Musician, hast been in Malta long?

BAR. Two, three, four month, madam.

ITHA. Dost not know a Jew, one Barabas?

BAR. Very mush; mounsier, you no be his man?

PILIA. His man?

ITHA. I scorn the peasant; tell him so.

BAR. [*aside.*] He knows it already.

ITHA. 'T is a strange thing of that Jew; he lives upon pickled grasshoppers and sauc'd mushrooms.

BAR. (*aside*) What a slave's this! The Governor feeds not as I do.

ITHA. He never put on clean shirt since he was circumcis'd.

BAR. (*aside*) O rascal! I change myself twice a day.

ITHA. The hat he wears Judas left under the elder when he hang'd himself.

BAR. (*aside*) 'T was sent me for a present from the great Cham.

PILIA. A masty [41] slave he is. — Whither now, fiddler?

BAR. *Pardona moy, mounsier,* [me] [42] be no well. *Exit.*

PILIA. Farewell, fiddler! — One letter more to the Jew.

BELL. Prithee, sweet love, one more, and write it sharp.

ITHA. No, I'll send by word of mouth now. — Bid him deliver thee a thousand crowns, by the same token that the nuns lov'd rice, that Friar Barnardine slept in his own clothes; any of 'em will do it.

PILIA. Let me alone to urge it, now I know the meaning.

ITHA. The meaning has a meaning. — Come let's in.
To undo a Jew is charity, and not sin. *Exeunt.*

ACT V — [SCENE I] [1]

Enter Governor [FERNEZE], Knights, MARTIN DEL BOSCO, [*and* Officers].

FERN. Now, gentlemen, betake you to your arms,
And see that Malta be well fortifi'd;
And it behoves you to be resolute;
For Calymath, having hover'd here so long,
Will win the town or die before the walls.

[1] KNIGHT. And die he shall, for we will never yield.

Enter Courtesan [BELLAMIRA *and*] PILIA-BORZA.

BELL. O, bring us to the Governor.

FERN. Away with her! She is a courtesan.

BELL. Whate'er I am, yet, Governor, hear me speak;
I bring thee news by whom thy son was slain:
Mathias did it not; it was the Jew.

PILIA. Who, besides the slaughter of these gentlemen,
Poison'd his own daughter and the nuns,
Strangled a friar and I know not what
Mischief beside.

FERN. Had we but proof of this ——

BELL. Strong proof, my Lord; his man's now at my lodging,
That was his agent; he'll confess it all.

FERN. Go fetch him straight. — [*Exeunt* Officers.]
I always fear'd that Jew.

Enter [Officers *with* BARABAS *the*] Jew [*and*] ITHAMORE.

BAR. I'll go alone; dogs, do not hale me thus.

[41] Burly. Some eds., perhaps rightly, emend *nasty* or *musty*.
[42] Cor. Reed; Q *we*.

[1] The senate-house.

ITHA. Nor me neither; I cannot outrun you, constable. — O my belly!

BAR. [*aside*] One dram of powder more had made all sure.
What a damn'd slave was I!

FERN. Make fires, heat irons, let the rack be fetch'd.

[1] KNIGHT. Nay, stay, my Lord; 't may be he will confess.

BAR. Confess! what mean you, Lords? Who should confess?

FERN. Thou and thy Turk; 't was you that slew my son.

ITHA. Guilty, my Lord, I confess. Your son and Mathias were both contracted unto Abigail; [he] [2] forg'd a counterfeit challenge.

BAR. Who carried that challenge?

ITHA. I carried it, I confess; but who writ it? Marry, even he that strangled Barnardine, poison'd the nuns and his own daughter.

FERN. Away with him! his sight is death to me.

BAR. For what, you men of Malta? Hear me speak:
She is a courtesan, and he a thief,
And he my bondman. Let me have law,
For none of this can prejudice my life.

FERN. Once more, away with him; you shall have law.

BAR. [*aside*] Devils, do your worst! I live in spite of you. —
As these have spoke, so be it to their souls! —
[*aside*] I hope the poison'd flowers will work anon.

[*Exeunt* Officers *with* BARABAS *and* ITHAMORE, BELLAMIRA, *and* PILIA-BORZA.]

Enter [KATHERINE].

KATH. Was my Mathias murder'd by the Jew?
Ferneze, 't was thy son that murder'd him.

FERN. Be patient, gentle madam; it was he;
He forged the daring challenge made them fight.

KATH. Where is the Jew? Where is that murderer?

FERN. In prison till the law has pass'd on him.

Re-enter [*an*] Officer.

OFF. My Lord, the courtesan and her man are dead;
So is the Turk and Barabas the Jew.

FERN. Dead!

OFF. Dead, my Lord; and here they bring his body.[3]

BOSCO. This sudden death of his is very strange.

FERN. Wonder not at it, sir: the Heavens are just;
Their deaths were like their lives; then think not of 'em.
Since they are dead, let them be buried;
For the Jew's body, throw that o'er the walls,
To be a prey for vultures and wild beasts. —
So now away, and fortify the town. *Exeunt.*

[SCENE II] [4]

BAR. What, all alone? Well fare, sleepy drink.
I'll be reveng'd on this accursed town;
For by my means Calymath shall enter in.
I'll help to slay their children and their wives,
To fire the churches, pull their houses down,
Take my goods, too, and seize upon my lands.
I hope to see the Governor a slave,
And, rowing in a galley, whipp'd to death.

Enter CALYMATH, Bashaws, [*and*] Turks.

CALY. Whom have we there, a spy?

BAR. Yes, my good Lord, one that can spy a place
Where you may enter, and surprise the town;
My name is Barabas; I am a Jew.

CALY. Art thou that Jew whose goods we heard were sold
For tribute money?

BAR. The very same, my Lord;
And since that time they have hir'd a slave, my man,
To accuse me of a thousand villainies.
I was imprison'd, but 'scap'd their hands.

CALY. Didst break prison?

BAR. No, no;
I drank of poppy and cold mandrake juice;
And being asleep, belike they thought me dead,
And threw me o'er the walls; so, or how else,
The Jew is here, and rests at your command.

CALY. 'T was bravely done; but tell me, Barabas,
Canst thou, as thou reportest, make Malta ours?

[2] Add. Reed.

[3] Barabas may have been carried on at this point; if so he was probably borne out at the end of this scene.

[4] Outside the city walls. Probably Barabas was "discovered," coming back to consciousness, on the inner stage.

BAR. Fear not, my Lord, for here against the [sluice][5]
The rock is hollow, and of purpose digg'd
To make a passage for the running streams
And common channels[6] of the city.
Now, whilst you give assault unto the walls,
I'll lead five hundred soldiers through the vault
And rise with them i' th' middle of the town,
Open the gates for you to enter in;
And by this means the city is your own.

CALY. If this be true, I'll make thee governor.

BAR. And if it be not true, then let me die.

CALY. Thou'st doom'd thyself. Assault it presently. *Exeunt.*

[SCENE III][7]

Alarums. Enter [CALYMATH, Bassoes,] Turks, [*and*] BARABAS, [*with* FERNEZE] *and* Knights, *prisoners.*

CALY. Now vail[8] your pride, you captive Christians,
And kneel for mercy to your conquering foe.
Now where's the hope you had of haughty Spain?
Ferneze, speak; had it not been much better
To kept thy promise than be thus surpris'd?

FERN. What should I say? We are captives and must yield.

CALY. Ay, villains, you must yield, and under Turkish yokes
Shall groaning bear the burden of our ire;
And, Barabas, as erst we promis'd thee,
For thy desert we make thee governor;
Use them at thy discretion.

BAR. Thanks, my Lord.

FERN. O fatal day, to fall into the hands
Of such a traitor and unhallowed Jew!
What greater misery could Heaven inflict?

CALY. 'T is our command; and, Barabas, we give
To guard thy person these our Janizaries;
Entreat[9] them well, as we have used thee.
And now, brave bashaws, come, we'll walk about
The ruin'd town, and see the wrack we made. —
Farewell, brave Jew; farewell, great Barabas.
Exeunt [CALYMATH *and* Bassoes].

BAR. May all good fortune follow Calymath. —
And now, as entrance to our safety,
To prison with the Governor and these
Captains, his consorts and confederates.

FERN. O villain! Heaven will be reveng'd on thee.

BAR. Away! no more; let him not trouble me.
Exeunt [Turks, *with* FERNEZE *and* Knights].
Thus hast thou gotten, by thy policy,
No simple place, no small authority.
I now am governor of Malta; true,
But Malta hates me; and, in hating me,
My life's in danger, and what boots it thee,
Poor Barabas, to be the governor,
Whenas thy life shall be at their command?
No, Barabas, this must be look'd into;
And since by wrong thou gott'st authority,
Maintain it bravely by firm policy;
At least unprofitably lose it not:
For he that liveth in authority,
And neither gets him friends, nor fills his bags,
Lives like the ass, that Aesop speaketh of,
That labors with a load of bread and wine,
And leaves it off to snap on thistle-tops;
But Barabas will be more circumspect.
Begin betimes; occasion's bald behind;
Slip not thine opportunity, for fear too late
Thou seek'st for much, but canst not compass it. —
Within here!

Enter [FERNEZE] *with a* Guard.

FERN. My Lord?

BAR. Ay, "lord;" thus slaves will learn.
Now, Governor; — stand by there; wait within. [*Exeunt* Guard.]
This is the reason that I sent for thee:
Thou seest thy life and Malta's happiness
Are at my arbitrament; and Barabas
At his discretion may dispose of both.
Now tell me, Governor, and plainly too,
What think'st thou shall become of it and thee?

FERN. This, Barabas; since things are in thy power,
I see no reason but of Malta's wrack,
Nor hope of thee but extreme cruelty;
Nor fear I death, nor will I flatter thee.

BAR. Governor, good words; be not so furious.
'T is not thy life which can avail me aught;
Yet you do live, and live for me you shall;

[5] Emend. Collier; Q *Truce.*
[6] Gutters.
[7] Unlocated, but evidently a place within the city.
[8] Lower.
[9] Treat.

And, as for Malta's ruin, think you not
'T were slender policy for Barabas
To dispossess himself of such a place?
For sith,[10] as once you said, within this isle,
In Malta here, that I have got my goods,
And in this city still have had success,
And now at length am grown your governor,
Yourselves shall see it shall not be forgot;
For, as a friend not known but in distress,
I'll rear up Malta, now remediless.

FERN. Will Barabas recover Malta's loss?
Will Barabas be good to Christians?

BAR. What wilt thou give me, Governor, to procure
A dissolution of the slavish bands
Wherein the Turk hath yok'd your land and you?
What will you give me if I render you
The life of Calymath, surprise his men,
And in an outhouse of the city shut
His soldiers, till I have consum'd 'em all with fire?
What will you give him that procureth this?

FERN. Do but bring this to pass which thou pretendest,[11]
Deal truly with us as thou intimatest,
And I will send amongst the citizens,
And by my letters privately procure
Great sums of money for thy recompense;
Nay more, do this, and live thou governor still.

BAR. Nay, do thou this, Ferneze, and be free;
Governor, I enlarge thee; live with me,
Go walk about the city, see thy friends;
Tush, send not letters to 'em, go thyself,
And let me see what money thou canst make.
Here is my hand that I'll set Malta free;
And thus we cast it: to a solemn feast
I will invite young Selim Calymath,
Where be thou present only to perform
One stratagem that I'll impart to thee,
Wherein no danger shall betide thy life,
And I will warrant Malta free for ever.

FERN. Here is my hand; believe me, Barabas,
I will be there and do as thou desirest.
When is the time?

BAR. Governor, presently;
For Calymath, when he hath view'd the town,
Will take his leave and sail toward Ottoman.

FERN. Then will I, Barabas, about this coin,
And bring it with me to thee in the evening.

BAR. Do so, but fail not; now farewell, Ferneze! — [*Exit* FERNEZE.]

And thus far roundly goes the business.
Thus, loving neither, will I live with both,
Making a profit of my policy;
And he from whom my most advantage comes
Shall be my friend.
This is the life we Jews are us'd to lead;
And reason too, for Christians do the like.
Well, now about effecting this device;
First to surprise great Selim's soldiers,[12]
And then to make provision for the feast,
That at one instant all things may be done.
My policy detests prevention;
To what event my secret purpose drives,
I know, and they shall witness with their lives. *Exit.*

[SCENE IV] [13]

Enter CALYMATH *and* Bashaws.

CALY. Thus have we view'd the city, seen the sack,
And caus'd the ruins to be new-repair'd,
Which with our bombards' [14] shot and basilisk
We rent in sunder at our entry; [15]
And now I see the situation,
And how secure this conquer'd island stands
Environ'd with the Mediterranean Sea,
Strong [countermur'd] [16] with other petty isles,
And, toward Calabria, back'd by Sicily,
[Where] [17] Syracusian Dionysius reign'd,
Two lofty turrets that command the town.
I wonder how it could be conquer'd thus.

Enter a Messenger.

MESS. From Barabas, Malta's governor, I bring
A message unto mighty Calymath;
Hearing his sovereign was bound for sea,
To sail to Turkey, to great Ottoman,
He humbly would entreat your Majesty
To come and see his homely citadel,
And banquet with him ere thou leav'st the isle.

CALY. To banquet with him in his citadel?
I fear me, messenger, to feast my train
Within a town of war so lately pillag'd
Will be too costly and too troublesome;
Yet would I gladly visit Barabas,
For well has Barabas deserv'd of us.

[10] Since. [11] Extendest, settest forth.

[12] Trisyllabic.
[13] Unlocated, but evidently another spot within the city.
[14] Large cannons'.
[15] Trisyllabic.
[16] Conj. Deighton; Q *contermin'd.* Cf. on I, ii, 383.
[17] Q *When;* cor. Robinson, who also corrects this line and the next, transposed in Q.

MESS. Selim, for that, thus saith the Governor:
That he hath in store a pearl so big,
So precious, and withal so orient,
As, be it valued but indifferently,
The price thereof will serve to entertain
Selim and all his soldiers for a month;
Therefore he humbly would entreat your Highness
Not to depart till he has feasted you.

CALY. I cannot feast my men in Malta walls,
Except he place his tables in the streets.

MESS. Know, Selim, that there is a monastery
Which standeth as an outhouse to the town;
There will he banquet them, but thee at home,
With all thy bashaws and brave followers.

CALY. Well, tell the Governor we grant his suit;
We'll in this summer evening feast with him.

MESS. I shall, my Lord. *Exit.*

CALY. And now, bold bashaws, let us to our tents,
And meditate how we may grace us best
To solemnize our governor's great feast. *Exeunt.*

[SCENE V] [18]

Enter Governor [FERNEZE], Knights, [*and*] DEL BOSCO.

FERN. In this, my countrymen, be rul'd by me;
Have special care that no man sally forth
Till you shall hear a culverin discharg'd
By him that bears the linstock, kindled thus;
Then issue out and come to rescue me,
For happily I shall be in distress,
Or you released of this servitude.

1 KNIGHT. Rather than thus to live as Turkish thralls,
What will we not adventure?

FERN. On then; begone.

KNIGHTS. Farewell, grave Governor! [*Exeunt.*]

[SCENE VI] [19]

Enter [BARABAS,] *with a hammer, above, very busy;* [Carpenters *also discovered*].

BAR. How stand the cords? How hang these hinges? Fast?
Are all the cranes and pulleys sure?

[CARP.] [20] All fast.

BAR. Leave nothing loose, all levell'd to my mind.
Why now I see that you have art indeed.
There, carpenters, divide that gold amongst you;
Go swill in bowls of sack and muscadine!
Down to the cellar, taste of all my wines.

CARP. We shall, my Lord, and thank you. *Exeunt* [Carpenters].

BAR. And, if you like them, drink your fill and die;
For, so I live, perish may all the world!
Now, Selim Calymath, return me word
That thou wilt come, and I am satisfied.

Enter Messenger.

Now, sirrah, what, will he come?

MESS. He will; and has commanded all his men
To come ashore and march through Malta streets,
That thou mayst feast them in thy citadel.

BAR. Then now are all things as my wish would have 'em;
There wanteth nothing but the governor's pelf,
And see, he brings it.

Enter Governor [FERNEZE].

Now, Governor, the sum.

FERN. With free consent, a hundred thousand pounds.

BAR. Pounds, say'st thou, Governor? Well, since it is no more,
I'll satisfy myself with that; nay, keep it still,
For if I keep not promise, trust not me.
And, Governor, now partake my policy:
First, for his army, they are sent before,
Enter'd the monastery, and underneath
In several places are fieldpieces pitch'd,
Bombards, whole barrels full of gunpowder,
That on the sudden shall dissever it,
And batter all the stones about their ears,
Whence none can possibly escape alive;
Now as for Calymath and his consorts,
Here have I made a dainty gallery,
The floor whereof, this cable being cut,
Doth fall asunder, so that it doth sink
Into a deep pit past recovery.
Here, hold that knife, and when thou seest he comes,
And with his bashaws shall be blithely set,
A warning piece shall be shot off from the tower,

[18] Unlocated; presumably the same as Sc. iv.

[19] A hall in the citadel. Barabas appears on the upper stage; the caldron is on the inner stage, concealed by its curtains till S. D. after l. 62.

[20] Q *Serv.*

To give thee knowledge when to cut the cord
And fire the house. Say, will not this be brave?
  FERN. O, excellent! here, hold thee, Barabas,
I trust thy word; take what I promis'd thee.
  BAR. No, Governor, I'll satisfy thee first;
Thou shalt not live in doubt of anything.
Stand close, for here they come. [FERNEZE *retires.*] — Why, is not this
A kingly kind of trade, to purchase towns
By treachery and sell 'em by deceit?
Now tell me, worldlings, underneath the [sun][21]
If greater falsehood ever has been done.

Enter CALYMATH *and* Bashaws.

  CALY. Come, my companion bashaws; see, I pray,
How busy Barabas is there above
To entertain us in his gallery.
Let us salute him. — Save thee, Barabas!
  BAR. Welcome, great Calymath!
  FERN. [*aside*] How the slave jeers at him.
  BAR. Will 't please thee, mighty Selim Calymath,
To ascend our homely stairs?
  CALY. Ay, Barabas. —
Come, bashaws, attend.
  FERN. [*coming forward*] Stay, Calymath!
For I will show thee greater courtesy
Than Barabas would have afforded thee.
  KNIGHT [*within*] Sound a charge there!

A charge [*sounded within.* FERNEZE *cuts*] *the cable:* [*the floor of the gallery gives way*]; *a caldron discovered,* [*into which* BARABAS *has fallen.*]

[*Enter* DEL Bosco *and* Knights.]

  CALY. How now! what means this?
  BAR. Help, help me. Christians, help!
  FERN. See, Calymath; this was devis'd for thee!
  CALY. Treason! treason! Bashaws, fly!
  FERN. No, Selim, do not fly;
See his end first, and fly then if thou canst.
  BAR. O help me, Selim! help me, Christians!
Governor, why stand you all so pitiless?
  FERN. Should I in pity of thy plaints or thee,
Accursed Barabas, base Jew, relent?
No, thus I'll see thy treachery repaid,
But wish thou hadst behav'd thee otherwise.
  BAR. You will not help me, then?
  FERN. No, villain, no.
  BAR. And, villains, know you cannot help me now. —
Then, Barabas, breathe forth thy latest fate,[22]
And in the fury of thy torments strive
To end thy life with resolution. —
Know, Governor, 't was I that slew thy son;
I fram'd the challenge that did make them meet.
Know, Calymath, I aim'd thy overthrow,
And, had I but escap'd this stratagem,
I would have brought confusion on you all,
Damn'd Christians, dogs, and Turkish infidels!
But now begins the extremity of heat
To pinch me with intolerable pangs.
Die, life! fly, soul! tongue, curse thy fill, and die! [*Dies.*]
  CALY. Tell me, you Christians, what doth this portend?
  FERN. This train he laid to have entrapp'd thy life.
Now, Selim, note the unhallowed deeds of Jews;
Thus he determin'd to have handled thee,
But I have rather chose to save thy life.
  CALY. Was this the banquet he prepar'd for us?
Let's hence, lest further mischief be pretended.[23]
  FERN. Nay, Selim, stay; for since we have thee here,
We will not let thee part so suddenly;
Besides, if we should let thee go, all 's one,[24]
For with thy galleys couldst thou not get hence,
Without fresh men to rig and furnish them.
  CALY. Tush, Governor, take thou no care for that;
My men are all aboard,
And do attend[25] my coming there by this.
  FERN. Why, heard'st thou not the trumpet sound a charge?
  CALY. Yes, what of that?
  FERN. Why, then the house was fir'd,
Blown up, and all thy soldiers massacred.
  CALY. O monstrous treason!
  FERN. A Jew's courtesy;
For he that did by treason work our fall,
By treason hath delivered thee to us.
Know, therefore, till thy father hath made good
The ruins done to Malta and to us,
Thou canst not part; for Malta shall be freed,
Or Selim ne'er return to Ottoman.

[21] Cor. Reed; Q *Summe.*

[22] Cunningham emends *hate.*

[23] Intended.

[24] It's all the same.

[25] Await.

CALY. Nay, rather, Christians, let me go to Turkey,
In person there to [mediate] [26] your peace;
To keep me here will naught advantage you.

FERN. Content thee, Calymath; here thou must stay,
And live in Malta prisoner; for come [all] [27] the world
To rescue thee, so will we guard us now,
As sooner shall they drink the ocean dry
Than conquer Malta, or endanger us. —
So march away, and let due praise be given
Neither to Fate nor Fortune, but to Heaven.
[*Exeunt.*]

[26] Conj. Collier; Q *meditate.*

[27] Emend. Reed; Q *call.*

The troubleſome

raigne and lamentable death of

Edward *the ſecond, King of* England: with the tragicall *fall of proud* Mortimer:

As it was ſundrie times publiquely acted *in the honourable citie of London, by the* right honourable the Earle of Pem-*brooke his ſeruants.*

Written by Chri. Marlow *Gent.*

Imprinted at London for *William Iones*, dwelling neere Holbourne conduit at the *ſigne of the Gunne*, 1594

INTRODUCTORY NOTE

With *Edward II*, probably produced in 1591–92, Marlowe carries the chronicle play to its highest level prior to Shakespeare's best "histories." Technically, though not imaginatively, it marks the culmination of Marlowe's dramatic powers. Characterization is now extended beyond one or two central figures, difficult problems of selection and condensation are surmounted with ease, and a masterly transfer of sympathy is accomplished. Whatever the King's faults, his death is affecting; to enlist the emotions of the audience for a monarch so weakly bad as Edward is a feat which does not suffer in comparison with Shakespeare's similar treatment of Richard II. On the greater dramatist's technical development Marlowe's most mature play may have exerted considerable influence. On the other hand, there are fewer lyrical outbursts than in the earlier works; it is curious that Marlowe's best play seems less Marlovian than the others.

The chief source of *Edward II* was Holinshed's *Chronicles*, though Fabyan's and Stowe's were also used for a few details. How popular the play was on the stage, and how long it remained in the repertory are unknown; but the number of early editions indicates considerable success. The title pages of the old editions state that it was acted by the Earl of Pembroke's company. It was revived, according to the Fourth Quarto, by Queen Anne's Men at the Red Bull.

Edward II was edited for the Malone Society by W. W. Greg (1925); for the Case Marlowe the editors are to be H. B. Charlton and R. A. Waller. Among other editions are those of A. W. Verity (1896) and W. D. Briggs (1914). The present text is based on the first edition, the best of the early texts of Marlowe, the octavo of 1594 (reprinted in quarto 1598, 1612, 1622), as reproduced by Greg and Brooke.

The latter was the first to observe that the Dyce copy of Q 1598 contains a transcript (supplying the absence of the first two leaves of that Quarto) dated, on the title page, 1593. This MS is given in facsimile by Greg. Since the text of the MS is closer to the first than to the second of the surviving editions, it rather looks as though an edition, now quite lost, had preceded them. Of the first surviving edition, but two copies are known; they are in the Landesbibliothek of Cassel and the Zentralbibliothek of Zurich.

THE TROUBLESOME REIGN AND LAMENTABLE DEATH OF EDWARD THE SECOND

BY

CHRISTOPHER MARLOWE

[DRAMATIS PERSONAE

KING EDWARD THE SECOND.
PRINCE EDWARD, his son, afterwards King Edward the Third.
EDMUND, EARL OF KENT, half-brother to King Edward the Second.
PIERCE DE GAVESTON, a Gascon courtier, afterwards Earl of Cornwall.
ARCHBISHOP OF CANTERBURY.
BISHOP OF COVENTRY.
BISHOP OF WINCHESTER.
GUY, EARL OF WARWICK.
THOMAS, EARL OF LANCASTER.
AYMER, EARL OF PEMBROKE.
EARL OF ARUNDEL.
EARL OF LEICESTER.
THOMAS, LORD BERKELEY.[1]
LORD MORTIMER, the elder, of Chirke.
LORD ROGER MORTIMER, the younger, of Wigmore, his nephew.
HUGH SPENCER, the elder, afterwards Earl of Winchester.
HUGH SPENCER, the younger, his son, afterwards Earl of Gloucester and Wiltshire.
ROBERT BALDOCK, a scholar.
HENRY DE BEAUMONT.
SIR WILLIAM TRUSSEL.
SIR THOMAS GURNEY.
JOHN, LORD MATREVIS.
LIGHTBORN.
SIR JOHN OF HAINAULT.
LEVUNE.
RICE AP HOWELL.
JAMES.
Abbot, Monks, Herald, Lords, Poor Men, Mower, Champion, Messengers, Soldiers, and Attendants.

QUEEN ISABELLA, wife to King Edward the Second.
Niece to King Edward the Second, daughter to the late Earl of Gloucester.
Ladies.]

[ACT I — SCENE I] [2]

Enter GAVESTON, *reading on a letter that was brought him from the King.*

[GAV.] "My father is deceas'd; come, Gaveston,
And share the kingdom with thy dearest friend."
Ah, words that make me surfeit with delight!
What greater bliss can hap to Gaveston
Than live and be the favorite of a king?
Sweet prince, I come; these, these thy amorous lines
Might have enforc'd me to have swum from France,
And, like Leander, gasp'd upon the sand,
So [3] thou wouldst smile and take me in thy arms.
The sight of London to my exiled eyes
Is as Elysium to a new-come soul;
Not that I love the city or the men,
But that it harbors him I hold so dear,
The King, upon whose bosom let me die,[4]
And with the world be still at enmity.
What need the arctic people love starlight,
To whom the sun shines both by day and night?
Farewell base stooping to the lordly peers;
My knee shall bow to none but to the King.
As for the multitude, that are but sparks
Rak'd up in embers of their poverty,
Tanti! [5] I'll [fawn] [6] first on the wind
That glanceth at my lips, and flyeth away.

[1] Old eds. *Bartley*.
[2] Unlocated; presumably a street in Westminster.
[3] Provided that.
[4] *I.e.*, swoon.
[5] So much for them.
[6] Cor. Robinson; old eds. *fanne*.

Enter three Poor Men.

But how now, what are these?

Poor Men. Such as desire your Worship's service.

Gav. What canst thou do?

1 P. Man. I can ride.

Gav. But I have no horses. — What art thou?

2 P. Man. A traveller.

Gav. Let me see; thou wouldst do well
To wait at my trencher and tell me lies at dinner time;
And as I like your discoursing, I'll have you. —
And what art thou?

3 P. Man. A soldier that hath serv'd against the Scot.

Gav. Why, there are hospitals [7] for such as you.
I have no war, and therefore, sir, begone.

3 P. Man. Farewell, and perish by a soldier's hand,
That wouldst reward them with an hospital.

Gav. [*aside*] Ay, ay, these words of his move me as much
As if a goose should play the porpentine,[8]
And dart her plumes, thinking to pierce my breast.
But yet it is no pain to speak men fair;
I'll flatter these, and make them live in hope. —
You know that I came lately out of France,
And yet I have not view'd my Lord the King;
If I speed well, I'll entertain you all.

Omnes. We thank your Worship.

Gav. I have some business; leave me to myself.

Omnes. We will wait here about the court.

Exeunt [*the* Poor Men].

Gav. Do. — These are not men for me;
I must have wanton poets, pleasant wits,
Musicians, that with touching of a string
May draw the pliant King which way I please.
Music and poetry is his delight;
Therefore I'll have Italian masques by night,
Sweet speeches, comedies, and pleasing shows;
And in the day, when he shall walk abroad,
Like sylvan [9] nymphs my pages shall be clad;
My men, like satyrs grazing on the lawns,
Shall with their goat-feet dance an antic hay.[10]
Sometime a lovely boy in Dian's shape,
With hair that gilds the water as it glides,
Crownets [11] of pearl about his naked arms,
And in his sportful hands an olive tree,
To hide those parts which men delight to see,
Shall bathe him in a spring; and there, hard by,
One like Actaeon peeping through the grove
Shall by the angry goddess be transform'd,
And running in the likeness of an hart
By yelping hounds pull'd down, and seem to die;
Such things as these best please his Majesty,
My lord. — Here comes the King and the nobles
From the parliament; I'll stand aside.

[*Retires.*]

Enter the King [Edward II], Lancaster, Mortimer Senior, Mortimer Junior, Edmund Earl *of* Kent, Guy Earl *of* Warwick, *etc.*

K. Edw. Lancaster.

Lan. My Lord.

Gav. [*aside*] That Earl of Lancaster do I abhor.

K. Edw. Will you not grant me this? — [*aside*] In spite of them
I'll have my will; and these two Mortimers,
That cross me thus, shall know I am displeas'd.

Elder Mor. [12] If you love us, my Lord, hate Gaveston.

Gav. [*aside*] That villain Mortimer! I'll be his death.

Young Mor. Mine uncle here, this earl, and I myself
Were sworn to your father at his death,
That he should ne'er return into the realm;
And know, my Lord, ere I will break my oath,
This sword of mine, that should offend your foes,
Shall sleep within the scabbard at thy need;
And underneath thy banners march who will,
For Mortimer will hang his armor up.

Gav. [*aside*] *Mort Dieu!*

K. Edw. Well, Mortimer, I'll make thee rue these words.
Beseems it thee to contradict thy king?
Frown'st thou thereat, aspiring Lancaster?
The sword shall plane the furrows of thy brows,
And hew these knees that now are grown so stiff.
I will have Gaveston, and you shall know
What danger 't is to stand against your king.

Gav. [*aside*] Well done, Ned!

[7] Almshouses.
[8] Porcupine.
[9] So MS (?1593); old eds. *Siluian.*
[10] Grotesque country-dance.
[11] Coronets; *i.e.*, bracelets.
[12] Speech-tags of old eds. *Mor. se.* and *Mor. iu.*, throughout.

LAN. My Lord, why do you thus incense your peers,
That naturally would love and honor you
But for that base and obscure Gaveston?
Four earldoms have I, besides Lancaster —
Derby, Salisbury, Lincoln, Leicester. —
These will I sell, to give my soldiers pay,
Ere Gaveston shall stay within the realm;
Therefore, if he be come, expel him straight.

KENT. Barons and earls, your pride hath made me mute;
But now I'll speak, and to the proof, I hope.
I do remember in my father's days
Lord Percy of the north, being highly mov'd,
Brav'd Mowbray[13] in presence of the King;
For which, had not his Highness lov'd him well,
He should have lost his head; but with his look
The undaunted spirit of Percy was appeas'd,
And Mowbray and he were reconcil'd;
Yet dare you brave the King unto his face? —
Brother, revenge it; and let these their heads
Preach upon poles, for trespass of their tongues.

WAR. O, our heads!

K. EDW. Ay, yours; and therefore I would wish you grant.

WAR. Bridle thy anger, gentle Mortimer.

Y. MOR. I cannot, nor I will not; I must speak.
Cousin, our hands I hope shall fence our heads,
And strike off his that makes you threaten us.
Come, Uncle, let us leave the brainsick king,
And henceforth parle[y] with our naked swords.

E. MOR. Wiltshire hath men enough to save our heads.

WAR. All Warwickshire will love him for my sake.

LAN. And northward Gaveston hath many friends. —
Adieu, my Lord; and either change your mind,
Or look to see the throne, where you should sit,
To float in blood, and at thy wanton head
The glozing[14] head of thy base minion thrown.

Exeunt [all but KING EDWARD, KENT, GAVESTON, *and* Attendants].

K. EDW. I cannot brook these haughty menaces.
Am I a king, and must be overrul'd? —
Brother, display my ensigns in the field;
I'll bandy[15] with the barons and the earls,
And either die or live with Gaveston.

GAV. [*coming forward*] I can no longer keep me from my lord.

K. EDW. What, Gaveston, welcome! — Kiss not my hand —
Embrace me, Gaveston, as I do thee!
Why shouldst thou kneel? Knowest thou not who I am?
Thy friend, thyself, another Gaveston!
Not Hylas was more mourned of Hercules,
Than thou hast been of me since thy exile.

GAV. And since I went from hence, no soul in hell
Hath felt more torment than poor Gaveston.

K. EDW. I know it. — Brother, welcome home my friend.
Now let the treacherous Mortimers conspire,
And that high-minded Earl of Lancaster;
I have my wish, in that I joy thy sight;
And sooner shall the sea o'erwhelm my land,
Than bear the ship that shall transport thee hence.
I here create thee Lord High Chamberlain,
Chief Secretary to the state and me,
Earl of Cornwall, King and Lord of Man.

GAV. My Lord, these titles far exceed my worth.

KENT. Brother, the least of these may well suffice
For one of greater birth than Gaveston.

K. EDW. Cease, Brother, for I cannot brook these words. —
Thy worth, sweet friend, is far above my gifts;
Therefore, to equal it, receive my heart.
If for these dignities thou be envied,[16]
I'll give thee more; for but to honor thee
Is Edward pleas'd with kingly regiment.[17]
Fear'st thou[18] thy person? Thou shalt have a guard.
Wants thou gold? Go to my treasury.
Wouldst thou be lov'd and fear'd? Receive my seal:
Save or condemn, and in our name command
Whatso thy mind affects, or fancy likes.

GAV. It shall suffice me to enjoy your love,
Which whiles I have, I think myself as great
As Caesar riding in the Roman street,
With captive kings at his triumphant car.

Enter the BISHOP OF COVENTRY.

K. EDW. Whither goes my Lord of Coventry so fast?

B. OF COV. To celebrate your father's exequies.
But is that wicked Gaveston return'd?

[13] Trisyllabic; old eds. *Mowberie.*
[14] Flattering.
[15] Contend.

[16] Accented on second syllable.
[17] Rule.
[18] Fearest thou for.

K. EDW. Ay, priest, and lives to be reveng'd on thee,
That wert the only cause of his exile.
GAV. 'T is true; and but for reverence of these robes,
Thou shouldst not plod one foot beyond this place.
B. OF COV. I did no more than I was bound to do;
And, Gaveston, unless thou be reclaim'd,
As then I did incense the parliament,
So will I now, and thou shalt back to France.
GAV. Saving your reverence, you must pardon me.
K. EDW. Throw off his golden mitre, rend his stole,
And in the channel[19] christen him anew.
KENT. Ah, Brother, lay not violent hands on him,
For he 'll complain unto the see of Rome.
GAV. Let him complain unto the see of hell;
I 'll be reveng'd on him for my exile.
K. EDW. No, spare his life, but seize upon his goods.
Be thou Lord Bishop and receive his rents,
And make him serve thee as thy chaplain:
I give him thee — here, use him as thou wilt.
GAV. He shall to prison, and there die in bolts.
K. EDW. Ay, to the Tower, the Fleet, or where thou wilt.
B. OF COV. For this offence, be thou accurs'd of God.
K. EDW. Who 's there? Convey this priest to the Tower. [*Enter* Guards.]
B. OF COV. True, true.[20]
K. EDW. But in the meantime, Gaveston, away
And take possession of his house and goods.
Come, follow me, and thou shalt have my guard
To see it done, and bring thee safe again.
GAV. What should a priest do with so fair a house?
A prison may best beseem his holiness.
[*Exeunt.*]

[SCENE II][21]

Enter both the MORTIMERS, WARWICK, *and* LANCASTER.

WAR. 'T is true, the Bishop is in the Tower,
And goods and body given to Gaveston.
LAN. What! will they tyrannize upon the Church?
Ah, wicked King! accursed Gaveston!
This ground, which is corrupted with their steps,
Shall be their timeless[22] sepulchre or mine.
Y. MOR. Well, let that peevish Frenchman guard him sure;
Unless his breast be sword-proof, he shall die.
E. MOR. How now! why droops the Earl of Lancaster?
Y. MOR. Wherefore is Guy of Warwick discontent?
LAN. That villain Gaveston is made an earl.
E. MOR. An earl!
WAR. Ay, and besides Lord Chamberlain of the realm,
And Secretary too, and Lord of Man.
E. MOR. We may not, nor we will not suffer this.
Y. MOR. Why post we not from hence to levy men?
LAN. "My Lord of Cornwall" now at every word!
And happy is the man whom he vouchsafes,
For vailing[23] of his bonnet, one good look.
Thus, arm in arm, the King and he doth march;
Nay more, the guard upon his Lordship waits,
And all the court begins to flatter him.
WAR. Thus leaning on the shoulder of the King,
He nods and scorns and smiles at those that pass.
E. MOR. Doth no man take exceptions at the slave?
LAN. All stomach[24] him, but none dare speak a word.
Y. MOR. Ah, that bewrays[25] their baseness, Lancaster;
Were all the earls and barons of my mind,
We 'll hale him from the bosom of the King,
And at the court gate hang the peasant up,
Who, swoln with venom of ambitious pride,
Will be the ruin of the realm and us.

Enter the [ARCH]BISHOP OF CANTERBURY [*and an* Attendant].

WAR. Here comes my Lord of Canterbury's Grace.
LAN. His countenance bewrays he is displeas'd.
A. OF CANT. First were his sacred garments rent and torn;

[19] Gutter.
[20] *I.e.*, you well may say "convey" (= steal).
[21] The same.
[22] Untimely.
[23] Doffing.
[24] Resent.
[25] Discloses.

Then laid they violent hands upon him; next
Himself imprisoned, and his goods asseiz'd.
This certify the Pope. Away, take horse.
[*Exit* Attendant.]

LAN. My Lord, will you take arms against the King?

A. OF CANT. What need I? God himself is up in arms,
When violence is offered to the Church.

Y. MOR. Then will you join with us, that be his peers,
To banish or behead that Gaveston?

A. OF CANT. What else, my Lords? for it concerns me near;
The bishopric of Coventry is his.

Enter the QUEEN [ISABELLA].

Y. MOR. Madam, whither walks your Majesty so fast?

Q. ISAB. Unto the forest,[26] gentle Mortimer,
To live in grief and baleful discontent;
For now my Lord the King regards me not,
But dotes upon the love of Gaveston.
He claps his cheeks, and hangs about his neck,
Smiles in his face, and whispers in his ears;
And when I come he frowns, as who should say,
"Go whither thou wilt, seeing I have Gaveston."

E. MOR. Is it not strange that he is thus bewitch'd?

Y. MOR. Madam, return unto the court again.
That sly inveigling Frenchman we'll exile,
Or lose our lives; and yet, ere that day come,
The King shall lose his crown; for we have power,
And courage too, to be reveng'd at full.

A. OF CANT. But yet lift not your swords against the King.

LAN. No; but we'll lift Gaveston from hence.

WAR. And war must be the means, or he'll stay still.

Q. ISAB. Then let him stay; for rather than my lord
Shall be oppress'd by civil mutinies,
I will endure a melancholy life
And let him frolic with his minion.

A. OF CANT. My Lords, to ease all this, but hear me speak.
We and the rest, that are his counsellors,
Will meet and with a general consent
Confirm him banishment with our hands and seals.

LAN. What we confirm the King will frustrate.

Y. MOR. Then may we lawfully revolt from him.

WAR. But say, my Lord, where shall this meeting be?

A. OF CANT. At the New Temple.

Y. MOR. Content.

A. OF CANT. And, in the meantime, I'll entreat you all
To cross to Lambeth,[27] and there stay with me.

LAN. Come, then; let's away.

Y. MOR. Madam, farewell.

Q. ISAB. Farewell, sweet Mortimer; and for my sake,
Forbear to levy arms against the King.

Y. MOR. Ay, if words will serve; if not, I must. [*Exeunt.*]

[SCENE III] [28]

Enter GAVESTON *and the* EARL OF KENT.

GAV. Edmund, the mighty Prince of Lancaster,
That hath more earldoms than an ass can bear,
And both the Mortimers, two goodly men,
With Guy of Warwick, that redoubted knight,
Are gone towards Lambeth; there let them remain! *Exeunt.*

[SCENE IV] [29]

Enter Nobles [LANCASTER, WARWICK, PEMBROKE, *the* Elder MORTIMER, Young MORTIMER, *the* ARCHBISHOP OF CANTERBURY, *and* Attendants].

LAN. Here is the form of Gaveston's exile.
May it please your Lordship to subscribe your name.

A. OF CANT. Give me the paper.
[*He subscribes, as the others do after him.*]

LAN. Quick, quick, my Lord; I long to write my name.

WAR. But I long more to see him banish'd hence.

Y. MOR. The name of Mortimer shall fright the King,
Unless he be declin'd from that base peasant.

[26] A metaphor, = "into seclusion," as Bullen notes.

[27] The archepiscopal palace, across the Thames.

[28] Unlocated; presumably at Westminster.

[29] London. The New Temple. It stood between Fleet Street and the Thames. Upon the fall of the Knights Templars Edward II had given it to Pembroke.

Enter the KING, GAVESTON, [*and* KENT].

K. EDW. What! are you mov'd that Gaveston sits here?
It is our pleasure; we will have it so.

LAN. Your Grace doth well to place him by your side,
For nowhere else the new earl is so safe.

E. MOR. What man of noble birth can brook this sight?
Quam male conveniunt! [30]
See what a scornful look the peasant casts!

PEM. Can kingly lions fawn on creeping ants?

WAR. Ignoble vassal, that like Phaëthon
Aspir'st unto the guidance of the sun!

Y. MOR. Their downfall is at hand, their forces down;
We will not thus be fac'd and over-peer'd.

K. EDW. Lay hands on that traitor Mortimer!

E. MOR. Lay hands on that traitor Gaveston! [*They seize* GAVESTON.]

KENT. Is this the duty that you owe your king?

WAR. We know our duties; let him know his peers.

K. EDW. Whither will you bear him? Stay, or ye shall die.

E. MOR. We are no traitors; therefore threaten not.

GAV. No, threaten not, my Lord, but pay them home.
Were I a king——

Y. MOR. Thou villain, wherefore talks thou of a king,
That hardly art a gentleman by birth?

K. EDW. Were he a peasant, being my minion,
I'll make the proudest of you stoop to him.

LAN. My Lord, you may not thus disparage us.—
Away, I say, with hateful Gaveston.

E. MOR. And with the Earl of Kent that favors him.

[Attendants *remove* KENT *and* GAVESTON.]

K. EDW. Nay, then, lay violent hands upon your king.
Here, Mortimer, sit thou in Edward's throne;
Warwick and Lancaster, wear you my crown.
Was ever king thus overrul'd as I?

LAN. Learn then to rule us better, and the realm.

Y. MOR. What we have done our heart-blood shall maintain.

WAR. Think you that we can brook this upstart pride?

K. EDW. Anger and wrathful fury stops my speech.

A. OF CANT. Why are you mov'd? Be patient,[31] my Lord,
And see what we your counsellors have done.

Y. MOR. My Lords, now let us all be resolute,
And either have our wills or lose our lives.

K. EDW. Meet you for this, proud overdaring peers?
Ere my sweet Gaveston shall part from me,
This isle shall fleet [32] upon the ocean,
And wander to the unfrequented Inde.

A. OF CANT. You know that I am legate to the Pope.
On your allegiance to the see of Rome,
Subscribe, as we have done, to his exile.

Y. MOR. Curse him, if he refuse; and then may we
Depose him and elect another king.

K. EDW. Ay, there it goes! but yet I will not yield,
Curse me, depose me, do the worst you can.

LAN. Then linger not, my Lord, but do it straight.

A. OF CANT. Remember how the Bishop was abus'd;
Either banish him that was the cause thereof,
Or I will presently discharge these lords
Of duty and allegiance due to thee.

K. EDW. [*aside*] It boots me not to threat; I must speak fair.—
The legate of the Pope will be obey'd.
My Lord, you shall be Chancellor of the realm;
Thou, Lancaster, High Admiral of our fleet;
Young Mortimer and his uncle shall be earls;
And you, Lord Warwick, President of the North;
And [*to* PEMBROKE] thou, of Wales. If this content you not,
Make several kingdoms of this monarchy,
And share it equally amongst you all,
So I may have some nook or corner left,
To frolic with my dearest Gaveston.

A. OF CANT. Nothing shall alter us; we are resolv'd.

LAN. Come, come, subscribe.

Y. MOR. Why should you love him whom the world hates so?

[30] How ill they agree!

[31] Trisyllabic.

[32] Float.

K. Edw. Because he loves me more than all the world.
Ah, none but rude and savage-minded men
Would seek the ruin of my Gaveston;
You that be noble born should pity him.

War. You that are princely born should shake him off;
For shame subscribe, and let the lown [33] depart.

E. Mor. Urge him, my Lord.

A. of Cant. Are you content to banish him the realm?

K. Edw. I see I must, and therefore am content.
Instead of ink, I'll write it with my tears.
[*Subscribes.*]

Y. Mor. The king is lovesick for his minion.

K. Edw. 'T is done; and now, accursed hand, fall off.

Lan. Give it me; I'll have it published in the streets.

Y. Mor. I'll see him presently [34] despatched away.

A. of Cant. Now is my heart at ease.

War. And so is mine.

Pem. This will be good news to the common sort.

E. Mor. Be it or no, he shall not linger here.
Exeunt [*all but* King Edward].

K. Edw. How fast they run to banish him I love.
They would not stir, were it to do me good.
Why should a king be subject to a priest?
Proud Rome, that hatchest such imperial grooms,
For these thy superstitious taper-lights,
Wherewith thy antichristian churches blaze,
I'll fire thy crazed buildings, and enforce
The papal towers to kiss the lowly ground,
With slaughtered priests [make] [35] Tiber's channel swell,
And banks rais'd higher with their sepulchres!
As for the peers, that back the clergy thus,
If I be king, not one of them shall live.

Re-enter Gaveston.

Gav. My Lord, I hear it whispered everywhere,
That I am banish'd, and must fly the land.

K. Edw. 'T is true, sweet Gaveston — O, were it false!
The legate of the Pope will have it so,
And thou must hence, or I shall be depos'd.
But I will reign to be reveng'd of them;
And therefore, sweet friend, take it patiently.
Live where thou wilt, I'll send thee gold enough;
And long thou shalt not stay, or, if thou dost,
I'll come to thee; my love shall ne'er decline.

Gav. Is all my hope turn'd to this hell of grief?

K. Edw. Rend not my heart with thy too piercing words.
Thou from this land, I from myself am banish'd.

Gav. To go from hence grieves not poor Gaveston;
But to forsake you, in whose gracious looks
The blessedness of Gaveston remains,
For nowhere else seeks he felicity.

K. Edw. And only this torments my wretched soul,
That, whether I will or no, thou must depart.
Be governor of Ireland in my stead,
And there abide till fortune call thee home.
Here, take my picture, and let me wear thine;
O, might I keep thee here as I do this,
Happy were I! but now most miserable!

Gav. 'T is something to be pitied of a king.

K. Edw. Thou shalt not hence — I'll hide thee, Gaveston.

Gav. I shall be found, and then 't will grieve me more.

K. Edw. Kind words and mutual talk makes our grief greater;
Therefore with dumb embracement let us part.
Stay, Gaveston, I cannot leave thee thus.

Gav. For every look, my Lord drops down a tear.
Seeing I must go, do not renew my sorrow.

K. Edw. The time is little that thou hast to stay,
And, therefore, give me leave to look my fill.
But come, sweet friend, I'll bear thee on thy way.

Gav. The peers will frown.

K. Edw. I pass [36] not for their anger. Come, let's go;
O that we might as well return as go.

Enter Edmund *and* Queen Isabell[a].

Q. Isab. Whither goes my Lord?

K. Edw. Fawn not on me, French strumpet! Get thee gone!

Q. Isab. On whom but on my husband should I fawn?

[33] Lout.
[34] At once.
[35] Emend. Dodsley; old eds. *may*.
[36] Care, am moved.

GAV. On Mortimer, with whom, ungentle Queen —
I say no more. Judge you the rest, my Lord.

Q. ISAB. In saying this, thou wrong'st me, Gaveston.
Is 't not enough that thou corrupts my lord,
And art a bawd to his affections,
But thou must call mine honor thus in question?

GAV. I mean not so; your Grace must pardon me.

K. EDW. Thou art too familiar with that Mortimer,
And by thy means is Gaveston exil'd;
But I would wish thee reconcile the lords,
Or thou shalt ne'er be reconcil'd to me.

Q. ISAB. Your Highness knows it lies not in my power.

K. EDW. Away then! touch me not! — Come, Gaveston.

Q. ISAB. Villain, 't is thou that robb'st me of my lord.

GAV. Madam, 't is you that rob me of my lord.

K. EDW. Speak not unto her; let her droop and pine.

Q. ISAB. Wherein, my Lord, have I deserv'd these words?
Witness the tears that Isabella sheds,
Witness this heart, that, sighing for thee, breaks,
How dear my lord is to poor Isabel.

K. EDW. And witness Heaven how dear thou art to me!
There weep; for till my Gaveston be repeal'd,
Assure thyself thou com'st not in my sight.

Exeunt EDWARD *and* GAVESTON.

Q. ISAB. O miserable and distressed queen!
Would, when I left sweet France and was embark'd,
That charming [37] Circes, walking on the waves,
Had chang'd my shape, or at the marriage day
The cup of Hymen had been full of poison,
Or with those arms that twin'd about my neck
I had been stifled, and not lived to see
The King, my lord, thus to abandon me!
Like frantic Juno will I fill the earth
With ghastly murmur of my sighs and cries;
For never doted Jove on Ganymede
So much as he on cursed Gaveston.
But, that will more exasperate his wrath,
I must entreat him, I must speak him fair,
And be a means to call home Gaveston.
And yet he 'll ever dote on Gaveston;
And so am I for ever miserable.

Re-enter the Nobles [LANCASTER, WARWICK, PEMBROKE, *the* Elder MORTIMER, *and* Young MORTIMER] *to the* Queen.

LAN. Look where the sister of the King of France
Sits wringing of her hands, and beats her breast.

WAR. The King, I fear, hath ill entreated her.

PEM. Hard is the heart that injures such a saint.

Y. MOR. I know 't is 'long of Gaveston she weeps.

E. MOR. Why? He is gone.

Y. MOR. Madam, how fares your Grace?

Q. ISAB. Ah, Mortimer! now breaks the King's hate forth,
And he confesseth that he loves me not.

Y. MOR. Cry quittance, madam, then; and love not him.

Q. ISAB. No, rather will I die a thousand deaths!
And yet I love in vain; he 'll ne'er love me.

LAN. Fear ye not, madam; now his minion 's gone,
His wanton humor will be quickly left.

Q. ISAB. O never, Lancaster! I am enjoin'd
To sue upon you all for his repeal;
This wills my Lord, and this must I perform,
Or else be banish'd from his Highness' presence.

LAN. For his repeal? Madam, he comes not back,
Unless the sea cast up his shipwrack['d] body.

WAR. And to behold so sweet a sight as that,
There 's none here but would run his horse to death.

Y. MOR. But, madam, would you have us call him home?

Q. ISAB. Ay, Mortimer, for till he be restor'd,
The angry King hath banished me the court;
And, therefore, as thou lovest and tend'rest me,
Be thou my advocate unto these peers.

Y. MOR. What, would ye have me plead for Gaveston?

E. MOR. Plead for him he that will, I am resolv'd.

LAN. And so am I, my Lord. Dissuade the Queen.

Q. ISAB. O Lancaster, let him dissuade the King;
For 't is against my will he should return.

[37] Able to enchant.

WAR. Then speak not for him; let the peasant go.
Q. ISAB. 'T is for myself I speak, and not for him.
PEM. No speaking will prevail, and therefore cease.
Y. MOR. Fair Queen, forbear to angle for the fish
Which, being caught, strikes him that takes it dead;
I mean that vile torpedo,[38] Gaveston,
That now, I hope, floats on the Irish seas.
Q. ISAB. Sweet Mortimer, sit down by me awhile,
And I will tell thee reasons of such weight
As thou wilt soon subscribe to his repeal.
Y. MOR. It is impossible; but speak your mind.
Q. ISAB. Then thus; — but none shall hear it but ourselves.
[*Talks to* Young MORTIMER *apart.*]
LAN. My Lords, albeit the Queen win Mortimer,
Will you be resolute, and hold with me?
E. MOR. Not I, against my nephew.
PEM. Fear not, the Queen's words cannot alter him.
WAR. No? Do but mark how earnestly she pleads.
LAN. And see how coldly his looks make denial.
WAR. She smiles; now, for my life, his mind is chang'd.
LAN. I'll rather lose his friendship, I, than grant.
Y. MOR. Well, of necessity it must be so. —
My Lords, that I abhor base Gaveston,
I hope your Honors make no question;
And therefore, though I plead for his repeal,
'T is not for his sake, but for our avail;
Nay for the realm's behoof, and for the King's.
LAN. Fie, Mortimer, dishonor not thyself.
Can this be true, 't was good to banish him?
And is this true, to call him home again?
Such reasons make white black, and dark night day.
Y. MOR. My Lord of Lancaster, mark the respect.[39]
LAN. In no respect can contraries be true.
Q. ISAB. Yet, good my Lord, hear what he can allege.
WAR. All that he speaks is nothing; we are resolv'd.

[38] Electric ray. [39] Consideration.

Y. MOR. Do you not wish that Gaveston were dead?
PEM. I would he were.
Y. MOR. Why, then, my Lord, give me but leave to speak.
E. MOR. But, Nephew, do not play the sophister.
Y. MOR. This which I urge is of a burning zeal
To mend the King, and do our country good.
Know you not Gaveston hath store of gold,
Which may in Ireland purchase him such friends
As he will front the mightiest of us all?
And whereas [40] he shall live and be belov'd,
'T is hard for us to work his overthrow.
WAR. Mark you but that, my Lord of Lancaster.
Y. MOR. But were he here, detested as he is,
How easily might some base slave be suborn'd
To greet his Lordship with a poniard,
And none so much as blame the murderer,
But rather praise him for that brave attempt,
And in the chronicle enroll his name
For purging of the realm of such a plague.
PEM. He saith true.
LAN. Ay, but how chance this was not done before?
Y. MOR. Because, my Lords, it was not thought upon.
Nay, more, when he shall know it lies in us
To banish him, and then to call him home,
'T will make him vail [41] the top-flag of his pride,
And fear to offend the meanest nobleman.
E. MOR. But how if he do not, Nephew?
Y. MOR. Then may we with some color [42] rise in arms;
For howsoever we have borne it out,
'T is treason to be up against the King.
So we shall have the people of our side,
Which for his father's sake lean to the King,
But cannot brook a night-grown mushroom,
Such a one as my Lord of Cornwall is,
Should bear us down of the nobility.
And when the commons and the nobles join,
'T is not the King can buckler Gaveston;
We'll pull him from the strongest hold he hath.
My Lords, if to perform this I be slack,
Think me as base a groom as Gaveston.
LAN. On that condition, Lancaster will grant.
WAR. And so will Pembroke and I.

[40] Where. [41] Lower.
[42] Excuse, show of reason.

E. Mor. And I.
Y. Mor. In this I count me highly gratified,
And Mortimer will rest at your command.
Q. Isab. And when this favor Isabel forgets,
Then let her live abandon'd and forlorn. —
But see, in happy time, my Lord the King,
Having brought the Earl of Cornwall on his way,
Is new return'd. This news will glad him much,
Yet not so much as me. I love him more
Than he can Gaveston; would he lov'd me
But half so much: then were I treble-blest.
[*They retire.*]

Re-enter King Edward, *mourning*, [*with* Beaumont *and other* Attendants].

K. Edw. He 's gone, and for his absence thus I mourn.
Did never sorrow go so near my heart
As doth the want of my sweet Gaveston;
And could my crown's revenue [43] bring him back,
I would freely give it to his enemies,
And think I gain'd, having bought so dear a friend.
Q. Isab. [*aside to the* Nobles] Hark how he harps upon his minion.
K. Edw. My heart is as an anvil unto sorrow,
Which beats upon it like the Cyclops' hammers,
And with the noise turns up my giddy brain,
And makes me frantic for my Gaveston.
Ah, had some bloodless Fury rose from hell,
And with my kingly sceptre struck me dead,
When I was forc'd to leave my Gaveston!
Lan. [*aside to the* Nobles] *Diablo!* What passions call you these?
Q. Isab. [*advancing*] My gracious Lord, I come to bring you news.
K. Edw. That you have parle[y]'d with your Mortimer!
Q. Isab. That Gaveston, my Lord, shall be repeal'd.
K. Edw. Repeal'd! The news is too sweet to be true.
Q. Isab. But will you love me, if you find it so?
K. Edw. If it be so, what will not Edward do?
Q. Isab. For Gaveston, but not for Isabel.
K. Edw. For thee, fair Queen, if thou lovest Gaveston.
I'll hang a golden tongue about thy neck,
Seeing thou hast pleaded with so good success.
Q. Isab. No other jewels hang about my neck
Than these, my Lord; nor let me have more wealth
Than I may fetch from this rich treasury.
O how a kiss revives poor Isabel.
K. Edw. Once more receive my hand; and let this be
A second marriage 'twixt thyself and me.
Q. Isab. And may it prove more happy than the first.
My gentle Lord, bespeak these nobles fair,
That wait attendance for a gracious look,
And on their knees salute your Majesty.
K. Edw. Courageous Lancaster, embrace thy King!
And, as gross vapors perish by the sun,
Even so let hatred with thy sovereign['s] [44] smile.
Live thou with me as my companion.
Lan. This salutation overjoys my heart.
K. Edw. Warwick shall be my chiefest counsellor;
These silver hairs will more adorn my court
Than gaudy silks, or rich embroidery.
Chide me, sweet Warwick, if I go astray.
War. Slay me, my Lord, when I offend your Grace.
K. Edw. In solemn triumphs, and in public shows,
Pembroke shall bear the sword before the King.
Pem. And with this sword Pembroke will fight for you.
K. Edw. But wherefore walks young Mortimer aside?
Be thou commander of our royal fleet;
Or, if that lofty office like thee not,
I make thee here Lord Marshal of the realm.
Y. Mor. My Lord, I'll marshal so your enemies,
As England shall be quiet, and you safe.
K. Edw. And as for you, Lord Mortimer of Chirke,
Whose great achievements in our foreign war
Deserves no common place nor mean reward,
Be you the general of the levied troops,
That now are ready to assail the Scots.
E. Mor. In this your Grace hath highly honored me,
For with my nature war doth best agree.

[43] Accented on second syllable.

[44] Add. Q 1612; om. earlier eds.

Q. Isab. Now is the King of England rich and strong,
Having the love of his renowned peers.
K. Edw. Ay, Isabel, ne'er was my heart so light.
Clerk of the crown, direct our warrant forth
For Gaveston to Ireland. Bea[u]mont, fly
As fast as Iris or Jove's Mercury.
Beau. It shall be done, my gracious Lord. [*Exit.*]
K. Edw. Lord Mortimer, we leave you to your charge.—
Now let us in, and feast it royally.
Against our friend the Earl of Cornwall comes,
We'll have a general tilt and tournament;
And then his marriage shall be solemnized.
For wot you not that I have made him sure [45]
Unto our cousin,[46] the Earl of Gloucester's heir?
Lan. Such news we hear, my Lord.
K. Edw. That day, if not for him, yet for my sake,
Who in the triumph will be challenger,
Spare for no cost; we will requite your love.
War. In this, or aught, your Highness shall command us.
K. Edw. Thanks, gentle Warwick; come, let's in and revel.
Exeunt [*all except the*] Mortimers.
E. Mor. Nephew, I must to Scotland; thou stayest here.
Leave now to oppose thyself against the King.
Thou seest by nature he is mild and calm,
And, seeing his mind so dotes on Gaveston,
Let him without controlment have his will.
The mightiest kings have had their minions:
Great Alexander loved Hephaestion;
The conquering [Hercules] [47] for Hylas wept;
And for Patroclus stern Achilles droop'd;
And not kings only, but the wisest men:
The Roman Tully [48] lov'd Octavi[u]s;
Grave Socrates, wild Alcibiades.
Then let his Grace, whose youth is flexible,
And promiseth as much as we can wish,
Freely enjoy that vain, light-headed earl;
For riper years will wean him from such toys.
Y. Mor. Uncle, his wanton humor grieves not me;
But this I scorn, that one so basely born
Should by his sovereign's favor grow so pert,
And riot it with the treasure of the realm.
While soldiers mutiny for want of pay,
He wears a lord's revenue on his back;
And Midas-like, he jets [49] it in the court,
With base outlandish cullions [50] at his heels,
Whose proud fantastic liveries make such show
As if that Proteus, god of shapes, appear'd.
I have not seen a dapper Jack so brisk;
He wears a short Italian hooded cloak,
Larded with pearl, and, in his Tuscan cap,
A jewel of more value than the crown.
Whiles other walk below, the King and he
From out a window laugh at such as we,
And flout our train, and jest at our attire.
Uncle, 't is this that makes me impatient.
E. Mor. But, Nephew, now you see the King is chang'd.
Y. Mor. Then so am I, and live to do him service;
But whiles I have a sword, a hand, a heart,
I will not yield to any such upstart.
You know my mind; come, Uncle, let's away.
Exeunt.

[45] Betrothed him. [46] *I.e.*, niece.
[47] Old eds. *Hector*. But note metre.
[48] Cicero; this allegation is pure invention.

[49] Struts. [50] Low fellows.

[Act II — Scene I] [1]

Enter [Young] Spencer *and* Baldock.

Bald. Spencer, seeing that our lord th' Earl of Gloucester's dead,
Which of the nobles dost thou mean to serve?
Y. Spen. Not Mortimer, nor any of his side,
Because the king and he are enemies.
Baldock, learn this of me: a factious lord
Shall hardly do himself good, much less us;
But he that hath the favor of a king,
May with one word advance us while we live.
The liberal Earl of Cornwall is the man
On whose good fortune Spencer's hope depends.
Bald. What, mean you then to be his follower?
Y. Spen. No, his companion; for he loves me well,
And would have once preferr'd me to the King.
Bald. But he is banish'd; there's small hope of him.
Y. Spen. Ay, for a while; but, Baldock, mark the end.
A friend of mine told me in secrecy
That he's repeal'd, and sent for back again;

[1] A room in the late Earl's residence at Gloucester. The historical Lady of Gloucester's brother, the Earl, was killed at Bannockburn.

And even now a post came from the court
With letters to our lady from the King;
And as she read she smil'd, which makes me think
It is about her lover Gaveston.

BALD. 'T is like enough; for since he was exil'd
She neither walks abroad, nor comes in sight.
But I had thought the match had been broke off,
And that his banishment had chang'd her mind.

Y. SPEN. Our lady's first love is not wavering;
My life for thine, she will have Gaveston.

BALD. Then hope I by her means to be preferr'd,
Having read unto her since she was a child.

Y. SPEN. Then, Baldock, you must cast the scholar off,
And learn to court it like a gentleman.
'T is not a black coat and a little band,
A velvet-cap'd cloak, fac'd before with serge,
And smelling to a nosegay all the day,
Or holding of a napkin in your hand,
Or saying a long grace at a table's end,
Or making low legs [2] to a nobleman,
Or looking downward with your eyelids close,
And saying, "Truly, an't may please your Honor,"
Can get you any favor with great men.
You must be proud, bold, pleasant, resolute,
And now and then stab, as occasion serves.

BALD. Spencer, thou knowest I hate such formal toys,
And use them but of mere hypocrisy.
Mine old lord whiles he liv'd was so precise,[3]
That he would take exceptions at my buttons,
And being like pin's heads, blame me for the bigness;
Which made me curate-like in mine attire,
Though inwardly licentious enough
And apt for any kind of villainy.
I am none of these common [pedants] [4] I,
That cannot speak without *propterea quod*.[5]

Y. SPEN. But one of those that saith *quandoquidem*,[6]
And hath a special gift to form a verb.

BALD. Leave off this jesting; here my Lady comes. [*They retire.*]

[2] Bows.
[3] Puritanical.
[4] Cor. Q 1598; O1 *pendants*.
[5] Because.
[6] Since. "In spite of his disclaimer, he *is* apt (Spencer hints) to give his reasons." (Verity.)

Enter the Lady [*of Gloucester, King Edward's* Niece.]

[NIECE.] [7] The grief for his exile was not so much
As is the joy of his returning home.
This letter came from my sweet Gaveston.
What need'st thou, love, thus to excuse thyself?
I know thou couldst not come and visit me.
"I will not long be from thee, though I die."
This argues the entire love of my lord.
"When I forsake thee, death seize on my heart."—
But rest thee here where Gaveston shall sleep.
[*Puts the letter into her bosom.*]
Now to the letter of my Lord the King.—
He wills me to repair unto the court
And meet my Gaveston. Why do I stay,
Seeing that he talks thus of my marriage day?—
Who's there? Baldock!
See that my coach be ready; I must hence.

BALD. It shall be done, madam. *Exit.*

NIECE. And meet me at the park pale presently.—
Spencer, stay you and bear me company,
For I have joyful news to tell thee of.
My Lord of Cornwall is a-coming over,
And will be at the court as soon as we.

Y. SPEN. I knew the King would have him home again.

NIECE. If all things sort out [8] as I hope they will,
Thy service, Spencer, shall be thought upon.

Y. SPEN. I humbly thank your Ladyship.

NIECE. Come, lead the way; I long till I am there. [*Exeunt.*]

[SCENE II] [9]

Enter [KING] EDWARD, *the* QUEEN [ISABELLA], LANCASTER, [Young] MORTIMER, WARWICK, PEMBROKE, KENT, [*and*] Attendants.

K. EDW. The wind is good; I wonder why he stays.
I fear me he is wrack'd upon the sea.

Q. ISAB. [*aside*] Look, Lancaster, how passionate [10] he is,
And still his mind runs on his minion.

LAN. My Lord.

K. EDW. How now! what news? Is Gaveston arriv'd?

[7] Speech-tags in old eds. *Lady*, or *Lad.*, throughout.
[8] Happen, befall.
[9] Tynemouth; presumably a hall in the castle.
[10] Sorrowful.

Y. Mor. Nothing but Gaveston! What means your Grace?
You have matters of more weight to think upon.
The King of France sets foot in Normandy.
K. Edw. A trifle! we'll expel him when we please!
But tell me, Mortimer, what's thy device [11]
Against the stately triumph we decreed?
Y. Mor. A homely one, my Lord, not worth the telling.
K. Edw. Prithee let me know it.
Y. Mor. But, seeing you are so desirous, thus it is:
A lofty cedar tree, fair flourishing,
On whose top branches kingly eagles perch;
And by the bark a canker [12] creeps me up,
And gets unto the highest bough of all;
The motto, *Aeque tandem.*[13]
K. Edw. And what is yours, my Lord of Lancaster?
Lan. My Lord, mine's more obscure than Mortimer's.
Pliny reports there is a flying fish
Which all the other fishes deadly hate;
And therefore, being pursued, it takes the air.
No sooner is it up, but there's a fowl
That seizeth it. This fish, my Lord, I bear;
The motto this, *Undique mors est.*[14]
K. Edw. Proud Mortimer, ungentle Lancaster,
Is this the love you bear your sovereign?
Is this the fruit your reconcilement bears?
Can you in words make show of amity,
And in your shields display your rancorous minds?
What call you this but private libelling
Against the Earl of Cornwall and my brother?
Q. Isab. Sweet Husband, be content; they all love you.
K. Edw. They love me not that hate my Gaveston.
I am that cedar — shake me not too much;
And you the eagles — soar ye ne'er so high,
I have the [jesses] [15] that will pull you down;
And *Aeque tandem* shall that canker cry
Unto the proudest peer of Britainy.
Though thou compar'st him to a flying fish,
And threatenest death whether he rise or fall,
'T is not the hugest monster of the sea,
Nor foulest harpy, that shall swallow him.
Y. Mor. [*aside to the* Nobles] If in his absence thus he favors him,
What will he do whenas he shall be present?
Lan. [*aside*] That shall we see; look where his Lordship comes.

Enter Gaveston.

K. Edw. My Gaveston!
Welcome to Tynemouth! Welcome to thy friend!
Thy absence made me droop and pine away;
For, as the lovers of fair Danaë,
When she was lock'd up in a brazen tower,
Desir'd her more and wax'd outrageous,
So did it, sure,[16] with me; and now thy sight
Is sweeter far than was thy parting hence
Bitter and irksome to my sobbing heart.
Gav. Sweet Lord and King, your speech preventeth [17] mine;
Yet have I words left to express my joy.
The shepherd nipp'd with biting winter's rage
Frolics not more to see the painted spring
Than I do to behold your Majesty.
K. Edw. Will none of you salute my Gaveston?
Lan. Salute him? yes. Welcome, Lord Chamberlain!
Y. Mor. Welcome is the good Earl of Cornwall!
War. Welcome, Lord Governor of the Isle of Man!
Pem. Welcome, Master Secretary!
Kent. Brother, do you hear them?
K. Edw. Still will these earls and barons use me thus?
Gav. My Lord, I cannot brook these injuries.
Q. Isab. [*aside*] Aye me, poor soul, when these begin to jar.
K. Edw. Return it to their throats; I'll be thy warrant.
Gav. Base, leaden earls, that glory in your birth,
Go sit at home and eat your tenants' beef;
And come not here to scoff at Gaveston,
Whose mounting thoughts did never creep so low
As to bestow a look on such as you.
Lan. Yet I disdain not to do this for you.
[*Draws his sword and offers to stab* Gaveston.]

[11] Painting on shield. [12] Cankerworm.
[13] Justly at length. [14] On all sides is death.
[15] The straps on a hawk's legs, to which the leash was attached. Old eds. *gresses.*

[16] Q 1622 and most mod. eds. *fare.*
[17] Anticipateth.

K. Edw. Treason! treason; where's the traitor?

Pem. Here! here!

K. Edw. Convey hence Gaveston; they'll murder him.

Gav. The life of thee shall salve this foul disgrace.

Y. Mor. Villain, thy life, unless I miss mine aim. [*Wounds* Gaveston.]

Q. Isab. Ah, furious Mortimer, what hast thou done?

Y. Mor. No more than I would answer, were he slain.

[*Exit* Gaveston *with* Attendants.]

K. Edw. Yes, more than thou canst answer, though he live.
Dear shall you both abye [18] this riotous deed.
Out of my presence! Come not near the court.

Y. Mor. I'll not be barr'd the court for Gaveston.

Lan. We'll hale him by the ears unto the block.

K. Edw. Look to your own heads; his is sure enough.

War. Look to your own crown, if you back him thus.

Kent. Warwick, these words do ill beseem thy years.

K. Edw. Nay, all of them conspire to cross me thus;
But if I live, I'll tread upon their heads
That think with high looks thus to tread me down.
Come, Edmund, let's away and levy men;
'T is war that must abate these barons' pride.

Exit the King [*with* Queen Isabella *and* Kent].

War. Let's to our castles, for the King is mov'd.

Y. Mor. Mov'd may he be, and perish in his wrath!

Lan. Cousin, it is no dealing with him now;
He means to make us stoop by force of arms.
And therefore let us jointly here protest,
To prosecute that Gaveston to the death.

Y. Mor. By Heaven, the abject villain shall not live!

War. I'll have his blood, or die in seeking it.

Pem. The like oath Pembroke takes.

Lan. And so doth Lancaster.
Now send our heralds to defy the King;
And make the people swear to put him down.

Enter a Post.

Y. Mor. Letters, from whence?

Mess. From Scotland, my Lord.

[*Gives letters to* Mortimer.]

Lan. Why, how now, cousin, how fares all our friends?

Y. Mor. My uncle's taken prisoner by the Scots.

Lan. We'll have him ransom'd, man; be of good cheer.

Y. Mor. They rate his ransom at five thousand pound.
Who should defray the money but the King,
Seeing he is taken prisoner in his wars?
I'll to the King.

Lan. Do, cousin, and I'll bear thee company.

War. Meantime, my Lord of Pembroke and myself
Will to Newcastle here, and gather head.[19]

Y. Mor. About it, then, and we will follow you.

Lan. Be resolute and full of secrecy.

War. I warrant you. [*Exit with* Pembroke.]

Y. Mor. Cousin, an if he will not ransom him,
I'll thunder such a peal into his ears,
As never subject did unto his king.

Lan. Content; I'll bear my part — Holla! who's there?

[*Enter* Guard.]

Y. Mor. Ay, marry, such a guard as this doth well.

Lan. Lead on the way.

Guard. Whither will your Lordships?

Y. Mor. Whither else but to the King?

Guard. His Highness is dispos'd to be alone.

Lan. Why, so he may, but we will speak to him.

Guard. You may not in, my Lord.

Y. Mor. May we not?

[*Enter* King Edward *and* Kent.]

K. Edw. How now!
What noise is this? Who have we there? Is't you? [*He starts to leave.*]

Y. Mor. Nay, stay, my Lord; I come to bring you news;
Mine uncle's taken prisoner by the Scots.

K. Edw. Then ransom him.

Lan. 'T was in your wars; you should ransom him.

[18] Pay for. O1 *abie;* other old eds. *abide.*

[19] Raise troops.